P. Piassetksy, J. Gordon-Cumming

Russian Travellers in Mongolia and China

in Two Volumes - Vol. 1

P. Piassetksy, J. Gordon-Cumming

Russian Travellers in Mongolia and China
in Two Volumes - Vol. 1

ISBN/EAN: 9783348054973

Printed in Europe, USA, Canada, Australia, Japan

Cover: Foto ©Andreas Hilbeck / pixelio.de

More available books at **www.hansebooks.com**

IN

MONGOLIA AND CHINA.

BY

P. PIASSETSKY.

TRANSLATED BY J. GORDON

IN TWO VOLUMES.

VOL. I.

LONDON : CHAPMAN & HALL, LIMITED.

1884.

LONDON:
PRINTED BY J. S. VIRTUE AND CO., LIMITED,
CITY ROAD.

CONTENTS OF VOL. I.

CHAPTER I.

CHAPTER II.

CHAPTER III.

CHAPTER IV.

CHAPTER V.

A JOURNEY IN CHINA.

CHAPTER I.

Departure from St. Petersburg—Siberia—Loss of the Chest—Arrival at the Frontier—Kiachta—First Acquaintance with the Chinese—Visit to the Mandarin of Kiachta—Departure—First night in Mongolia.

AFTER several weeks of preparation, I left St. Petersburg on the 14th of March, 1874, and stopped at Moscow to take leave of my relatives. In this town I was overtaken by two of my fellow-travellers, M. Sosnowsky, the head of the expedition, and M. N——, a photographer; but as the health of the latter broke down, he was obliged to leave us at Omsk, and was replaced by M. Boiarsky. We left Moscow for Nijni Novgorod, and from thence had to post 6,000 versts before reaching Kiachta, on the Chinese frontier. In these days of railroads, I had almost forgotten the prose and poetry of a journey on sleighs.

We crossed the Volga, went through the towns of Kasan and Perm, and over the Oural Mountains.

As spring was at hand, the snow melting and streams overflowing, we left the sleighs, took a carriage, and at length reached Siberia, halting in Tiumen, its first town.

Sosnowsky, who had described our expedition as scientific and commercial, considered this halt indispensable in the interests of our commercial affairs.

The merchants seemed to agree with him on all points until pecuniary offerings in favour of the expedition came into the question, when they were always ready with excellent reasons for refusing their aid. And, what was still worse, they perfectly infuriated Sosnowsky by spreading abroad that so far from our being official envoys of the Government, we were nothing but vagabonds and amateur artists.

I must, however, mention that the merchants at Tiumen presented us with excellent cases for our photographic apparatus; those which we had brought with us from St. Petersburg being utterly worthless, and quite unfit for our purpose. On leaving Tiumen we went through several small towns, and crossed various rivers on rafts before arriving at Omsk, the administrative centre of Western Siberia. And here we were overtaken by M. Matoussowsky, our topographical surveyor.

From the town of Omsk the road followed the river Irtysch as far as Semipalatinsk, the principal place in the district of that name.

Although this town was not on our road, Sosnowsky had decided that the last preparations for our journey were to be completed there, and the Cossacks (Pawlow, Smokotnine, and Stepanow) who were engaged to accompany us there, awaited our arrival.

We spent twenty-three days at Semipalatinsk in the

month of May, just the hot season, and were quite sorry to leave this little town, formerly surrounded with woods, but now by an arid and sandy desert. The departure from Semipalatinsk took place during a beautiful night, dark but starlit, the Cossacks, with the luggage, having left half-an-hour before us; and then we settled. ourselves back to back in a two-wheeled vehicle. I occupied the back seat and, absorbed in thought, was mechanically watching the road vanish behind us, when suddenly I heard a horseman, at full gallop, trying to overtake us, and hailing us at the top of his voice. We then waited, and great was our astonishment on beholding the Cossack Stepanow. On inquiring where he came from, and how he happened to be behind us on horseback, he replied that "A misfortune had happened, and that our money was lost : the weight of the chest had smashed the bottom of the carriage, the chest had come to pieces, and all the silver was scattered on the ground."

"Just what I said would happen," growled Matoussowsky waking up. And, indeed, I well remembered that at Semipalatinsk Matoussowsky argued for the best part of two days with Sosnowsky, trying in vain to convince him how unsuitable a wooden chest was for carrying about 15 poods (600 pounds) of silver, but he had only been requested not to teach those who were as wise as himself.

The Cossack explained that having lost their way, they heard the bell on our carriage, and thus getting on the right track again, came upon our scattered silver. Two of them had remained to guard our treasure, whilst the third rode

on to overtake us. "Thank God," added he, "that the
devil led us astray; else we had ere this reached the
station, and to-morrow the first passer-by had picked up the
silver."

Conceive our position; had we only discovered the
absence of the chest and the consequent loss of the silver
later on, here at one blow would our journey to China have
been at an end. How overwhelmed with shame we should
have been! After ordering the Cossack back to rejoin his
comrades, we continued our road to the station, whence we
despatched two men, armed with lanterns, to help our people
to pick up the silver, which was afterwards apportioned
between our three vehicles. Glad and truly thankful that
this first accident had not been followed by disastrous consequences, we again set out, through thick forests and across
rivers, such as the Obi, the Tomi, and the Yenissei, this last
so wide that we could hardly see the opposite bank. We
then came to the town of Tomsk. A little farther on was
the small town of Mariinsk, with its Hôtel de Paris; then
Kansk, with one solitary stone-built house; and then
Irkoutsk, capital of Eastern Siberia. Here our company
was increased by a new member, M. Andreïewsky, who had
been previously engaged as interpreter, but who soon
admitted that he knew the Chinese language very imper-
fectly, adducing in self-justification that his salary was only
to be 600 roubles.

We crossed the great Lake Bïkal in a steamer, passing
Selenguinsk, a small town lying forgotten in the desert; at
Troickosawsk we heard the bells of a Russian church for

the last time, and on a beautiful July morning we entered Kiachta, the frontier town.

M. Sokolow, a merchant of this town, having put his house at our disposal, we proceeded to install ourselves in the rooms allotted to us, and even before we had time to change our attire there entered four Chinese belonging to Maï-Maï-Tzeng. They saluted us in Russian, and held out their hands as to old friends, and as if they saw us every day of their lives. Their entry was accompanied by a strong and disagreeable odour of garlic and opium; nevertheless this visit charmed me, and I entertained them with as much curiosity and coolness as they showed towards us. The conversation begun in Russian, for although the Chinese of Maï-Maï-Tzeng speak our language, they murder it so frightfully that it is a little difficult to understand them; consequently their version of it has been rightly called the " Kiachtien " language, or the dialect of Kiachta. After exchanging several questions, we should have been glad if they had taken themselves off and allowed us to complete our toilet, but as they did not stir we told them we must change our clothes.

" It is true," they replied, without disturbing themselves. " There is a great deal of dust on the roads."

It only remained for us to request their departure, which they took with the best grace possible, again shaking hands with us. Notwithstanding the difficulty we had in coming to an understanding with them, their visits never ceased during the fortnight we spent at Kiachta. They entered our rooms at any moment, sometimes in considerable num-

bers, tranquilly seated themselves, put questions to us and
offered us their merchandise, or else remained sitting there
without uttering a word. These children of nature had no
shyness; they cared not where they seated themselves, on
the chairs or on the beds, and effectually prevented our
continuing our occupations, or even taking our meals, or
going to sleep. Eventually we were obliged to admit them
at certain hours only   I must admit, however, that this
freedom in visiting strangers is not characteristic of the
Chinese people; it is peculiar to the inhabitants of Maï-
Maï-Tzeng, and the Russians themselves are to blame for
having allowed them to get into these habits.

I had determined to get to Maï-Maï-Tzeng as soon as
possible, which I may here mention is not a noun substan-
tive, but means "small commercial town." It is for this
reason that the Chinese, in their relations with the Russians, call Kiachta "Your Maï-Maï-Tzeng," and supposing
Kiachta has the same meaning in Russian, designate Maï-
Maï-Tzeng by the name of " Your Kiachta," which they
pronounce Tzaketou.   Thus I went from our Maï-Maï-Tzeng
to visit the Chinese Tzaketou.

On leaving the only street in Kiachta, I came upon a
waste piece of ground about 250 yards wide, which consti-
tutes the frontier boundary between Russia and China. It
appeared strange that two old wooden posts, covered with
mud, and without any mark or inscription, should be all
that denoted the limits of the frontier; and I marvelled
that two powers like Russia and China had not treated
themselves to something grander. Had it depended on me,

a beautiful Russian temple should have been built by
Kiachta, and a no less beautiful pagoda by Maï-Maï-Tzeng.

During our journey I perceived the black and dirty tent
of some beggars, farther on a row of windowless huts,
surrounded by palings, and next to these the clay house of
the official stationed at the gate of Maï-Maï-Tzeng. I was
now joined by a Chinaman who had come to see us the
evening before, and who had undertaken to be my
cicerone.

On entering the street I was struck by the singularity of
the scene, for I seemed as if transported to another world.
Nothing I saw had the slightest resemblance to anything I
had ever beheld in Europe. The very narrow street, with
its tower at the end, the roofs, the façades of the houses, the
wide-open doors giving peeps into their courtyards and
gardens, the flowers, and the quantities of birds in cages, all
were new to me. My guide gave me some explanations
which I could not take in, and showed me the house of the
chief, or Tzargoutzi, a house hidden at the bottom of courts,
and of which I could see nothing but the surrounding wall
and two soldiers on duty at the door. Next we reached the
temple, and my brain whirled with the multitude of new
impressions which passed before my eyes—objects, forms,
and colours. In the interior I was again struck by the
originality of the monster idols and ornamented lamps, and
by the darkness which surrounded the statue of Confucius
and the smaller idols at the end of the temple. I could hear
the melodious sound of little bells placed in the angles of
the roof and played on by the wind. But words fail to

describe such a spectacle; drawing can best reproduce what strikes the eye. On my return I got ready to pay a visit with my colleagues to the Tzargoutzi. In the first court we found a group to do us honour; the second court was bounded by low buildings and surrounded by a gallery. The Tzargoutzi came forward to receive us, accompanied by his suite, and the Russian Commissary for Kiachta presented us one after the other, on which the mandarin, who was somewhat civilised, shook hands all round; but he did it like an archbishop giving his benediction right and left. He then invited us to enter his abode. We went through the first room, where there was a stove, and on it a copper kettle full of boiling water; the second, which served as a reception-room, was divided into three compartments by glazed and dimly-lit partitions. There were inscriptions on the walls, lanterns on the ceilings, and at the end of the room was the kang, covered with mats, which answers the purpose both of bed and sofa. A table was placed in the middle, on which was a lacquer box in divisions, full of bonbons; and around it were three wooden stools covered with red cloth.

We took our places at the table, and whilst tea was handed to us, the conversation opened with the usual questions upon our health and upon our arrival; it then passed on to our farther travels in Mongolia, the preparations necessitated thereby, and everything that might render it easier or less dangerous. It was during this conversation that I was able to examine my mandarin. He wore a straw hat, conical in shape, ornamented by a tuft of red horsehair, and surmounted by a blue button. Chinese etiquette forbids the master of the house to remain uncovered before his guests, who would also be considered guilty of rudeness if they took off their hats. So we carefully kept them on. At last the Commissary asked him to uncover, to which he immediately assented, and at once proposed that we should do the same, ordering one of the officers to take off his hat for him. This duty·the individual performed with great gentleness, raising the chief's head-gear with with both hands, as if it were a precious vase, and depositing it with much precaution in its appointed place.

The mandarin might have been forty years old. He spoke fast and energetically, and when anyone addressed him in Russian, he fixed his eyes on the speaker as if he was listening intently, or even as if he understood what was being said to him. Only when the speaker had ceased did he turn to the interpreter, and while answering addressed the speaker, not the interpreter. This was required of Chinese politeness, but Sosnowsky, not being able to accustom himself to this habit, always spoke to the interpreter, visibly annoying the mandarin, who to conceal his annoyance, changed the conversation, and offered us something to eat. Business over, the mandarin turned to me, saying that he was very happy to see a doctor in his house, and complained of the bad state of his health. I proposed that we should adjourn to a private room that I might examine him, and went with him into his small sleeping-room, which was almost entirely filled by the bed, draped in blue silk curtains. Various members of his suite, who seemed afraid that I might do

him a bad turn, assisted at this consultation. I counselled
him to abstain from smoking opium, to which he replied that
he never smoked it, leaving me nevertheless convinced that
the use of opium was the cause of his suffering.

In my turn I begged his permission to go over his house.
He immediately consented, ordering one of his officers to
accompany me. Here was a real labyrinth of passages,
corridors, and courts. I even ascended the roof, from whence
I obtained a bird's-eye view of the whole town, which presented a succession of clean red roofs made of clay and
chopped hay. By means of these roofs, which touched each
other, one might have traversed half the town, divided from
the other half by the principal street. A fire, which broke
out in 1869, destroyed Maï-Maï-Tzeng, as it had done
Kiachta; and though no traces of this disaster were now
visible, it was asserted that the town was formerly larger
and prettier.

The following day the Tzargoutzi sent to ask us when we
should be disposed to receive him, as he desired to return
our visit. He came in a carriage drawn by a mule, which
was unharnessed at the porch of our house, and the soldiers
who accompanied him dragged the vehicle at a running pace
as far as the steps, where he was taken out and supported
under the arms like an archbishop. He stayed with us more
than an hour. Champagne was served to him, and various
objects shown that might interest him; and before taking
his departure he consented to sit whilst I drew his portrait
in my sketch-book. As I shall have occasion to come back
upon the Chinese repasts, I will say nothing at present about

the dinners to which we were invited, and only mention the entire absence of strong drinks and wines. The best that they produced was spirits of wine warmed with essence of roses, which was served in microscopic cups during dinner.

I awaited the hour of our departure with some impatience, as the continual invitations of our compatriots during our stay at Kiachta quite prevented my working; and I barely succeeded in taking two sketches, one of the Temple of Maï-Maï-Tzeng; and the other of the frontier zone, with a part of the town of Kiachta on the one hand and of Maï-Maï-Tzeng on the other.

Whenever I went to Maï-Maï-Tzeng to draw, I always took care to ask permission of the Chinese to pass through this court or that passage, knowing their repugnance to letting a stranger see their family life. Great was my astonishment on being told in their Kiachta dialect that "Here one may walk everywhere." Not only was I unquestioned on any subject whatsoever, but as soon as I began working a group collected around me and examined all my artistic apparatus, beginning with the camp-stool, which was the special object of their admiration, so much so that the mandarin charged a workman to take a model of it. They also lavished praise on my drawings, stating that they were of the first quality; that they could not be executed except by a superior mind. "You are very clever." "Men like you are rare," &c. Whether these praises were false or sincere I cannot say, but what pleased me greatly was their natural taste for painting, for I hoped that this art might render me good service in my connection with the Chinese of all classes.

At last the moment came for quitting the hospitable town of Kiachta, where the Russian merchants were good enough to offer 3,000 roubles in gold to the expedition, and, in addition, samples of all sorts of merchandise to the value of 1,000 roubles. They provisioned us besides with eatables, wines, bonbons, &c.

After the farewell dinner at the house of the Commissary, who with his family and numerous others was to accompany us to the next station, we set off, a large party, and leaving Kiachta and Maï-Maï-Tzeng behind, saw spread out before us the immense green steppe of Mongolia, intersected by reddish and sandy paths. The weather, at first splendid, overclouded suddenly, and before arriving at the station we were soaked by a heavy shower. The rain was still falling in torrents when we reached some nomad tents, which gave us shelter. The Mongols, men and women, crowded forward to the entrance, looking on us with as much fear as curiosity.

The weather having cleared, two tents were erected and tables arranged, and this last meal accomplished, our compatriots returned to Kiachta, with thousands of good wishes for our safe journey.

We passed the night at this place, and continued our journey on the following day to the town of Owrga, where we saw some Mongolian chariots harnessed with oxen or horses, but there were no camels. A great log having been lit, our beds were prepared, and everyone longed for repose.

I myself, being unable to sleep, spent my time examining the Mongolian ïourta under which I was passing my first night. It was composed of a slight framework of wood covered with felt, and as a habitation was on the whole tolerably endurable. One must not be too exacting on the subject of cleanliness, or pay any heed to the insects swarming on the ground, which are simply the flooring of the ïourta.

CHAPTER II.

July 13*th*, 1874. A beautiful morning. We take tea on a carpet spread on the grass; around us ragged Mongols, with their almond-shaped black eyes; their children squatting or lying about, gaze intently at our slightest movement.

There was no need to hurry, as our baggage, being drawn by oxen, could only advance slowly, and we had still time to overtake it. At length we had to take our places in three two-wheeled Chinese carriages, one of which the Commissary of Kiachta had given us, and the other two were lent us by a Maï-Maï-Tzeng merchant; we were to leave them all at Kalgan. Each of these carriages is usually drawn by two horsemen, who are again joined by two, four, or even a greater number of others, according to the difficulty of the journey; for instance, they may help to drag the carriage up the hills, or to support it in the descent. This is why, during a journey in Mongolia, the convoys are always accompanied by a considerable number of men and relays of horses; and our three vehicles were further escorted by a whole cavalcade of Mongols, sometimes by their wives as well. These *ladies* are also on horseback, and if needful they help to draw the carriages.

On our departure from the station of Gilan-nor, our cavalcade was therefore composed of about twenty Mongols, of
two Mongolian women about twenty years of age and rather
pretty, five Russian horsemen, and two functionaries, the
one Chinese, the other Mongolian, who escorted us according
to custom; and we had a reserve of fifteen horses. To complete this rapid sketch, I must add two words on the attire
of the Mongols, who are for the most part very poorly clad,
and all exceedingly dirty. Men and women are dressed
nearly alike; that is, in wide trousers and a brilliantly
coloured dressing-gown, the collar crossing on the chest.
From their girdle hangs a knife, a spoon, and chopsticks,
besides their pipe and tobacco-pouch—the whole of Chinese
manufacture. They wear boots, and a hat with turned-up
brim, to which blue or red ribbons half a yard long are
attached at the back. They wear their hats on the back of
their heads, with the strings under their chins. The men,
as Chinese subjects, shave their heads, leaving a tail at the
back; the women wear two plaits, which fall on the chest or
on the shoulders.

A plain separated Gilan-nor from the station of Ibitzyk,
and we crossed it trotting or galloping as fast as we could.
At Ibitzyk we were received by two Mongols more cleanly
in their dress than the rest, who after saluting us, invited us
to enter the ïourta, where tea awaited us.

I had ridden the whole way on a horse saddled Mongolian
fashion, with very short stirrups; consequently I felt intense
fatigue, and was not sorry to stretch my legs. Whilst waiting for our baggage, I thought I would take the portrait of

one of the two women, who were still on horseback; the moment she discovered this she whipped up her horse and set off at full gallop. I then began the portrait of the other when the first, arriving most inopportunely, whipped up her companion's mount, and they both disappeared, but returned a moment later. Nevertheless I succeeded eventually in sketching the portrait. It was here that camels were brought to us for the transport of our baggage, and whilst they were being loaded I entered the ïourta to take a cup of tea. My thirst was so great that, regardless of the copper teapot, the wooden cup, the tea in tablets,* and the milk of doubtful complexion, I swallowed the beverage with avidity.

At this station I got into a carriage which could only be entered by climbing up the shafts before the horse was harnessed, and next by creeping on all fours and headforemost into the interior. I eventually achieved the desired position in it. One might remain recumbent or sit cross-legged like a Turk; but these chariots have no seats, and no well for one's legs. It is possible to sit with them dangling outside, but it is also dangerous, as one runs the risk of being thrown out at the first jolt. A mattress, my fur, and my greatcoat, covered the boards at the bottom of my carriage, and as I also had my cushion, the couch was less hard than it otherwise would have been. The interior of the carriage was lined with blue cotton material, having deep pockets at each side, and at the entrance mats were hung for curtains, which could be hermetically closed against rain. In case of need

* Tea manufactured out of the coarsest leaves, and the small twigs pressed with a grindstone; it then takes the form of bricks or tablets.

our apron could furthermore be lowered, and was tied down
and rolled up above the place of entrance; outside the carriage was covered by felt, and mats falling over the door to
give shade. The mats reflect the rays of the sun, and felt
is, as everyone knows, a non-conductor of heat, the result of
which is that a certain amount of cool air is always secured
for the inside compared with the outer temperature, which
on that day was 37 degrees, whilst inside the carriage it was
only 20 degrees Reaumur. Thus it may be seen that I was
fairly comfortably installed. The stage from this station
was more varied : hills covered with boulders, deep valleys
and ravines. The ground became more and more stony, and
quitting the main road, our Mongols started at a gallop
across the steppe. The jolts became so frequent and so
violent that I ordered them to stop that I might ride ; but
owing to the stirrups being too short, I was soon forced to
get back into the carriage.

It was here that we had to cross the Yre-Gol River, a
tributary of the Orchonte, which in its turn empties its
waters into the Selenga. The Yre-Gol, at the place we had
to cross it, was not wider than the Neva, not deep, but very
rapid. We were to cross it on a raft, which I now saw
before me, and which consisted of three hollow little joists
tied to each other in three places.

When everyone was assembled and the camels unloaded,
two Mongols in the costume of acrobats *minus* the tights,
that is to say, quite naked, entered the water to push the
boat (I can call this nautical apparatus by no other name)
towards the shore, holding it up and sustaining it by the

end. Two others pushed the carriage, shafts foremost, until it was on the raft, the half of its wheels being in the water, while it left quite a small place at the back for the boatman or ferryman. The naked Mongols placed themselves at the extremities of this most original raft, and armed with long poles breasted the current, pushing with their boathooks against the bottom of the river. They managed it with astonishing dexterity, resisting the current, which did its best to carry them off, pushing their feet against the wood of the raft so firmly that one could have believed them rivetted to it, perpetually shifting their poles from side to side, and always sure of what they were about. I quite trembled for them; a false step had sufficed to throw them into the river. But this false step they never took; and, contrary to their habit of chattering incessantly, they performed all this in silence.

When they had gone far enough they gave their raft a twist, utilising the current to steer for the opposite bank, and landed exactly at the spot where we were awaited by the men and horses that were to conduct us further. They then unshipped the carriage, returning to ply their occuation, and this mode of crossing a river interested me so much that I went over several times with them, my admiration for their strength and agility increasing with each journey. This passage of the Yre-Gol and the reloading of the baggage on different carriages took a certain amount of time, so we decided on spending the night beside the water. A fire was lit, and after supper, whilst waiting for tea, our Mongols, with some persuasion, consented to sing to us,

Without wishing to offend our guides, I must say that their songs resembled nothing so much as the howling of dogs or the whistling of the wind. I could catch no melody, and I imagine that they improvised as they went along.

Then our Cossacks sang in their turn, and were listened to by the Mongols with an altogether infantile astonishment, and a smile on their lips. I would like to have known what they thought of these songs, for, if I mistake not, they did not at all appreciate them. The Cossacks followed the transport, and we gave ourselves up to repose, some of us under the stars, others under a tent, but in perfect confidence as to our personal safety, and that of our baggage, the honesty of the Mongols in this part of the country being an excellent safeguard.

July 14th, 1874. A beautiful morning. Boïarsky tried unsuccessfully to photograph a group of Mongols with their horses. It was much ado about nothing, as it was not possible to get them to stay quiet a single instant. Entreaties, explanations, encouragement, nothing had any effect. " Stay quiet, do not move," we said to them. " Saïn baïna " (it is well) they replied. In vain did the photographer open the apparatus and count the seconds; invariably one of the Mongols would suddenly rise, and run towards the negative to see what was taking place, inducing confusion, cries, and abuse, and thus, after five attempts, it had to be given up. To-day we have travelled quicker than usual.

The Mongols are generally of a gay and careless disposition; they talk during the whole of the journey, and to-day had taken it into their heads to overtake the baggage transport, which had left before we did. Behold them, therefore, all at once become silent and thoughtful; they bend over their horses, which, seeming to understand the manœuvre, begin to trot quicker and quicker; at a given moment they start off full gallop, with impossible .cries. You have only to look out for yourself. The drivers of the carriages they are trying to overtake perceive this manœuvre when too late. In vain do they whip on their horses, for they are beaten, to the delight of the victorious. We follow a beautiful wide valley, shut in between two verdant mountains thickly covered with shrubs. At the station of Kouitoun, in addition to the tea and its traditional milk, they give us a drink called airyk, a sort of koumiss, but much more sour, and therefore better calculated to quench the thirst.

The transit between the two stations cost us a cake of tea and three roubles of money each, without counting the Cossacks; in all, fifteen roubles. It is the usual pay; and I do not know why the Mongols at this station demanded more, which was, however, refused them, as there was no reason for their demand.

From this point I started on horseback. The Mongolian official who received us at Ourmouktouï accepted a piece of plush and two handkerchiefs with gratitude as a gift, and, raising them above his head, bowed himself to the earth.

The day waned; but, notwithstanding Matoussowsky's and my advice, we did another stage in the darkness, and during a very cold night; and we had only just settled to repose when it began to rain.

July 15*th.* Grey day—mist. We have to cross the mountains. The rain having loosened the soil, the road is strewn with stones and granite, and the carriages proceed with difficulty, notwithstanding the number of horses being doubled, and even trebled. Whilst passing the baggage carriages drawn by oxen, I was distressed at the way these poor beasts were struggling along. At last, however, we were at the top of the mountain, and the horses were allowed to rest. I got out of my carriage to see the view, but a thick mist hid even the nearest objects. The descent was even more fatiguing than the ascent; we had to cross streams and ravines, and often man and beast had to stop short to avoid taking a false step.

Once on the plain we started at a canter for the Bain-Gol station, where we were received by a big, grave Mongol: a rich man, holding the rank of general in the Chinese service. His duties consisted in rare visits to Court, there to present gifts and receive others in return. He wore a light grey dress and a regimental cap with the red button. After saluting us in Mongolian, "Amrkhan saïn baïna" he greeted us in Russian. He had been at Kiachta, and knew some words of our language. He made us enter the felt-covered ïourta, in the midst of which stood a tripod. The rubbish that burned in it filled the room with a thick, acrid smoke; one could neither see nor breathe in it. Although this species of heating apparatus was a mark of attention on his part, we begged him to remove it at once, saying that we were not cold. I tried to make him understand how disagreeable the smoke was, and how it was the sole cause of the weakness of the eyes from which they all suffer, and advised him to use chimneys to conduct the smoke away; but he did not appear to understand me, and listened gazing into space.

Here we had to wait some time for the arrival of the baggage, which we had outstripped; and our interpreter got into a blue rage, scolding the Mongolian general for his want of forethought, as caravans never go out of a foot-pace. It was very disagreeable to me to see this elderly Mongol, who was so respected by his fellow tributaries, thus roughly called to account before every one. I observed as much to the interpreter, telling him that his conduct appeared most unsuitable to us civilised Europeans. He replied that he knew them well, that they could not be treated otherwise, and that he looked upon the Mongols as his own brothers. I answered nothing, but inwardly considered this mode of fraternising to be most singular.

The rain continued falling, time was getting on, so we left during the night for the next station, accompanied by the General.

July 16*th.* I am on horseback alongside of the interpreter, who relates some peculiarities of the life of the Mongols, amongst whom he has lived for a long time. Cleanliness is unknown to them ; the men seldom wash, the women never. In summer they change their linen once a month, in winter not at all. Their principal nourishment is tea with milk and airyk, a sort of koumiss, made out of cow's milk ; khourout, or curdled milk dried and boiled, sour or tastless, fatty or without butter ; and *ourium,* the skin of boiled milk. The

Chinese sell flour to them, with which they make unleavened
bread. They also make soup with millet and milk. Their
meat is chiefly mutton, and accessible to the rich alone; the
poor only eat the flesh of animals that have died. If a
Mongol loses a cow, a sheep, a camel, or a horse, he will
certainly not waste his property, but will consume the dead
animal.

The Mongol is nomad, and passes from one place to another
with his flocks as soon as the pasture is exhausted. His
only occupation is to strike his tent and transport it to the
spot where he intends to sojourn for some time. Once
installed, he has no further care : he is free from morning
till night, until necessity forces him to go and pitch his
tent farther on.

His flock is his fortune. In exchange for his horses and
sheep he obtains clothing, saddles, hats, shoes, knives, pipes,
and all his household requirements from the Chinese;
utensils in copper or iron, his bench, chest, &c. The woman
busies herself with the housekeeping; the man wanders un-
occupied round the ïourta, sings, and squats or lies down in
the sun, and if he wants variety he goes some versts off and
sees a neighbour.

When they meet they dismount, squat down in front of
each other, and talk over their pipes of their flocks, or
of some extraordinary event, such as, for instance, our
journey.

After passing Khara-Gol and two other stations, we saw a
salt lake in the distance, and on it a quantity of swans and
a good many ducks and woodcock. We halted for the night

at the station of Kouï, where there were a considerable number of nomad tents.

Kouï was the last stage before the town of Ourga, called Kourène or Da-Kourène by the Mongols, which means monastery. To get there we had to cross high mountains, and on one of them we saw the *obo* of the Mongols, which, however, is found on all heights.

The obo is only a cairn of stones, sticks, branches, bones, rags, sometimes handkerchiefs with images or prayers upon them. They have a religious meaning, and are formed in the following manner. The first-comer collects a heap of stones on the summit of a mountain or hill, and every passer-by throws a stone, or anything that comes to hand, on to this heap, meanwhile invoking the deity supposed to haunt the spot. Thus real pyramids of stones and all sorts of other things gradually accumulate, until they are sometimes ten feet high.

Whilst I gazed on the landscape unfolded before my eyes, the Mongols were muttering prayers and throwing stones on to the obo, stretching out their hands towards it. According to their belief, prayers and offerings before the obo preserve the traveller from all harm.

Situated in a plain surrounded by mountains, the town of Ourga can be seen from a distance of fifteen versts. We began to meet a considerable number of people, men and women, covered with rags, some bareheaded, notwithstanding the excessive heat, others adorned in hats of sheepskin dyed yellow, looking as if they were surrounded by an aureole.

I now reached the principal square of the town, consisting of clay huts only, which are railed round, excepting three edifices with gilded roofs of eccentric shape, and embellished by symbolical figures : these are the temple; the palace of Khoutoukta, a spiritual personage who represents the deity; and lastly the Mongolian school belonging to the lamas. Such is the town of Ourga; I confess that I expected something better.

Having lingered behind my companions, I made my entry alone. The streets I rode along were crowded with Mongols and Chinese, ragged and dirty men and women, with their children completely naked. In the square were a quantity of shops, which were only tents or felt huts; then pedestrians and riders, carriages and camels; enormous heaps of dung; also bones, some of them human ; and with it all a hideous noise. Such is the aspect of this place, which I went through without attracting the least notice.

Outside the town I continued to follow my guide, wondering where the Russian Consulate could be, and presently I perceived a two-storied house, with outhouses and a garden, surrounded by a wall. This turned out to be the Consulate, where I was received by the secretary. A little later we all went to call upon M. Schichmarew, the Consul, who received us most politely, and invited us to share his meals during our stay in Ourga. He at the same time recommended us to go and see the local authorities.

The next day a messenger was sent to the Prefect to know at what hour he could receive us, and while waiting for the answer we went into Ourga to visit the palace of Khoutoukta and the temple of the god Maïdar. The lamas on guard at the door of the palace would not permit us to enter, and I could barely cast a glance at the first courtyard, which was dirty and deserted, and seemed to resemble an ancient circus. The temple of Maïdar is open at certain hours, so we were enabled to see it. At the entrance there are four wooden pillars, with penthouses, the whole ornamented with an original design in the most glaring colours. Inside is an enormous bronze statue of the principal deity, attired in yellow satin, and perhaps seventy-five feet high. This statue, cast in Thibet, was removed to Ourga in separate bits, and when it was complete the temple was constructed.

At the feet of the idol is the altar, with candelabra on it, and cups full of meat and drink, ornamented by sixteen symbolical signs painted in red and blue, and arranged in two rows, meeting in the centre. To the right and left of the altar are two other bronze statues; on each side of the hall, along the walls, are low divans, with filthy cushions, and small tables placed in front of them. It is on these divans that the lamas sit to chant their prayers and beat their drums. Here also is Khoutoukta's arm-chair, covered with a saddle-cloth. The lama who was our guide, and who judged us unworthy of visiting the temple, refused to withdraw the saddle-cloth. But the receipt of a rouble speedily induced him to do so, and he even invited us to sit down in the arm-chair. This temple has a choir, or rather a gallery, all round it; and from this point the head of the idol can best be seen, as it is considerably higher than the gallery. There are a number of idols along the walls, great and small, seated in arm-chairs or on cushions, like Turks. Amongst others is one representing the *White Czar* (Tzagan Darkhi). There are also glass recesses where they guard thousands of bronze statues arranged in rows, and on the walls are drawings of horrible monsters, who, we were informed, are saints. In every corner of the sacred edifice members of the clergy paraded about with nothing to do, their faces shining with grease, and their heads shaved; they were attired in red and yellow *chlamys*, and mumbled their prayers and told their beads, looking at us all as if we were inferior beings. However, they have invented an effective method by which they curtail the time necessary for the recital of these prayers. In the towns, as well as on the principal roads, may be seen cylinders revolving on two vertical axes. Printed prayers are glued on to the cylinder, and all that is necessary is to put it in motion, so that each turn counts as if the glued-on prayers had been recited. Just as we were leaving, I saw an ordinary Mongol or *black* (hara) enter the temple; the laymen are thus named to distinguish them from the lamas. It is possible that the *black* had not the right to enter the temple at this hour, as he received a sounding blow from our guide, and took himself off with all speed, without showing the least fight, as though he had only come there to receive a benediction administered in the guise of a blow. This comic scene took place in the most solemn manner, and without a word being exchanged on either side.

At the same moment a band of young lamas (pupils) swarmed into the temple, dispersing in every direction.

Each saluted his favourite idol by touching it with his forehead. They did it mechanically, without the smallest trace of
piety, staring at us, and just as often as not making their bow
into space instead of to the idol.

From the temple we proceeded to the camp of the Chinese
garrison, where the commanding officer had promised our
Consul to execute manœuvres in our honour. The soldiers
I saw at the entrance of the camp were dressed in vests of
black cloth, with round patterns of red or white on their
breasts embroidered with letters or figures to indicate their
subdivisions or companies; they wore wide black trousers,
white canvas shoes and gaiters, and on their heads black
handkerchiefs twisted like turbans. The house of the commanding officer was at the bottom of the second court, and
the barracks were on each side. The chief stood on the
step with his aides-de-camp, and we alighted some paces off
and went to salute him. He shook hands with us both, and
invited us to take tea and Russian marmalade. A man of
simple bearing, he was of a gay and communicative disposition, and altogether most likeable.

The conversation was nevertheless difficult, as our interpreter frankly confessed to not understanding a word of
Chinese; but, to console us, he assured us of his knowledge
of Mongolian. The chief showed us several articles which
were precious to him but of no interest to us, such as a
watch, a binocular, a revolver, &c.

We were afterwards present at their sword exercise. At
a thrice-repeated blast of the trumpet, the camp became
suddenly animated; the soldiers emerged from the barracks,

and ran right and left; some carried flexible pikes, others
guns; there were even some of huge dimensions, requiring
two men to carry them, and there were three great flags
with seven colours.

As soon as they were collected in the principal court a
signal was given, the soldiers changed front, left the yard,
and after describing a semi-circle, on their return formed two
lines on either side, and a half-circle facing us. The drum
beat, the copper *lo* resounded; a halberdier advanced from
the ranks and saluted us, as might an acrobat, beginning
his drill by showing the offensive and defensive manner of
using a weapon.

He advanced running, jumping, twisting, whirling, and
flourishing his weapon about, all the movements being those
of a practised gymnast.

When the drum stopped beating, the soldier saluted and
resumed his place in the ranks. Another replaced him,
very ugly, squinting, and with protruding teeth. He held
a long knife in each hand. The drum and the *lo* set up
their noise again. Executing various antics, the soldier
began his knife practice, which he whirled round his body
and at times brought so near his neck that I trembled for
his safety, as he appeared to have decided to put an end to
himself before our eyes, and I could not refrain from thinking how unpleasant it would be to meet such a performer in
a secluded spot, and without a revolver.

Others succeeded him, and we witnessed a dozen exer-
cises of all sorts. The commanding officer being a great
judge of arms, wished to examine the carbines our Cossacks

carried. The mechanism was explained to him and the firing and the action of the ball ; he was quite stupefied, and all the more as he appeared thoroughly to understand that in presence of these guns, all their tricks and contortions with knives and halberds would be quite unavailing. For my part, I was surprised at the ignorance of this military chief as to the manipulation of a gun, which he did not even know how to hold. After the drill, I visited the barracks, the kitchens, and other peculiarities of the camp. The buildings are of unbaked brick, furnished with stone beds, which are heated in winter, and the windows pasted up with paper. Six men are lodged in each division of the barracks ; it is kept clean and the air is pure ; the barracks are open from morning till night.

On our return from the camp, we stopped to see Khoutoukta's summer palace, which stands apart on the river Ouliassoutaï; it is surrounded by a wall, and has eight doors, with penthouses (in Chinese style). In the courtyard some poplars shelter the earthly deity's bath, a sort of wooden basin or tank sunk in the ground. The palace is three-storied, and all its rooms, big or little, are perfectly empty, like those of a deserted house. Not a chair, or a table, or a bench. On the walls are carefully executed drawings in miniature, representing scenes in the lives of the gods, some of which are most indecent. I noticed that our guide, the lama, singled these out to touch with his forehead. "But how can Khoutoukta lodge here ? " I inquired. I was informed that when he came, a tent was prepared for him in the courtyard, in which he lived, and that he only

went into the palace for prayer. There was, however, some
thing more than met the eye in all this; but it is not give:
to a stranger to find out all that goes on behind the scenes
the mystery is the power of the lamas over the ignoran
multitudes. This summer palace seemed to be more like
mausoleum, desolation reigned everywhere, and there wa
nothing in it worthy of note.

The following day we paid the governor a visit, and then
it was I saw Chinese women for the first time, as they ar
forbidden by law to inhabit Maï-Maï-Tzeng. There wer
two of them, one old and one young, and they walked roun(
the garden without appearing disconcerted by the presenc
of strangers. Whether they were mother and daughter, o
the two wives, I could not find out. Wishing to visi
Ourga by night, I started off in a little carriage with th
interpreter and Matoussowsky. The town was plunged ir
absolute silence, but whilst driving along we heard tw
shots. Next day we were told at the Consulate that th
watchers at the Russian shops fire blank cartridges to keej
off robbers.

During our stay here, I made acquaintance with severa
Russian merchants, who traffic in tea, flour, grain, furs, &c
One of them, who had lived for nine years in the town o
Ouliassoutaï, informed me that he made a profit of 50, 60
and 75 per cent. on his leather transactions; but the lif
there is insupportable, as strangers are not allowed to build
a house, but are forced to hire one, and the Chinese houses
without windows or flooring, are uninhabitable in cold and
damp weather. "It was with difficulty," he said, "that]

obtained leave to lay down flooring or to put in windows; the landlord forbids you to touch anything, as his house would then be contrary to the law." And it is the case that in China the rules as to building are strictly observed. Nevertheless the Russians at Ourga succeeded in making them build some quite small houses with windows; and this was a real victory over the Chinese.

I always hoped, during my walks about the town and its suburbs, to come upon some corpse thrown to the dogs, according to Mongolian custom; for they never bury their dead, but carry them outside the town, and throw them down anywhere. The dogs, which from this very cause are so numerous, are not long in collecting and beginning to devour the body, but if they have not finished it in three days, the family of the deceased are overcome by grief, as it is a sign that the gods were displeased with him, and prayers are offered up for the remission of his sins. The prayers are always granted, as the dogs never fail to come and resume their prey. I did not succeed in seeing this curious and repulsive spectacle, but in my walks I often stumbled over skulls and human bones in the streets as well as in the country, and no one heeded them. My fellow-countrymen have assured me that sometimes packs of wild dogs, which subsist entirely on human flesh, attack both pedestrians and horsemen. Neither did I succeed in making acquaintance with a certain lama in Ourga, who practiced medicine according to the school of Thibet. I had heard of him at Kiachta. My loss was not great, for, judging by the tales I heard, I made up my mind that this lama-doctor was a vulgar charlatan. Amongst other things, he prescribed mixtures composed of seventy different herbs ; and he recommended a lady, in Kiachta, who had consulted him about a headache, to lie down in bed with her feet pressed against the wall in a vertical position, and so to remain six or eight hours, even were she to bleed at the nose, ears, and mouth.

We left Ourga the 24th of July, after spending nine days there instead of three, as we had fixed to do. Our compatriots accompanied us as far as the river Toula, which we had to ford; and such was the rapidity of this limpid stream, that I had to shut my eyes to prevent myself falling from my horse from absolute giddiness. Mongols, naked or half-naked, and chattering as usual, helped with the transit of the carriages and baggage. We had a thousand versts to travel across the plain of Mongolia and the desert of Gobi, before reaching the first town, which is Kalgan. The plain, as I could distinguish from a distance, is watered by the Toula, which divides itself into two branches. Here and there was the smoke of various ïourtas ; and flocks of black-faced sheep, cattle, and horses were scattered about. Far in the distance a string of camels wended their way down the hill. As we journeyed on, I saw a goodly number of skulls bleached by the sun and rain, and I picked up one for my anthropological collection. When we arrived at the station, all the Mongols assembled to see us, and all screamed in a deafening fashion, without the least knowing why.

July 25th. Nothing worthy of note. Drenched by a shower, we stopped at Djargalanta to dry ourselves. In the night I saw a splendid meteor rush through the sky, leaving a straight and luminous trail behind it, which lasted three minutes; before disappearing the trail took a curve. In the morning I had succeeded in sketching some Mongolian portraits, and as a reward I gave them some Chinese meats and sugar-candy that had been given me at Maï-Maï-Tzeng.

July 26th. This morning, I have been able to sketch, to the great satisfaction of the Mongols, who had plenty of leisure for examining me and my implements, such as my camp-stool, the burning-glass with which I lit my pipe, &c. If I happened to whistle while drawing, they looked into my mouth to see if there were not some instrument hid in it.

The plain became poorer and poorer in vegetation, a sign that we were nearing the desert called Gobi by the Mongols, and Cha-Mô by the Chinese. The heat was suffocating; no wind; the only chance of a little cool air was while passing over the dark patches cast by the shadow of the clouds. I noted a slab of stone a yard long, inscribed with a Mongolian prayer. At the halting-place, called Tola-Boulyk, there were about twenty nomad families, as poor as the soil they inhabit; their tents were small and dirty, and the few beasts of their herds were very thin. One of these tents, inhabited by an old beggar, was so low that when this short-statured old woman stood upright in the middle of it, her head protruded through the opening at the top. Among the Mongolians there was one afflicted with a harelip; a quarter of an hour's operation and subsequent dressing would have cured the evil. I offered to perform the operation, and he made them ask me how many of his sheep I would take for doing it, but on hearing that I would do it for nothing, he refused to be operated upon. It was a proof to me that their clergy (the lamas), who dabble in medicine, never practice gratuitously; greed of gain makes them follow the profession, and not the love of science. I repeated my offer, but the Mongol refused, doubting my ability and suspecting that I wanted to do him a bad turn.

While waiting to start, I tried to enter the tent of the old beggar of whom I spoke. Profiting by her absence, I crept inside: on the ground there was a piece of old felt, a tripod with a small copper, a few leathern bags for water hung on a string, and a small chest locked up. I would have given something to know what the chest of an old woman covered with rags could contain; perhaps some sacred object, or handkerchiefs with prayers or pictures on them.

I returned to the carriage. The soil is clay, covered with pebbles, the vegetation poor, not a human being to be seen. At the station of Naroun, is a small salt lake, the reservoir for two springs. There is a great quantity of the grass called tchii, the presence of which, in the steppes, indicates the existence of salt or of subterraneous springs; likewise, when they require it, the Mongols seek for water where the tchii grows. The places here are called saline where the earth contains a sufficient quantity of salt to deposit it on the surface, which then looks as if it were covered by a slight layer of flour or powdered chalk; or the salt would remind one of recently fallen snowflakes, were it not difficult in suffocating heat to conjure up snow to the imagination.

Generally we make one meal a day, before going to bed, which is contrary to every rule of health; and in my capacity

of doctor I tried several times to draw attention to this object-
ion. But it would appear that to some the rules of science
are of no value.

As for me, I had every opportunity of getting to know the
pretended laws of the steppes, to which our chief, Sosnowsky,
perpetually referred. Have the nomads any ? I doubt it ;
perhaps later on I may expect to understand them.

July 27th. The same scenery. I had a very communicative guide to-day, who never ceased talking, although he
knew perfectly that I could not understand him. If I had
had an interpreter, what might I not have learnt ! He often
repeated the word *orso*, Russian, and imitated the gestures
of a person playing the accordion ; then he imitated the
Russian national dance, by executing various movements, and
this seated on his horse going at full speed.

July 28th. In proportion as we advanced, the vegetation
grew poorer. I saw some lizards and grasshoppers. A bad
day for the Mongols, often unseated and thrown to the
ground by their horses, and my carriage was also upset. As
soon as they are on their legs again, these poor people look
with fear at the *ambohan*, or gentleman, seated in the carriage,
and ask his pardon. It appears that these accidents are not
overlooked when they have to drive Chinese mandarins, who
behave with considerable cruelty.

The station of Saïr Oussou is tenanted by a Chinese
official ; perhaps it is to this that we may attribute the
solemn reception that greeted our arrival. At a certain distance from the ïourta prepared for us, four Mongols, having
unharnessed the horses, dragged the carriage by the shafts

as far as the tents, and then knelt before each of us, their
hands folded on their breasts. I arrived last, and the official
came to salute me, offering his snuff-box. This being a sign
of politeness, I accepted a pinch, and in my turn presented
some tobacco to him. He took a bit of it, which he put to
his nose. Others then approached us, likewise offering their
snuff-boxes, and saluting with their "Amrkhan saïn baïna."
In the tent a small divan with several mattresses was
arranged.

July 29th. I got up early, and went to explore the surroundings of the picket. Not far from the tents, camels and
horses surrounded the well, where a Mongol drew water
with a bucket, and emptied it into a trough. The beasts all
pressed against each other, and without the aid of some of
the men, not one of them would have been able to drink by
reason of the pressure. One could easily see how much they
suffered from thirst, and it appeared to me that none had
drunk their fill. They left the trough because they were
driven away, and went off to seek another. I turned away
from this sorry spectacle, and went to see horses captured by
an *arcan*, formed by a long stick with a knotted-fast cord,
which the Mongol threw to the right and left till he had
caught one. As soon as the horse felt the string on his neck
he stopped short without stirring.

When I went back to our tent, I found the Mongol official
who had come with us, who now revealed for the first time
that he was a musician and a singer. Seated cross-legged on
the felt, he held a violin with a long handle like a violoncello,
and sang to his own accompaniment. The sounds he

extracted from the instrument resembled the buzzing of a blüebottle in a room. His voice was monotonous and disagreeable, passing from baritone to soprano.

July 30*th.* Nothing of importance.

July 31*st.* Various casualties having occurred to Sosnowsky during the day, he declined to proceed any farther, but recommended that I should go on without him, were I so minded; on which I started off with two mounted Mongols, taking with us an extra horse. Just when I was at full gallop, my horse fell and threw me ; I picked myself up and was going to remount, when the horse started off full speed and disappeared in the steppes. My two Mongols dashed off after him, taking the spare horse with them, and here was I in the middle of the night, forsaken in the midst of the steppes.

What was I to do, or attempt? I decided to walk up and down, and await the return of the Mongols. From time to time, I heard the race in the distance, and cries of "Aïe! aïe ! " which showed that the horse was still at large. After waiting for half-an-hour, a Mongol came back to me, who turned out to be the one who led the spare horse, which I now mounted. Shortly after we caught up the other Mongol, who had succeeded in capturing my beast, and soon we met our carriages, with Matoussowsky in one of them. We slowly continued our way, and at last arrived at the station, which was the thirty-third since leaving Ourga.

August 1*st.* The heat was overpowering ; sandy deserts, sometimes bushes of *Nitraria Schoberi*, the branches of which retain the sand blown about by the wind, and in this way form hillocks of considerable height. During our journey I moreover noticed various marshes in which snipe were to be found. At the next station there was a monastery for lamas. It does one good to recall the pleasure experienced on coming across an inhabited nook in the midst of a desert, quiet though it was.

Hardly had we arrived, before we were surrounded by a crowd of Mongols with shaven heads, that is to say, by members of the clerical body. These lamas of an inferior order were as simple and *naïf* as the *khara* or ordinary Mongols, who are equally numerous here. They all stared us out of countenance; and all my odds and ends, from the pencil and burning-glass, to the air-cushion, were objects of astonishment to them. I regretted that so short a time was at my disposal for observing all these types and costumes.

Most of the lamas had nothing on but a petticoat fastened round the waist by a sash, to which were suspended a knife, spoon, and chopsticks. The knife may be of some use, but what use do they make of the chopsticks? The Mongol never uses them to eat with; he dips his five fingers into the dish, then licks them, and wipes them on his head or on his dress. One lama would be draped in a mantle, one arm naked to the shoulder; another would be in a dressing gown; some were only covered by a simple piece of stuff. The colour chosen for the lamas' dress is usually red or yellow; I have however seen some in blue or grey. They shave their heads or cut their hair, and wear skullcaps, or hats with ribbons at the back. Some had simply wound a handkerchief round their heads, like the old

women in Russia. Others wore two plaits stuck together
with glue such as cabinet-makers use, and which makes the
hair as hard as wood; to this they add several adornments—
coral, turquoises, copper, &c. Their dress consists simply of
a tight-fitting chemise, with narrow sleeves raised with
puffs at the shoulders. Young girls are permitted to walk
about freely, but the children are as wild as little wolves.
The least of our movements put them to flight, but they
would return smiling a moment after. All this crowd
chattered, screamed, and laughed. I saw very few who
looked sad. The lamas seemed even more joyous than the
rest, for as they belonged to a privileged class, they led a
more peaceful existence. They played with each other like
children, giving each other sounding blows on their shaven
heads without taking the least offence. I went to the
monastery, which is surrounded by a high brick wall. In
the interior is a colonnade, at the bottom of which stands
a statue of Buddha; between the pillars are two rows of
seats, on which the lamas sit during the service. They
were reciting their prayers in a loud and monotonous voice,
from time to time accompanying this exercise with drums
and copper cymbals. At given periods, some of them
extracted prolonged sounds and kind of flourishes from
trumpets five yards long. There were other little temples
where the same service was going on, for it never ceases in
the Buddhist temples; but what a service! I could discover
no sign of inward devotion among them. It was more like
a factory, only the workmen's task consisted in uttering
prayers, beating drums, and blowing trumpets. Work being

over, the lama's crowded out of the temple, pushing each
other, and rushing to the kitchens, where dinner awaited
them, after which they dispersed right and left, till the
signal recalled them to prayer.

I looked upon them as parasites, and working like the
Danaides and producing nothing. My fellow-travellers
had already left when I returned from the monastery.
Along the road I met three caravans, two of which were
going to Russia with tea. It is rare in the Gobi to meet so
many in one day.

August 2nd. To-day we skirted sacred mountains, which
are numerous in Mongolia. These are a series of mounds
like a railway embankment. This long range, which
vanishes on the horizon, ends up by an escarpment on the
plain, and I can hardly believe it to be natural. As there
was an obo at the highest point I wanted to see it, although
the little path leading to it was very steep, and my horse
was very nearly perpendicular several times, quite leading
me to expect it to fall back upon me. On reaching the
summit, with some difficulty, I was sorry I had taken the
trouble, as the obo presented nothing of interest. According to Mongolian legends, the forges of Djenghis-khan
were on this mountain; but it appears that several places
in Mongolia claim the honour. We were much surprised to
find no living creature. On arriving at the station of Toli,
where there were about thirty tents, which always means
a certain number of inhabitants; it turned out that a
Khoutoukta had just arrived from Thibet, on a visit to the
neighbouring monastery, and as the greater number of the

inhabitants of Toli are lamas. duty, piety, or simple curiosity had taken them all to see him.

Although we were quite aware how difficult it was to obtain sight of this personage, the representative of the Deity, we sought nevertheless to obtain an interview, and concocted the following message : " Russians travelling to Pekin salute you, and crave your benediction. Can you receive them ? " To our great surprise, we received a favourable reply. Khoutoukta awaited us, and begged us to come at once, as he was retiring to rest. Without an instant's delay we accepted his invitation, attended by three lamas, one of whom carried a lantern. The monastery reached, we crossed a dark court, lit up by the lights from the temple, whence resounded the cymbals, drums, and trumpets.

On our left was a dim light, towards which our guide led us, and then bade us go through such a low and narrow door, that we had to creep, one by one, into the interior of the tent; for it was only an ordinary ïourta ; and I was much astonished on finding myself face to face with the important personage we had come to see, seated on a divan, two paces from the door.

Khoutoukta received us simply and pleasantly, begged us to be seated, and ordered tea, which two lamas at once brought in cups. While conversing, I could examine the personage surrounded by lamas squatted around the divan. He might be forty, was of middle height, and thin and yellow. His shaven head, his bright and intelligent black eyes, his pleased and interested expression, were more characteristic of the Caucasian than of the Mongolian race.

A dark yellow mantle thrown over one shoulder covered his whole body, except one shoulder and arm, and he wore a cinnamon-coloured robe under his mantle. A bolster on his divan, a small table beside it, on which were a lamp and some glass cases containing little copper idols; on another table a bundle of papers with prayers, and his snuff-box which he used perpetually; these completed his furniture.

Simple in manner, he was very dignified, and seemed more like a European, or even a man of the world, than a barbarian from the deserts of Asia.

He shook hands with each of us, and ordered his lamas to take us back to our tents, whence Sosnowsky sent some boxes of bonbons to the high-priest, and a clasp knife to each of the lamas who had accompanied us.

August 3rd. At break of day I was up, and hastened at once to the temple. Crossing the first court, I noticed a beautiful Mongolian girl on the steps of the temple, her eyes lowered, her hands clasped on her forehead, kneeling from time to time and praying earnestly.

I found Khoutoukta quite ready for the sitting. He was in full dress, yellow satin dressing-gown with wide sleeves; on his head a yellow *klobouk* with a turned-up brim and ending up in a point. I saluted him, and made him understand at the same time that I could not speak his language. I then showed him my book, with the sketches I had succeeded in making during our journey, and he and his lamas examined them with mingled interest and curiosity. After this I proceeded to take his portrait in water-colours, and when it was finished they all leisurely examined it, marvelling at the likeness, and chuckling with satisfaction.

Khoutoukta, seeing the bit of indiarubber that I used for

rubbing out pencil drawing, imagined that it was a cake of colour, and took it up to try and make a stroke, but as soon as he felt its elasticity he threw it down frightened, and shaking his fingers as if he had touched something repulsive. I could not help laughing ; the frightened lamas started up crying " Fire ! burning ! " and then Khoutoukta began to laugh himself, and reassured his acolytes. The indiarubber went from one to another, and they all wondered at its efficacy in removing pencil marks. I had my indiarubber goblet in my pocket, so I showed it to them, and turned it outside in ; but they looked at it with repugnance. After which, thanking the great personage for his goodness in sitting to me, I took my leave.

Our interpreter told us that a discussion had taken place among the lamas as to whether they had done right in allowing the features of so saintly a person to be reproduced. They asked themselves why the portrait had been wished for, and whether unpleasant consequences might not result from it. Khoutoukta appeased their anxiety on this head, explaining to them that his portrait had been taken to transmit to their fellow-worshippers in Russia, who have no means of coming so far to greet him. For this reason his portrait would be a welcome gift to them. Nevertheless Khoutoukta would not permit the photographer to take a view of the temple while the lamas were at prayer. He said that, personally, he saw no harm in it and had no objections to make, but that the superstition of the lamas was so great that he would not like to risk their reproaches or incur their displeasure.

August 4th. In the midst of the desert ; population sparse and extremely poor ; no cattle ; the horses frightfully thin ; famished dogs wandering round the camels, and licking traces of blood on the saddles which have just been taken off. The camels are mere skin and bone, and their backs are covered with sores and full of flies. Even a crow, sometimes profiting by the absence of the attendants, comes to peck at the wounds—a horribly repulsive but quite authentic fact.

I was glad at the next station to see the camels unloaded and our luggage put into Chinese carriages, the presence of which was a welcome token that we had nearly reached the end of the desert.

August 5th. Station of Chara-Mouren, the forty-third since Ourga. Neither horses nor carriages ready. I guessed we should not start very soon.

After dinner we went to take our places in the carriages. Cries, threats, and oaths fell thickly upon the Mongolian factotum (*hundé*) and orders were given that everything should be got ready forthwith. Runners were sent in every direction to search for what was needful, but it was now getting dark.

We waited. The noise subsided, then began again louder than before. I heard blows from the nabaïkha, inevitable in the administration of the laws of the steppes. Cries, excuses —but all these did not further our cause in the least. Nine o'clock, ten, eleven, we were still there. The Cossacks and Mongols, dead tired, remained standing about, and not one of the messengers returned. At last Sosnowsky, the interpreter,

and the photographer, who had all pronounced in favour of
continuing the journey, perceiving that their yells and both
had produced no result, consented to remain where they
were.

August 6th. A cold morning. I shivered in my winter
greatcoat. However, the thermometer was at 10° Reaumur.
This is the worst of getting accustomed to 35° Reaumur, the
heat we had in the middle of the day.

As we went along, the Cossack Stepanow came to inform
me that " Not far off were a thousand wild goats behind the
hill." Knowing that he was a keen sportsman, I stopped
the carriage, got the rifles out, and we then climbed the hill
that hid a herd of antelopes. They saw us, and fled. "Fire,
Stepanow!" He fired, and missed; and here we felt painfully conscious that we were not very expert with our rifles.

Station of Tzagan-Choudouk. A quite small tent, with
a new felt on the ground. This is all that is necessary to
shelter us from the sun. I had already lost civilised habits,
and had become as thoroughly a nomad as if I had spent my
whole life wandering. After tea we started again, and I
went to sleep in the carriage, but was soon awakened by the
most frightful jolting over a very stony road ascending the
mountain. Two Mongols on horseback, one old the other
young, who dragged my carriage, were nearly exhausted;
the latter could scarcely keep back his tears, so I ordered
another to replace him. On the other side of these mountains the vegetation becomes richer—a plain carpeted with
flowers, chiefly Siberian asters.

August 7th. A great many inhabitants at the station

re were even some Chinese. The tents in groups of
s and threes, others apart; in the distance some fine
ures, with herds of horses and cattle. Not far from our
s was a field of potatoes surrounded by a wall. I offered
uy some from the owner, who happened to be at the
s, but she obstinately refused, because the law forbids
n to sell what is unripe.

ut the brightness of a silver rouble had such effect that
sold her potatoes and broke her laws, and so we dined
new potatoes in Mongolia. After this repast we con-
ed our journey without having to remain, as usual,
gry till the evening.

o-day we saw the big Lake of Tzagan, now on our left.
he evening we came upon a rather populous town, if one
r judge by the number of ïourtas. It was the town of
gan. Its tents were very clean and well-constructed,
ounded by walls, and ornamented by gardens. We saw
vision for firing—dead branches and brushwood; and
ep grazing all around.

ight had fallen, the air was cool, and the Mongols
med themselves round the logs on which food was being
pared. My guide stopped, not at the door of a tent,
at a porch, and I saw our carriages in a courtyard,
ounded by a curious throng. Everything in this abode
new. In the courtyard were four little Chinese houses
travellers. I entered the one already occupied by our
ow-travellers, and settled myself in a small room with a
dow pasted up with paper; under this was a couch ot
r, covered with a carpet, round the sides benches along

the walls and a little low table. The whitewashed walls
were covered with drawings of deformed horses, or of scenes
that the censor had certainly not examined. There were
also several Chinese and Manchu inscriptions, which were
incomprehensible to us, as our guide understood neither
language. The ceiling of bamboo trellis-work was covered
with paper, torn in various places.

August 8th. It is a very long time since I slept beneath a
roof. We left early. The lake of Tzagan-Nor was still
visible. Our road skirted a smaller one, the low and muddy
banks of which are covered by a quantity of solid foam,
forming a sort of wrack. The water of this lake, which is
salt, is thick, and looks like a mixture of milk and water.
Cranes, snipes, and ducks frequent its banks.

While waiting for relays I took notes, and inquiring
minds observed my writing, and commented on its rapidity.

August 9th. The photographer has taken some views. I
profited by this to sketch some types of Mongols of the
Tzacker race. They differ from the Khalkas, whose country
we have come through, by their cheek-bones being less high,
their eyes less almond-shaped, and the profile more regular.
They also differ in costume, and the women in their head-
dress. We had a visit from a singer and itinerant musician,
who played the flute and an instrument I can only call a
violin because he played on it with a bow. The tone of
his song was gay, bright, and energetic. It is needless to
add that I did not understand a word of it.

The locality became more and more hilly. We could see
that we were about to cross a range of mountains, but it

was difficult to make out how high the road ascended in front of us. To our right was a range of hills, with ruined towers, vestiges of the ancient Great Wall. To our left a wall, about the height of a man, behind which, I fancied, a terrible precipice. Perhaps a river flowed beneath, watering the plain now steeped in mist, and on the horizon of which we could still just see the distant blue mountains. This was all that I could distinguish, and I regretted more than ever that we were obliged to travel by night.

Our equipage now entered a courtyard crowded with carriages, horses, and mules. Chinese and Mongols bustled about in all directions. There was a row of little buildings on each side of the courtyard, with the kitchen in a separate little house at the end, and this was the hotel of Nor-Dian. A boy of about fifteen, with shaven head and dressed in white, ran towards us. He talked to us without my being able to recognise one of the words we had learnt during our journey.

"Ah! my dear boy," I said to him, "vainly do you chatter; I should understand you quite as well if you said nothing."

"What do you say?" replied the boy with astonishment, and then seeing that we did not understand Chinese, he pointed out a door to us and took us to it. We entered a sort of room only as wide as the door and window alongside of each other. To the right of the door was the wall that separated the two adjacent rooms, and to the left was the bed. There was only space for three people; if a fourth wanted to come in, one of the three would have to get

on the bed. The paper of the window hung in strips, and
the room was lit up by a night-light. Our companions, who
had fallen behind, had not arrived yet, and the interpreter
was with them. We were hungry, and had to make ourselves understood as best we could. We therefore searched
our dictionary, and pronounced the words, eggs, bread, salt,
cup, in Chinese, and just as they are written, which, after
all, does not seem difficult—*tsi-dan, mó-mo, yan, van.* The
boy could understand nothing, so we then shewed him the
book with the same words written in Chinese. When he
had read them, he exclaimed to the effect "that we might
have said it long ago." Then he asked us the quantities,
which were easily described on our fingers. He soon brought
us boiled eggs, salt, and bread, or rather spiced wafers.

August 10*th.* I got up early to take a look round the
neighbourhood, which I had not been able to see during the
night. I went to a place admired by all former travellers,
and from whence I could see China itself for the first time.
I could also see bluish mountains hid in mist.

Of the ancient Great Wall, only a low rampart remains,
with square towers diminishing towards the top. These
towers are generally placed on the summits of the mountains across which the wall winds. I ascended one of them,
the better to contemplate the view, but had no one with
whom to share all the admiration that I felt at this moment.

It is quite impossible to describe all that the eye took in :
mountains, valleys, gorges, grass-covered slopes, pastures,
farms, lakes. The presence of man is to be felt; everything
is full of life; not of the local village or town life, but the

life of a great State. I would fain have sketched or taken notes, but I was so entranced that it was impossible.

To the east a superb valley, dotted over with Chinese villages surrounded with bushes and trees; farther off, on several levels, chains of mountains, the tops of which were on a level with my eyes. To the west, the ground undulates gradually towards the plain, beyond which are more mountains. On the south, magnificent pasture-land, intersected by the Great Wall with its ruined towers.

En route! It is to-day that we are to reach the town of Kalgan, on the Chinese frontier. We descended the mountain by such a narrow road that two carriages could scarcely pass each other. On our right the Great Wall, cracked and destroyed by centuries, and covered with plants; on our left a slope towards the plain, laid out in artificial terraces, with fields of millet, oats, potatoes, and hemp. As to the Chinese, they are to be seen everywhere, with long plaits, and bareheaded, attired in a white shirt and blue trousers. The women are nearly naked, and only wear one petticoat and braces; the children, whose heads are decked with flowers, are naked, or nearly so. What strikes one most is the sudden transition from the barren desert of yesterday to the fertile and populous country of to-day. It seems like a never-ending village of small houses, covered with verdure, gardens, and flowers, the whole extremely tidy and pleasant to the eye. This, then, is that swarming human ant-hill, China!

At the foot of the mountain we reached a gorge, which in the rainy season becomes a rapid and dangerous torrent.

When this occurs, the town of Kalgan is without communications till the waters subside. To-day the bed was dry and full of stones.

I saw some Chinese threshing corn with flails similar to ours, and in measured time, as we do. Elsewhere the inhabitants, sitting in the shade of the trees, saw us pass with indifference. Probably the sight of strangers is no novelty to them.

Pausing frequently to look around, I had got far behind with my guide, who with a sign pointed out Matoussowsky seated on the terrace of a house with glass windows and a Chinese roof. It was that of a Russian merchant who had invited us to stay with him—a welcome and agreeable rest after the privations of the desert of Gobi. It was situated in a secluded spot outside the town, and had the advantage ████████████et. Strangers having no right to build, it ██████████on the condition that, on the death of the ██████████it should lapse to the landowners. ██████████hich in one of our country towns would be ██████████er roubles (nearly £800), cost only 1,500 ██████████ Living is very cheap at Kalgan. A dinner of three courses costs 5 roubles (15s. 10d.) a month; in Chinese money this is 12,000 sapeques. The best places in the theatre cost 1,500 sapeques—little more than 2s.

CHAPTER III.

August 11th. Farewell to the steppes of Mongolia! Their memory will not take long to fade before the impressions of populous China.

The Mongols who had accompanied us thus far came to bid us farewell, and were now to return to their homes. One of the lesser officials had done half the route with us, so I wished to take his likeness as a souvenir. I took his portrait, and in return gave him some trifles, such as a burning-glass, which had always enchanted him, a packet of needles, a copy-book, a pencil, and a clasp-knife, which he made me understand by signs he should use for shaving his head. After breakfast we went to call on such of our fellow-countrymen as are to be found here, amongst others, on the postmaster of the route between Kiachta and Tien-Tsinn, after which we all walked to Kalgan, or Tchang-Tzia-Koou* in Chinese. This town is in a gorge formed by rocky moun-

---

* In "Madame de Bourboulon's Travels" this name is spelt Tchang-Kia-Keou.

tains, at the foot of which are rows of small houses and shops, which form the suburbs, or, rather, the *extra muros* quarter of the town.

We noted the crumbling wall of the town and its tower ; it comes vertically down the hillside, and crossing the defile surrounds the town, and but for the gate, Kalgan would be impenetrable. Here, then, correctly speaking, is the actual entrance to China, and this is the reason that both Chinese and Mongols call Kalgan " gate " or " passage." At the end of the gorge this wall is supported by a quay built of compact blocks of limestone strengthened by cement and bars of iron, so as to resist the pressure of the water during the inundations. This quay, though only about one-half the height of a man, is so wide that we could not see anything at the base of it.

The defile of which I have just spoken joins another, which in the same way answers the purpose of a road at one season, whilst at another they both form beds for the two mountain streams, which rapidly become torrents of sufficient volume to carry away such men or animals as may happen to be in their course.

After examining this quay we turned our steps towards the gates of the town, of which there are two, the one wide and modern—the other small and ancient, a regular hole, through which one has to crawl to get past it.

This ancient *koou* (opening) is a characteristic monument of the past, testifying to the terror inspired by the barbarians of the North in the breasts of the Chinese, and the precautions which they took in their intercourse with them.

I was attracted by this historic hole, and therefore directed my steps thither with one of my compatriots. Behind this entrance was another very high wall, which had to be got round before we could find a street into the town. The wall of the town was crowned at this spot by a pretty temple, and about eighty. stone steps led up to it. A boy of about fifteen, most probably attached to the service of the temple, obligingly offered to show us the way to it. My attention was at once drawn to the deformed, wicked-looking idols in it, represented in martial attitudes, with their weapons in their hands or their fists clenched, ready, it seemed, to crush the first who should venture past them. I never could understand how they could put monsters of this sort into their temples, and still less how they could address their prayers to them.

A European, who is accustomed to see large open spaces in churches, in which hundreds and thousands of believers may meet together, is at once struck by the absence of an aisle ; but this is explained by the Chinese having no general worship. The Chinaman says his prayers when he feels the need of them, just when he likes, and not at fixed hours or on a special day. In the temple of which I speak there was scarcely room fôr fifty people.

On the altar were some cups and a cake, wax candles, and some ornaments, which I had no time to examine. I could only linger on the terrace, which was adorned with plants and tanks containing the little red fish so much sought after in China.

We returned to the house, where a Russian dinner awaited

us prepared by a Chinaman. It appears that formerly a Russian cook at Pekin had taken pupils, whence sprung a whole generation of Chinese experts in the Russian culinary art.

August 12th. To-day we were invited to dine with a Chinaman to whom we had consigned several poods* of silver from his correspondent at Maï-Maï-Tzeng. He came himself to thank us and to ask us to dinner, and had even sent carriages to drive us to his house.

The only Chinese equipage is a carriage on two wheels. Their carriages for town use are even smaller than their travelling-carriages; you have to double up your legs in them, and they shake you to pieces. I therefore declined to get into one, and went on horseback. The dinner took place at an hotel, and consisted of forty-five delicious and dainty courses. One could not desire better, but it annoyed me greatly to be unable to carry on any conversation. After dinner we adjourned to our host's own house, but of his inner and private life I can say nothing, as we only saw the reception-room and the servants.

I seized the opportunity and took a portrait of our host, which gave him great pleasure. The servants held their sides with laughter, and he himself, to show me how pleased he was, held his hands together with the fingers upraised, which is their highest expression of satisfaction.

Afterwards we went out on foot to see the town. We entered some fruit-gardens and vineyards, where the proprietors gave us grapes, but would accept no money. The

* A Russian weight.

vines grow like small creepers, forming graceful arbours, and are not on vine-stocks, as in Europe.

Going along the road we stopped at a tailor's establishment, where there were about thirty workmen, cutters and ironers, who used hollow irons full of live coals, and others who gummed the collars to stiffen them. All these workmen are paid by the day and fed. I asked to taste their food; the master consented, and ordered one workman to take me to the kitchen, and another to hold a fierce watch-dog that was in the yard. Two pans on the fire, one containing vermicelli, the other pork and vegetables, or rather vegetables and pork, seeing that there was very little of the latter, and some little pâtés made with garlic and lard, is what I saw there. This nourishment, without being very tasty, is relatively suitable enough, but I learnt that they were only allowed meat every five days. .

It was difficult to distinguish the masters from their workmen. Some of them seemed in bad health; most of them had weak eyes, for, owing to the absence of chimneys, the rooms as well as the streets are dense with smoke.

We also went to a locksmith's establishment, where they were roughly forging some large copper vases; and to a butcher's, where I sought in vain for dog's flesh.

The crowd in the street was as great as it is with us on a market-day. The inhabitants are generally thin and of middle height; their skin swarthy, but by no means yellow. There were no whites, but I saw a good many women painted red and white, but—great heavens!—like our masks in the time of the carnival. In one of the less-frequented streets I saw a woman of forty or fifty years old dressed so peculiarly that I stopped to sketch her. The Chinese noticed this, and attracted the woman's attention to it, which made me fear that she would disappear; but, on the contrary, she remained, and even appeared flattered by it. She had a band on her head, a small bodice without braces, very wide trousers, and quite tiny boots; her bosom and arms were entirely naked.

The town itself is very badly kept. In certain parts the air is not fit to breathe from the smells and miasma. The streets are not very narrow, but in the lanes two carriages can scarcely pass each other; therefore when a driver enters at one end, he screams at the top of his voice to prevent any one coming in from the other. Notwithstanding this precaution, two carriages often do meet each other. The horse must then be unharnessed, the carriage put on end with the shafts in the air and turned, or else the horse has to be backed to the opening of the lane. The streets are paved, or rather they once were, but the pavement has never been repaired. There are great retail shops of all sorts. I never saw one shop where tea was sold, but there are wholesale tea warehouses. On the other hand, garlic may be seen in every corner, laid out in heaps, or hung in bunches under the roofs and windows. The Chinese eat an enormous quantity of it.

Numerous signboards are hung perpendicularly or nailed over the doorways of the houses, with inscriptions or symbolical signs; this gives the whole a most picturesque effect. They sell everywhere: in the shops, in the streets, in the market-places; and every sort of merchandise; above all, fruits and slices of melon covered with dust.

To finish up, I must add that I met no sick people in the town; and my fellow-countrymen assured me that there exists neither hospital, infirmary, nor asylum for children.

On our way home we chanced to see an itinerant theatre established on an open space; a crowd of men hurried towards it, the women looked on from their carriages. All through the play the same noise prevailed. The actors perspired at every pore in their attempts to make themselves heard; a noisy band increased the hubbub of the crowd, and the bird-fanciers trysted each other at this spot, convinced that in the midst of all this row their birds would improve their singing powers. I am even told that the very knowing go up to the top of the mountain, from whence the distant hum of the town may be heard, to educate their birds to a more agreeable note.

August 14th. Many discussions as to our start, during which a Chinaman arrived on the scene, rather tidily dressed, and with velvet boots, and saluted us in Russian. Having heard of our journey at Kalgan, he came to offer his services as interpreter, or as an ordinary servant. I was quite enchanted with this good fortune, which seemed sent straight from heaven. We should thus have two interpreters, and I should now have some one with whom I could explore the towns; I should be able to ask questions, and examine and hold conversation with the Chinese. The man was a Christian, for whilst still a child he had been taken to Siberia, where a Russian merchant had him baptised and named Theodor.

He made no bargain. "Take me with you," he said. " I will stay a month with you, or two months, by which time you will see what I am worth, and then you can pay me according to my deserts. If you are satisfied with me, perhaps you will take me with you to Russia, where I should like to go, as I have no family, and have nothing to do here." We consented to engage him, and he then ran for his things. Our fellow-countrymen knew him a little; they imagined his only fault to be that he never stayed long in one place, and often changed his abode.

We started after dinner, and as we went through the town noticed a greater stir in the squares and streets, and a compact crowd everywhere, on which we learnt that this was a holiday. A carriage occupied by four Chinese women followed us for some time. The coachman walked along leading the horses, and the oldest of the women held the reins. The other three, who were younger, were inside the carriage, but we could see them quite well. They were all smoking, and were caked with red and white, and looked as if they had masks on. From the elegant carriage and the coachman's get-up, one could guess that they belonged to the higher classes, and they were in fact the Governor's family. In the crowd some Chinese greeted us with their habitual *hao*, without our being able to discover why; one even greeted us in Russian.

Leaving the town, we again entered the mountain pass and reached the station, where we changed our horses and continued on our road all night. Before dawn we saw the crumbling wall of Suen-Hoa-Fou, and fording a stream, reached the gate of the town. The wall is very thick, and the gateway is positively a tunnel; behind this first boundary

there was a higher but older wall in ruins, and covered with
weeds. We followed the space left between the two walls,
which was about fifty paces wide. We then went through a
door in the inner wall, and found ourselves in a little square
court. An official, on crying "Who goes there?" was
answered that "The gentlemen had come," and being satisfied with this answer, allowed us to pass. It was like lords
of the manor entering upon their own. This seemed strange
to me, as we expected difficulties and delays, visits and
inquiries, on the part of the suspicious Chinese.

Nothing of the sort: we passed through a town plunged
in absolute silence; no one but a night-watcher walked up
and down, and from time to time struck his copper gong.
One solitary house was lit up, and we could hear music and
singing, drums and cymbals. Theodor informed us that
they watched over a corpse. After much twisting and turning through this silent city, we arrived at the inn, in a
narrow and muddy little street, although, according to the
interpreter, it was the inn patronised by the officials. Having
travelled a whole day and night, I was so tired that, without
waiting for supper, I threw myself upon a kang and went to
sleep.

August 15th. Perhaps the gentle reader may imagine
that a Chinese hotel somewhat resembles its equivalent in
Europe—a vast two-storied house with endless rooms and
beds, washing-hand stands, linen, &c. He will soon find
that he must perform his ablutions in the courtyard with
a cup; linen and soap are unknown quantities, neither
will he see looking-glasses or brushes. In his cham-

ber the walled couch (kang), covered with a mat as an apology for a bed, a table, and some chairs or stools, neither bottle or water, or still less pegs on which to hang his clothes. The establishment is totally deficient in these things. It only undertakes to supply his meals and to boil the water for his tea.

Our interpreter Andreïewsky, who had been here once before, proposed that we should visit the Catholic Church belonging to the French Mission House. We only found one of the fathers at the Mission House. He was still a young man, and looked exactly like a Chinaman. He wore their costume, shaved his head, and wore a pigtail, but his stand-off manners were neither French nor Chinese. Whether he had special reasons for behaving thus, I know not. If he questioned us about our journey and its object, it was merely out of politeness. On our asking whether the Mission had gained many proselytes, he replied, "About four thousand."

We proposed that he should show us the church, but he made some excuse for not doing it. Our company evidently embarrassed him, so we cut short our stay, on which this reverend father of austere and surly mien, invited us to taste wine of his own manufacture, which was a real treat, as the Chinese make no wine.

The town which was so silent during the night was now really lively and full of people; we ought at least to have spent one day in it, and seen more of those houses with their brilliant signs, their triumphal arches; those temples and their roofs ornamented with figures; this crowd of men, some laden with clothes, others half-naked; some in straw

or bamboo hats, others with nothing on their heads, notwithstanding the suffocating heat; and then all this crowd
of pedestrians and horsemen, carriages and palanquins,
umbrellas, fans, &c.

We left the town by the south gate, and followed a road
hewn out of granite and slate, almost impracticable for
carriages, but we were all on horseback. Around us were
fields, with family burying-grounds distributed over them.
The surrounding mountains were of the wildest character.
They were covered with accumulations of yellow sand, and
on their summits we could see buildings which turned out
to be the monasteries of Chinese hermits. Looking at these
solitary habitations, one asked how men could exist there.
Have they the necessaries of life? Have they water and
fields, so as not to require to come down? I could have
wished to pass some days there, but not having time even to
make the ascent, I tried to scan them with my opera-glass.
I could see little houses, terraces, and balconies, a suspension-
bridge over a precipice, but I could not distinguish human
beings from such a distance.

We then came on to the town of Tzy-Min-Y,* the ruined
walls of which were in sight. The mountains were now of
a pale grey tint and devoid of vegetation. Quantities of
partridges in the valleys and on the slopes, and we shot a
few. Man's presence does not frighten them much; they run
off at a great pace, but they fly very little, and are evidently
gone after, for amongst those we picked up there was one
minus a claw. It was getting late when we entered the

* Probably Ky-Min-Y, according to Madame de Bourboulon.

town of Tzy-Min-Y, but our chief gave orders that we should go on.

Going along, I entered into conversation with the Chinese interpreter, Theodor, who spoke French pretty well, and a little English into the bargain. He had learnt these languages whilst in the service of foreigners at Shang-hai and at Tien-Tsinn. Not altogether devoid of intelligence, he unfortunately had never been educated. He told me that his principal reason for becoming a Christian was that he might go to Russia. I found that he had no religious opinions.

The gospel was known to him by hearsay, but he knew no prayer.

I asked him if the Chinese willingly embraced Christianity, and questioned him as to the number of native Christians. There are very few, he said, and these let themselves be baptised because the missionaries bribe them to do it; but they are not liked, especially the Catholic missionaries, because they torment the people with their religious books, and run down the Chinese faith, whilst exalting their own.

I then questioned him as to the price of various articles, and having no idea of our suprise at the cheapness of everything here, Theodor tried to console me by telling me that although everything between Kalgan and Pekin was very dear, further on everything would be very cheap.

August 16th. I have got hold of Theodor again, and am trying to learn some words of Chinese; it does not sound unpleasant, and seems slightly to resemble Italian. One day, when two Chinese were quarrelling, I thought they were singing, by the intonation they gave to the last syllable of their sentences. Another time, when we were dining at a station, every now and then I heard what I thought was a short song, but it was the waiter calling up the dishes from the cook, standing at the end of the yard.

I must not omit to mention a stone bridge by which we crossed the river Tzin-Tzy-Kho. This bridge is of ancient construction, with five arches and parapets, one of which is in ruins, but the bricks with which it is paved are very well preserved.

August 17th. We now followed a sandy road, strewn with little blocks of granite and quartz, and shut in on either side by a chain of mountains which seemed to meet in the distance and close in the valley.

An arm of the Great Wall was before us, which we reached by a narrow pass leading to the gate of Gouan-Goou. We had to climb rocks hard as iron, and might almost have thought that no one had ever attempted this road before, had it not been for the deep ruts cut in the rocks, which testified to its antiquity ; and one wondered inwardly how it was that the Chinese could put up with such roads. It could not be from idleness. The Chinese are known as the most laborious people on the earth. Nor could it be from ignorance, for in the interior they have admirable roads. Nor could it be from want of means. The Great Wall, which they assert to be 10,000 *li* in length, is there to testify to their resources, and what an amount of science, material, and labour must have been required for its construction!

But I have heard a very possible reason given, namely, that the Chinese leave their roads in this primitive condition in obedience to an ancient law which commands them by all the means in their power to prevent the Mongols, or northern barbarians, from entering their country.

When we arrived at the gate of Gouan-Goou, I prepared to take a sketch of this part of the monument, and then to examine its details. My companions were already far ahead; a single guide waited for me; but I had forgotten everything in the satisfaction of beholding this monument, unique of its kind, and of the remotest antiquity. At its base, the great wall is constructed of huge blocks of granite and of reddish quartz. To get to the top of it, I had to pass through the gate into China, so to speak, and find the staircase which gives access to the bastions. I went up and followed the wall in a northerly direction; it is seven paces wide at the top and paved with brick-tiles about 16 inches square, and about 3½ inches thick. The parapet on the northern side—that is, on the outer side—is about the height of a man; that on the south side is only half as high. In some places the tiles are missing, and the space is covered by red, yellow, and black lichen, but the whole terrace is hidden in thick, tall grass, through which it is difficult to force a path. There are various specimens of the grass tribe, bulbous and cruciferous plants, &c. They cover the cast-iron cannons, which are a yard long, and circular in shape, cast with three bands.

Some of these cannons are still in their embrasures on the

north side of the wall. Some have perhaps been loaded for centuries.

Following the wall in the same direction, I reached a tower, which seemed like a little house with several rooms in it, connected with each other by windows and having a passage on the south side. Its walls were in ruins and filled the rooms with gravel, and the wild vine grew as luxuriantly in it as in a hothouse. Bricks fell out of the walls, or were on the point of doing so. I feared that even my movements might do some mischief. Certain parts were, in fact, quite in ruins, and left perfectly preserved beams exposed to view. Examining this tower in detail, I came to the conclusion that, apart from its defensive properties, it had great architectural value, everything in it being artistically combined. The bricks over the doors and windows were in regular semi-circles, the parapet above was of bricks placed sideways, and the thresholds of the doors were of granite, with designs engraved on the stone. The stone eaves which finish up the gutters were worked into dragons' heads, and the stairs were well designed. All this proves that the construction was not undertaken in haste or solely with a view to the defensive.

The Great Wall at this place was of uniform height. Therefore it followed the surface of the ground on which it was constructed. It rose and fell, and in this way its outline sometimes took a very steep incline, rendering its ascent most difficult. These gradients were impossible on horseback. All along the walls were heaps of gravel from the ruins, and anyone undertaking a journey along the Great

Wall can only have done so on foot, for even then he must have been obliged to go down to avoid the obstructions.

Standing on the tower, I looked upon the silent and lonely scene, going back in thought to the far-off past and the period when this wall was built, and I pictured to myself the swarming ant-hill of workmen, carrying bricks and blocks of granite, mortar, and beams, &c. Tradition tells us that a million men at a time were employed during the building of it.

I was now obliged to rejoin my fellow-travellers, and therefore left the wall, following my guide in silence, as we had no means of understanding each other.

· We met caravans with loaded mules, and in a narrow lane something on one of the mules caught in a parasol which I had fastened to the saddle. The mule-driver set himself at once to repair the evil. It was the first proof of delicate attention I had received from a Chinaman. Farther on a Mongol recognised me as a Russian, and greeted me as if we were old acquaintances.

The road was terrific; it might have been the ruins of a great town after an earthquake. It got dark, and I began to feel cold. Our horses slipped and stumbled, but went slowly along, although stopping every now and then to look right and left, that they might avoid false steps, which they always did succeed in doing, notwithstanding the darkness of the night. At last we arrived, quite exhausted but without misadventure, at Tziui-Youn-Guang, which my companions had already reached.

August 18*th*. We left the station at seven in the morning,

.and passed under a monumental gate of the Great Wall ornamented with bas-reliefs.

Here the villages are quite thickly populated, the vegetation is rich, quantities of fruit, and also of fruit sellers and first-class jujube merchants. Not a house or terrace without heaps of jujubes drying in the sun on mats.

At length the road leaves the pass and goes out on to a plain. We see cultivated fields, millet, garlic, onions, and are struck by the cleanliness and prosperity of the villages and farms that we come across, the carefully swept courtyards and streets, the little houses and walls adorned by brick or tile ornaments, the stone wells most carefully kept, surrounded by a little wall ; and the troughs for the cattle are equally clean, and often hewn out of a block of granite.

We now reached the town of Tchang-Ping-Tcheou, where we had to wait three hours before carriages were found for our baggage. Wandering through the town, I stopped in front of a Chinese who was plaiting bamboo with the greatest dexterity. Beside him a boy, afflicted with an eye disease, attracted my attention, and the Chinese who were around me guessed that I was a doctor.

I heard the word *dai-fou* repeatedly, but without understanding their talk.

The one who was weaving the plaits left his work and disappeared, returning a moment after with his little girl, whom he presented to my notice, bowing before me and saying something by which I understood him to ask for my advice. The child was suffering from rickets ; I signed to him to follow on to the hotel, and through the interpreter prescribed treatment. A few minutes later I was assailed by a crowd of invalids, who all had their complaints and asked me to come to their aid. Unfortunately, it was impossible to bring immediate relief to most of them. Many had goîtres, and I was assured that in a neighbouring village every creature, not excepting the children, suffered from the same thing.

Not having been able to procure carriages, it was decided to change all the baggage on to horses and mules. My horse being incapable of keeping up with the rest, I remained behind and alone with my guide, the two interpreters being always attached to the person of the chief. I pursued my road as peaceably as if I had been in the suburbs of St. Petersburg, and very shortly entered the populous village of Cha-Kho, which lined the road on both sides. Raised pavements ran along houses covered with inscriptions in large letters, and there were a good many inns with their doors standing open, which doubtless were well known to my Rosinante. The poor beast, which was going at a foot-pace, seeing one of these doors, quickened its pace and made straight for it. With the greatest difficulty I checked it and turned its head. I was, however, unable to persuade it to go on. Whip and spur could not induce this famished and exhausted horse to advance another step. The Chinese who happened to be in the street laughed, and a half-naked strong young fellow took the animal by the bridle to force it to go on; but it was useless; it stuck out its head without advancing an inch. There was nothing left for me to do but to get down and wait for my guide, who had got behind, and I installed myself on the bench of a neighbouring inn. I was immediately surrounded by a crowd of Chinese, and the first comers settled themselves opposite me, leaning their elbows on the table and their heads on their hands, examining me curiously. I submitted to this examination with a certain amount of enjoyment, and taking my tobacco from my pocket, I proceeded to roll up a cigarette. The spectators then began to discuss among themselves whether I was going to eat it or smoke it. They examined every-thing—the tobacco, the cigarette, the paper, and cigar-case ; all these were strange to them, as they only smoke pipes. At last I took out my flint and steel, a small wheel revolving by means of a spring, which in turning produced a sound from the friction against the flint, the sparks then lighting up the wick. This sound frightened them at first, but as soon as they saw the lighted wick all their right hands were stretched out towards me with their fingers raised, their sign of approval, and I could hear the word *hao*, which means good. Whilst awaiting my guide I wrote out my notes; my writing interested them greatly, and they stooped over me examining it attentively, as if they were able to read what I had written. I sat there as comfortably settled as if I were at home ; no one came to ask if I needed anything, or why I stopped there without ordering anything. At last a waiter addressed me by signs, and from his discourse I gathered two words, *ma fou*, " guide," and *tzau*, " fusil," which made me understand that my guide had passed with-out noticing me in the crowd.

I got back on to the horse to try and overtake him, but

the horse would not stir. A Chinaman tried to help me,
and ended by pulling off the bridle, to the untold satisfaction
of at least a hundred spectators. Not wishing any longer to
be a laughing-stock for this crowd, I got down, and having
re-adjusted the bridle I went on foot, leading the horse,
which this time allowed me to have my way. At the end of
the road, taking advantage of a lead from another horseman,
I again mounted, and this time the horse condescended to
follow the rider.

Further on I detected my guide looking everywhere for
me, and we both arrived somewhat late at the station where
we were to spend the night.

August 10*th*. Thus we shall not make our entry into
Pekin in the dark.

Sheltered by the shadow of weeping willows and larches,
we at last entered a wide, and at present, owing to the
floods, a very muddy street in the suburbs of Pekin, at the
end of which, surmounted by enormous and curious bastions,
we could see the walls which surround the capital. No
sooner had we entered this street than I could perceive a
change in the air; it was so charged with unpleasant emana-
tions that for the time I longed to be deprived of the sense
of smell. The Chinese, their children and male-nurses,
horses, donkeys, and mules, all form one seething and
brawling mass. Coal merchants, undertakers, butchers,
blacksmiths, hawkers crying or chanting their wares. Woe-
ful beggars with unshaven heads begging for alms; a
dead horse in the middle of the street; camels chewing
their food; an enormous bazaar, through which we rode

towards the walls ; this was the picture unfolded before our eyes.

The tower, with four rows of empty embrasures, was already visible. Two or three of them had been boarded up, and had black and red circles painted on them, probably representing cannon mouths. The walls which surround Pekin are very high, and even at some distance one has to throw one's head back to enable one to see its crenelated edge. A canal skirts the wall, over which some bridges are thrown. We went through a gate which gave us an opportunity of proving the thickness of the wall, and entered a space surrounded by similar walls. This space is planted with trees, and on it a temple built of yellow tiles.

We entered the town through another gate, of which there are sixteen, each surmounted by a tower ; and followed a wide, unpaved, dusty street, in which an immense crowd hurried to and fro, some on foot, and many on asses adorned with bells.

Under the trees, and sheltered by parasols, shopkeepers sold fruit in plates and cups, and dressed dishes ; the whole covered with a good layer of dust.

Farther on the neighbourhood changed; the shops and the crowd suddenly disappeared, the houses seemed deserted, and only occasionally a man or a woman might be seen peeping out of a half-open door.

We next passed under a red tower newly painted, and built of wood on stone foundations; at the top it had a gallery and colonnade supporting a tiled roof; two streets crossed each other at right-angles beneath it. We then

turned down another street to the right, the middle of which
seemed raised like an embankment.   The houses sloped
down from it and were only one-storied.   They all had
artistically decorated shops or warehouses ; the *façades*
carved with fretwork, gilt, or simply lacquered.

The designs of these carvings were very varied and elaborate.   Entire poems were represented on some of the houses ;
others were embellished with flowers, bouquets and garlands,
fruit, branches, and some were ornamented with foliage,
animals, and arabesques.

One could not fail to admire the patience of their artists
when one examined all this work in detail, and one may
conclude that the charge for sculpture, which is so heavy in
our country, must be very much less in China.

But besides these splendidly gilt shops, there were rows
of booths covered with rags, and on their threshold filth and
dirt in every direction.   These booths, for the sale of meat,
vegetables, and herbs, have all sorts of different signs, such
as bits of stuff, coloured feathers, &c.

Another wall, and then the street becomes a double arcade.
Under the penthouse between the two gates or arcades, and
in the open air was a restaurant, which must have driven a
thriving trade.   A row of tables with smoking-hot dishes,
fruits, tea-pots full of boiling water, and a great quantity of
china ; this was the bar, and at the sides were tables for the
customers.   Numerous waiters ran about the streets, taking
orders and carrying dishes.   We rode so close to the tables
that we required to be careful not to upset the plates with
our feet.

The air was impregnated with the smell of cooking, tobacco, and opium, and the dust was suffocating. Every-

body screamed at the top of their voices to insure attention.

This gate admitted us into the Imperial City, the central

part of Pekin, also surrounded by a wall. The Tartar army was quartered in this street, and at the end of it a pink wall surrounded that part of the town called the "forbidden quarter," Tzing-Tzen, and enclosed the gardens and palace of the "Son of Heaven." A canal runs along this wall, and over it one can just see the tops of the trees and the artistic roof of several of the buildings of the palace. At one spot a hill rises above the wall, on which are three kiosks covered with enamelled tiles. According to tradition, the hill is composed of coal, and represents the amount consumed in the palace during the siege of Pekin by the Manchus. It was on this hill that the last Emperor of the Ming dynasty committed suicide.

This is all that the traveller is permitted to see of the principal object of interest in this part of the town. I confess that I was rather disappointed, for I had not imagined the Emperor of China to be thus hidden from the eyes of the world. I did not expect to find a neighbourhood of such tottering old houses or such crowds of sordid beggars so close to the palace, &c.

We went through a good many more streets, and over bridges across canals or small streams, and saw a great many walls, which entirely hid the Chinese houses and their home life. We passed the English and French Embassies, and next saw the Russian flag waving over an imposing portico. This was our Embassy, having that of the United States just opposite. M. Popow, the dragoman of our Embassy, was the first to receive us. He showed us where we were to lodge, and then sent us several Chinese servants, who spoke a little Russian, to help us to settle ourselves. We went in full dress to our Ambassador, M. Butzow, who was good enough to give an unofficial tone to this official reception.

He invited us to dinner, and as we had still some time on our hands, we called on several members of the Embassy, amongst others, on the secretary, who informed us that the Embassy had received no notice of our expedition.

The Russian colony in Pekin is divided into two parts, at a considerable distance from each other. The Embassy is in the quarter known as the South Court, and the other quarter, occupied by the religious mission, is known as the North Court. The premises of the Embassy, which are of considerable dimensions, are divided into two parts, the court and the garden. The former is given up to the household, the Cossacks attached to the Embassy, the stables, the kitchens, &c.; and the latter to the Ambassador's house, those of other members of the Embassy, and to the chapel.

Next morning I rose early, and lost no time in making for some eminence, so as to get a general view of the town. I had been advised to go up the wall which separates the Manchu or Tartar quarter in Pekin from the Chinese. I went to it with M. Popow, who was kind enough to accompany me in my walks. This wall is thirty feet high and twenty-five feet thick, a little narrower at the summit than at the base. Inclined planes in the walls give access to the ramparts, but the gate is always locked. The porter opened it with alacrity for a matter of fifteen kopecks, and we followed the ramparts, which were paved with tiles, and here and there covered with flowers and grasses. We proceeded along the wall, whence I hoped to see all the splendours of the town unfolded.

My companion showed me the palace of Bohdokhan, which, as far as I could judge, by no means came up to my dreams or expectations. A grass-grown space; a paved path leading through a sort of shed with three doors into another court, and in the centre of this another edifice, more beautiful than the last, having again three doors; farther on gardens, half hiding a row of unpretentious buildings with blue, yellow, and green roofs. This was about all; distance prevented the study of detail.

My friend pointed out some of the more remarkable monuments, but they were at a great distance, and did not stand out from the rest, so that no very salient point could strike the eye.

From a height Pekin has none of the ordinary characteristics of a great town, but is more like a collection of suburbs, or a large village, divided into thickly planted gardens, in the midst of which one can just barely see the tops of the houses. Its extent can best be understood from the towers on the surrounding walls, which are seen far in the distance. The town is built on a plain, and its northern and western boundaries reach the mountains of Inn-Chan.

I went along the wall about five versts, and came across a considerable number of houses belonging to the men in charge, without being able to discover what they were sup-

d to take charge of. These little houses had courts and
ens, and domestic animals about the doors.

he noise of the town scarcely reached the top of the wall,
from time to time I heard a sound which I was at a loss
account for. My companion explained to me that this
inal music was produced by the flight of pigeons, to the
s of which were fitted whistles made out of bamboo-bark.
y were little pipes which passed under a feather in the
, and the resistance of the air produced the sound in the
es.

hey say that these pipes were originally meant to keep
ds of prey off the pigeons, but after a time they developed
o musical instruments. The Chinese seemed very fond
his music, as one heard it everywhere, and it was by no
ans unpleasing.

s we returned home we came to the principal street in
in, called Ho-Da-Min, and went up the tower over a gate,
t we might see a great funeral procession. It was
ttered over nearly three quarters of a mile, without being
unbroken mass of people. Those who took part in it were
ded into groups at regular intervals. Some carried
bolical signs, others flags and parasols of a particular
d, to denote the rank of the deceased; others held copper
bals, which they performed upon with vigour, but the
se of the cymbals could not overpower the heartrending
entations of the hired mourners. Another group accom-
ied the carriage and the palanquins belonging to the
eased. Another bore the corpse on a bier, placed on an
rmous and heavy litter. This last group numbered at

least sixty people, all dressed in green, with brilliant coloured spots. The hearse was followed by carriages containing the family and the friends of the deceased, who were all in mourning, that is to say, in white. Thanks to all this noise and pageant, this usually sad ceremony had something rather joyous than solemn in its nature. The hearse, draped with scarlet silk, had gilt ornaments on the top, and four large flat gilt chains came down the sides, and were held by the men.

All these funeral trappings and symbolical signs and vestments can be hired, including the mourners, who are only beggars. To these a burial is a real treat; they cover their rags with beautiful garments, their dirty heads with dress-caps, and gaily march across the town, jesting or talking with each other, and looking forward to the pay of the tzy-fan, or dinner, which awaits them when the ceremony is over.

When we got back I found Chinese merchants in the Embassy yard, who pay the strangers a visit every day to offer them rare articles which it would be difficult to find in the shops, and this also saves them the trouble of going into the town. Their prices were enormous, so we simply turned them out of doors, forbidding them to return. The Chinamen do up their parcels and go away, only to return next day with the same articles, and others besides, still sticking to their original prices. At last they give in, but even in the end they secure a huge profit. The following day we visited the home of our mission in the North Court, four miles distant from the South Court. Surrounded by walls like the Embassy, it comprises a garden, a chapel with a small belfry, and a building in which dwell the members of the mission. The Superior at this time was the archimandrite, Father Palladine,* well known to the learned world by his works on the Chinese language and literature.

They all wear the Russian and not the Chinese costume, as the missionaries from other nations are in the habit of doing. They lead a very retired life, having very little intercourse with the natives, for they are convinced of the futility of forced conversions. Their doors are open to all those who desire religious discussion with them; consequently the Chinese hold them in greater respect than the Catholic missionaries, who torment them, and try to impose their religion upon them.

I ought to say something on the arrangements for watering the streets of Pekin, which I had an opportunity of seeing on my way home. It is done with water taken from the puddles and ponds at the corners of the streets. These ponds are first filled with rainwater, and all the sewage goes into them as well; this muddy, dirty, stagnant water, covered with film and decaying matter, contains organic detritus and gases that collect and rise from its surface. The Chinese water the streets from these ponds to get rid of the dust, which towards evening becomes suffocating. The gases and miasma fill the air, the odour becomes intolerable, and never in my life was my sense of smell put to such suffering as during this process of hygienic watering. I

* Died at Marseilles the 6th Dec., 1878, when returning to Russia.

thought I should suffocate, whilst the Chinese, as if totally unconscious of it, appeared absolutely indifferent to these smells. The poor creatures buy their experience with their health and their lives: epidemics of small-pox and typhus carry them off by thousands, and most of the population suffer from sore eyes. But Pekin had once a network of sewers, of which some vestige may still be traced. They are canals formed by masonry and cement, not very far below the surface of the earth.

Everything in this town is going to rack and ruin, if one may judge by what one sees on every side—trumpery side by side with gold, ruins next to marble bas-reliefs and precious carvings; but the artistic and noble remains of antiquity put all that is modern into the shade. This town is not, however, less full of interest, as it is the centre to which the life of this people converges, and the mainspring of all its material and intellectual riches.

Two Catholic missionaries having called upon us, politeness required us to return their visit, and to reach their mission-house we had to go across part of the imperial town, through a quarter somewhat remarkable for its beautiful gates, like triumphal arches; we also crossed an enormous marble bridge, Youï-He-Tziao, with two triumphal arches. It is thrown across a great pond called Lian-Hua-Tchi. The banks of the pond are masses of greenery, and planted with trees, under the shade of which are built a variety of small houses, kiosks, temples. Steep bridges span the streams which empty their waters into the pond. But all these do not combine to make so interesting a landscape as the reader might perhaps imagine, for the buildings are diminutive, and the pond is very large.

At the Catholic mission-house we were received by Father Favier, a very pleasant French missionary, who took us into the reception-room, which was tolerably comfortable, and ornamented with pictures and all sorts of Chinese curios.

The reverend father was highly, I may say intensely, interested in our future journey, and, with the aid of a map, examined in detail the route we intended taking. He seemed to have some anxiety as to the designs of Russia, and asked us if we did not intend to make a railway between Russia and China. Then he took us over the library, as well as over the natural history museum, chiefly formed from the careful collections of Father Armand David.

This tolerably large hall is full of stuffed birds, mammalia, reptiles in bottles, and cases of insects and minerals. From the museum we went to the light and pretty but modest church. On the left side of the colonnade stood four Chinese women, and others were seated on square cushions. Although our entry disturbed them slightly, they continued their prayers; a young girl we especially noticed remained on her knees, with her head in her hands. Father Favier went up into the gallery and played on the organ. I was deeply impressed by the silence which reigned throughout the temple, the great voice of the organ, and the sight of these women, belonging to a nation that for centuries had resisted all external influences, praying before the image of Him who has said that there shall be one fold and one Shepherd.

Some days later M. Popow kindly joined me to wander

about the Chinese quarter. We went through the gate already known to the reader, leading to a square with houses and shops. This is divided by the Hou-Tzeng-He River, protecting the town, which is crossed by a triple stone bridge, well known to Europeans as the Beggars' Bridge, because beggars make it their shelter and meeting-place.

At this moment no small number of the members of this confraternity were present. To tell the truth, it was difficult to pass them without an exclamation of pity and fear. Even the young ones of about five-and-twenty are all dreadful to look upon, and they are emaciated to a degree that I have rarely seen, even amongst the dying in hospitals. Their dirty and sunburnt skin shows through the few rags that cover them, and the cries of these living corpses cut one to the heart. Their faces express impotent rage or shame, but sometimes light up with a spark of the life that is ebbing from them. Having seen many of these beggars on the road to Pekin, I could not but wonder what impression the appearance of such a type would produce in a European town, for the Chinese do not heed them at all. They lie crouching on the ground, and the crowd walks round them without so much as looking at them.

Just as I passed under the Tzian-Min Gate, which is always blocked with a crowd of people and carriages, a boy of about twelve years old rolled in the dust as if seized with convulsions, and screamed loudly; but the passers-by took no notice, except to avoid treading on him. Even a mule put its head down and threw itself back, carefully picking its steps to avoid crushing him. I know not whence proceeds this indifference to wretchedness on the part of the Chinese. Is it hardness of heart or selfishness, inability to aid them, or contempt for the vices that have brought them to this pass? Europeans who begin by being charitable become hardened at last, for if you give to one, you have the whole band at your heels. Later on, we went down a very narrow side street full of shops, warehouses, and rows of booths, where all sorts of things are sold retail; at every other step we came upon open-air kitchens and smelt butter and grease frizzling in pots into which the cooks threw cakes, pancakes, and cracknells of a fixed weight. And although all these preparations contain a certain amount of dust, they are in such demand that the cooks can hardly supply their customers. We next visited several warehouses which displayed beautiful things, especially faïence and enamelled metals, lacquer, &c. But everything was very dear, and one had to go armed with, not hundreds, but thousands of roubles. Naturally the fixed price at first demanded does not really exist; the article is eventually ceded to you for a fifth or sixth of the original sum. These fictitious prices are not general in China; it is only in Pekin that the Europeans had themselves got the natives into this habit, as they throw about money by way of cultivating the good graces of the Chinese.

On the 30th of August we started on an expedition to the suburbs of Pekin. Fifteen versts to the north-west of the town, at some distance from each other, are three imperial parks: Ouan-Choou-Chan, Youi-Tziouan-Chan, and Sian Chan, comprehensively known under the one name of

Youan-Ming-Youan. These formerly magnificent parks are now neglected, though ruined or partially injured buildings recall their ancient splendour, and likewise the visit of two civilised western nations, France and England, who pillaged the temples and palaces, and then set fire to them. We dined there, on the shore of the lake, in the Ouan-Choou-Chan Park, and we spent the night in the Y-Gouan-Sy temple on beds brought on purpose from Pekin. Only a large volume with pictures in it could satisfactorily describe all that may be seen here. I will give a mere list of the chief features : paths paved with pebbles ; gardens, courts great and small ; circular doors, or shaped like a leaf or vase ; triumphal arches ; a marble boat of huge dimensions (like an island) ; terraces, statues of gods or symbolical animals, staircases and marble balustrades, subterranean passages through the mountains ; canals, ponds, cascades ; kiosks and pavilions with terrific names, such as " Thunder-clouds," or " Gathering Clouds," covered galleries ; lakes, tanks full of red fish, islands leading to each other by bridges ; hills, ravines, grottoes ; endless towers and temples, in which the Emperors have apartments when they come to stay here.

A mass of white marble, enamel, tiles, precious woods, artistic ornaments, the accumulation and toil of centuries, and the whole reduced to ruins by the hand of man. This is what one sees at Ouan-Choou-Chan. Sian-Chan, with its troops of antelopes, is a still more beautiful park.

Next morning we went and visited the monasteries and temples of the neighbourhood, situated in a beautiful spot

at the foot of the mountains.   The peculiarity of the Chinese
monasteries is that very few monks inhabit them.   The
buildings are large, but appear deserted.   They are rarely
visited, and one wonders for whom they and their numerous
temples could have been erected.   The monasteries are
generally well kept up; well-swept, brick-paved, courts are
shaded by venerable chestnuts, salisburies, and other trees ;
the terraces are adorned with plants and rare flowers, but
there is no animation.   The deformed idols in the temples
bear witness to the knowledge of art, as regards sculpture,
being still in its infancy.   Thus in the temple of Ouo-Fo-
Sy, which means Buddha in Repose, he is really lying down
—but in what way ?   The statue, which originally represented the god standing up, has been placed in a horizontal
position, so it is not in the least the attitude of a person in
repose, but merely a statue placed horizontally, and which
gives no feeling of repose, notwithstanding the enormous
pair of slippers placed by its side and corresponding to the
size of its feet.   In two halls of the Bao-Tzian-Sy, the
sufferings of hell and the joys of paradise are represented
by numerous drawings, including twenty-eight infernal
prisons and twelve dwellings in paradise.   In the first
division, the figures grouped in various scenes represent the
most refined tortures of hell.   In paradise they are simply
seated, and seem to rejoice in idleness.

   The monastery of Bi-Youn-Sy, situated higher than the
others, is built in a style which reminds one of the monuments of India.   The temple of this monastery, built entirely
of white marble, is surrounded by three galleries, the highest

of which looks out on a magnificent view. From it the distant mountains and the plain below may be seen, covered with villages and farms, gardens, woods, and pastures, parks, and imperial palaces, and at the feet of the spectator a wood of silver cedars and thuyas.

The monks led us into an enormous building containing five hundred gilded wooden idols, as large again as life-size. They are arrayed as if in a shop, and each has a symbolic sign; some hold cups or teapots in their hands, others animals, or such-like. Some have smiling faces, and others are of terrible and threatening mien.

The shaven and emaciated priest who guided us tottered in his gait, and was apparently a confirmed opium-smoker. He would gladly have received his gratuity and gone off peaceably, but Doctor Bretschneider particularly wished to show me a court in this monastery where he had once spent some days. Accordingly he asked the monk's permission, who pretended not to understand, although the Doctor spoke Chinese quite well. It was, however, a different matter with Popow, and willing or unwilling, he had to give in. We crossed several courts, and he opened the door into the one we wished to see. This basin in the rocks was a charming retreat for a lover of solitude. A spring of limpid water filled a small pond, and around it were masses of moss-covered rocks, wild vines, and shrubs, which were prettily reflected on its surface. The sun penetrated it very seldom, and the trees shadowed it darkly. On an island in the middle of the pond there is a house with surrounding gallery. The strangers resident in Pekin are beginning to hire the temples from the monasteries as summer resorts, but there are very few places where such a romantic little nook is to be found.

At length we had to take the road and again start homewards. We soon lost ourselves in the small village streets and the paths through the fields, which were little known to our guides. Even Popow was obliged to " borrow some intelligence," to use the Chinese expression for asking for information. The Chinese were very willing to direct us, and two young men noticing that we did not know our way, accompanied us, showing us every turn to take. This is done in hopes of a reward, which strangers never refuse. These guides start up even when not required, and when they are told you have no money, they say they will trust you, and guide you all the same, quite certain that the debt will not be allowed to stand.

Continuing our road, we entered the park of Youi-Tziouan-Chan, that we might see an enormous tower on the top of a high hill. A very inconvenient flight of slate steps is the only means of reaching it. This tower is hexagonal and six-storied, connected by a spiral staircase. Every story is of equal height, and has a chamber with three windows or doors, as they are down to the ground. There is no parapet or balustrade, and the least imprudence or passing giddiness would precipitate you below. Three niches are arranged down each side of every room, adorned with hideous figures of idols, and before them a small table serves as an altar to place offerings upon.

This tower, which is constructed with much care, is quite

new, but full of filth and dust. From the windows of the
sixth floor a splendid view is to be seen, but I could not
have stayed there without something to lean on ; my head
began to go round and my breath to fail me, and I hastened
to rejoin the others, who awaited me below.

After dining on the same terrace as yesterday in the
Ouan-Choou-Chan Park, we quickened our pace so as to be
back in Pekin before the gates were shut, that is before
sunset. We should otherwise have to spend the night outside
the town. M. Popow and I were on horseback, but the
Embassy doctor and Matoussowsky were on donkeys. The
former, who could not endure the braying of an ass, happened
to be on one which simply never ceased braying. This, as our
conductor explained, was because he heard another donkey
to the east (the Chinese describe the right and left by the
cardinal points). Night was drawing nigh, and all those we
met recommended us to get on as fast as we could ; so
putting on all speed, we were finally able to avoid being
locked out.

At length a flash of lightning darted from the sky, a clap
of thunder rent the heavens, and the rain began to fall in
large drops. The merchants installed near the gates began
to collect their wares and rush into the gate as fast as
possible, with a whole crowd of others. We managed to get
shelter under it without getting off our horses, thinking the
rain would only last a few minutes. The width of the wall
of Pekin is so considerable that a whole crowd can take
shelter under it or its penthouse. There were two carriages
and several loaded mules and donkeys, besides ourselves.

The rain fell in torrents ; bursts of thunder succeeded each other rapidly, resounding under the roof and mingling with the terrific cries of the crowd, which can never resist setting up a noise. The metallic sound of a gong now warned us that the gate would soon be closed. Then the noise and turmoil only got louder. All of a sudden I heard a cry from an individual which sounded as if some horrible accident had happened to him.

" What is the matter? What is the meaning of that scream ? " I asked my companion, who seemed to pay no attention to it.

" It is the order to close the gate ; that is their usual way of expressing it."

" Is that all ? I thought someone was being assassinated."

The gatekeepers closed the two wings with some difficulty, and I heard the lock creak.

To be imprisoned with this screaming crowd, and not be able to understand a word of their talk, had a very disagreeable effect, and my thoughts flew to the massacre of Europeans in June, 1871, suggesting how easy it would be for them to get rid of two strangers if they took it into their heads.

Meanwhile the rain fell steadily, the sky remained overcast, and the night was dark, so I proposed to my companion that we should go to an hotel.

" But we have no money with us," said he, " and you do not know what the Chinese hostelries are. We should arrive there soaked, and should find neither beds, nor sheets, nor anything else, and that is how we should have to spend the night. The best we can do is to try and get home, but on this dark night I might lose the way in the lanes, and I should find no one 'to borrow intelligence' from; I will ask if someone will be good enough to accompany us."

He addressed this question to the Chinese who surrounded us, but not one of them responded. He repeated his proposition, this time raising his voice, and promising a liberal recompense; no one moved, no one was willing. The situation was not cheerful, and we shivered in our thin greatcoats. At last a Chinese consented to lead us, and without alluding to the promised recompense, he came out from under the roof and told us to follow him. It crossed me that he might play us a trick, and at some moment leave us alone in the rain, and I confided my fear to M. Popow. "It is quite possible," he replied, "but what can we do? Even were this to happen, we should still get home somehow."

We followed him through the streets; the rain continued falling, and in a few minutes we were soaked to the skin. Flash after flash of lightning changed darkness into light. We could see the lighted lanterns in the shops and the tradesmen playing chess, drinking tea, and talking together. But these lanterns did not light the streets. We had to take care not to fall into some pond, for it is well known that men as well as horses and mules come to their death in these sloughs. Thanks to the continuous lightning, we were able to see some steps in front of us and advance slowly. As to the poor Celestial, he had nothing but a pair of trousers on, and carried his shoes in his hand that he might not lose them in the mud, sometimes going up to his knees into the water.

The rain still continued, and as a climax to our woes, a cold wind got up. Our teeth began to chatter, but this was only temporary and we soon got over it.

A little farther on our guide began to complain of the cold. We were sorry for him, but his iron constitution and his fortitude filled us with astonishment ; we agreed to give him 12,000 sapeques—quite a fortune to a Chinese, to whom a good dinner only costs 100 sapeques.

At last we reached the Marble Bridge, and my companion, now seeing that we had gone nearly an hour out of our way, began to reproach the guide, who replied that he had not followed the straight road because he feared he might have got lost in the labyrinth of small streets, and our necks might have been broken over its inequalities, therefore he preferred going farther round so as to lead us by a road less fraught with peril. " Good man," said M. Popow, " his prudence deserves an addition of 6,000 sapeques to his pay." There is a straight road across the imperial city which considerably shortens the way, but unfortunately it is forbidden to Europeans since an Englishman wantonly destroyed a statue. On consulting the guide, he advised our going that way, but begged us not to betray ourselves by uttering a single word, and then he ran on well in front so as to disarm all suspicion of collusion, and should we be stopped we agreed to plead ignorance of the prohibition.

As we advanced, I felt my heart beating violently from

a sense of trespassing on forbidden ground, but probably at this hour and in such weather the officials did not expect trespassers. Perhaps, as often happens in China, they had sought refuge from the rain and the cold somewhere in the depths of the gateway. As we passed it we heard talking; my heart beat still louder. No one saw us, no one hailed us, and in the interval of two flashes of lightning we got safely past.

"Now catch us if you can," said my companion; "we shall soon be at home."

Our guide told us that the voices we heard had only been those of the ordinary Chinese taking shelter, but that the officials slept. At last we reached the final bridge, and came to our own street and the door of the Embassy. Under the penthouse several beggars were asleep, having no other resting place, and on such a bad night the dormitory was in even greater request than usual.

Some days after, Sosnowsky started for Tien-Tsinn, taking the interpreter Andreïewsky with him. I took advantage of this to spend some days in the parks and do some sketching. We were in September, the best season in Pekin. The weather was beautiful, and on the 3rd, with Theodor and two guides, I set out for the temple of Y-Gouan-Sy, where I intended to establish my headquarters, so as to be able to get to the other parks. Our two donkey-drivers helped to carry my small baggage.

Going along the road, I was surprised at the cleverness of the animals, the name of which, "lini," is an abusive epithet in China as well as in Europe. I listened attentively to the driver's conversation with his donkey, and it understood all he said and obeyed without any whip.

"I, I, I!" cried the driver, on which the ass went to the left. Further on the man imitated an old man's cough. "O-ho! o-ho!" and the ass turned to the right. "Trr, Trr, · Ou!" the beast forced the pace and began to trot. "Houaa!" (thou wilt slip), or "Ker-doou!"(a hole, take care), the donkey slackened speed and carefully inspected the road. During our journey we bought maize and potatoes, and just as we had our mouths full of these vegetables, a whole cavalcade of mandarins passed us. It was one of the uncles of the Emperor with his suite, but they passed so quickly that I could only distinguish horsemen completely attired in silk.

Leaving Pekin, we followed a now deserted old road covered by a layer of cement, and unmended, owing to the ruined parks never having been visited by the Emperor since the war. Nevertheless the traffic on it is greater than in most of the provincial towns in Russia. After travelling for four hours we arrived at the temple, and were received by a bright-eyed and eager little old priest with a shaky head. Through the kind thought of my fellow-countryman, a cook had been dispatched the night before, who was to remain with me during the whole of my stay. Directly after dinner I arranged all my things and went to bed early, so as to be up at sunrise next morning.

The paper ceiling of my room was torn in various directions, so I quite expected scorpions to fall upon and sting me. They are very numerous, and the Chinese catch them easily. I asked a Chinese servant at the Embassy for a specimen one day, and in a quarter of an hour he brought me back five. They catch them in the following manner: when they see one on a wall, they blow upon it, and the scorpion immediately puts itself into a fighting attitude, raising the pointed tip of its tail; the Chinese then take it by this appendage, above the sting, and in this position the scorpion can do no harm. Its sting is very painful, and produces a tremendous swelling, but I have never heard of its being mortal.

I stayed ten days at Y-Gouan-Sy, favoured by continuous fine weather. The first thing in the morning, I betook myself to some park where I spent the day collecting insects or drawing, and returned at nightfall to the temple. All the inhabitants of the park knew directly of my arrival, and as it was hinted all over the park in which direction the foreign artist had gone, the whole community was enabled to collect around me. The children came running to see, the old men dragged themselves breathlessly along, painfully climbing the hill, and I was able to satisfy myself of their taste for painting as well as of their respect for artists.

About twenty or thirty grouped around, gazed fixedly on the paper, so long as the drawing was incomplete. They shut one eye to look at it, which the children did too, in imitation of their elders, and spoke in whispers, explaining the drawing to each other, amazed at the rapidity of execution and the likeness, and lavishing their praises upon it. "Hen-Hao! Tzen-Hao, Hua-dy-hao! Tzen-tzen-hao! Igo-yan!" which means, "Very well done; really well done! Well drawn! Very, very well! An exact copy!" And their right hands were raised towards me on every side. They were quite annoyed if their occupations called them elsewhere. "It is time for us to go," said one. "We must go.; time is up," replied another. But they still remained where they were. "Tzoou; let us go," and then off they went, returning several times to repeat "hao," and show me the upright finger.

I soon had so many proofs of their kindness and attention that all my prejudices vanished. I might have been their master, so much did they all seek to obey and be useful to me. I was soon convinced that their hatred for strangers is not so great as is generally supposed, and that it only depends on these strangers to make it disappear entirely.

Thus, one of the mandarins who lived in the park and was at first very haughty, eventually became most kind to me, and other rich or well-to-do people, who had previously passed without taking any notice, subsequently went in search of me and asked the park-rangers where I was, or found out from Theodor whether I had dined and had a good dinner, and all I wanted, &c.

These people, at first so stand-off, afterwards ran up more than once with their teapots in their hands, offering tea to quench my thirst, and shyly asking me to show them my collection of drawings, would say to each other, "It is very well done; never since strangers have had leave to come here have we seen anything so good."

Sometimes the dinner I took with me being more than I wanted, I shared it with Theodor and one of the guides who carried my things. This greatly astonished the Chinese, and they went nearer their compatriot to watch him eat the slice of mutton which he held in his fingers.

The days on which I got back earlier to the temple, I amused myself by joining in a Chinese game, to which my interpreter, Theodor, is devoted. This original game is a fight between crickets, just as cocks or quails fight. This species of amusement, which is very common in Pekin and its environs, gives rise to an important branch of commerce, owing to the different implements required in pursuit of the crickets, namely scissors to loosen the earth or to enlarge the cracks in the walls in which the insects are hidden; wire bells; tubes several inches long and open at the ends; and for each game, two cups, the larger of which has a cover. Those in which the crickets are kept have two little plates for rice and water, and a sort of small sentry-box which serves as a refuge for the insect. A hole is bored in the cover, and by blowing through this the cricket can be forced to come out. The bell and the little tube are indispensable for capturing the insect without touching it, as it might get hurt, and thus disabled for the fight.

More than once I observed Theodor devoting whole hours to searching for and hunting crickets. When he had hunted one from its lair, he carefully covered it with the bell, and when the insect climbed on to the top he presented the tube, into which it immediately entered. Then putting the little tube on to the cups, he would blow into it, and thus upset the cricket: he did the same with the rest of the insects, imprisoning each in a cup.

And now begins the tournament. The owners of the

crickets first settle the conditions of the combat, and above all at what moment the victory is to be declared. The prize which is to be awarded to the winner is also decided, and then the two heroes are let down into an open, flat-bottomed box with perpendicular walls.

These insects, as soon as they come in contact, engage in battle, seize each other by the body, just as men do, and direct blows at each other with their pointed mandibles. They fight till one has to retire or is hurled out of the box. On this depends the joy of the victorious backer, or 'the shame and confusion of the owner of the vanquished cricket. Sometimes the victor is replaced in the box to encounter another opponent. On other occasions both are changed. If the conquered cricket gives hopes of greater prowess in another fight, it is retained, or otherwise restored to liberty with a good deal of abuse.

For instance, Theodor was heard thus to address one of his little wrestlers, "Little villain! thou art not worth the trouble of having nourished thee!"

He greatly amused me by the spirit and earnestness which he put into this game. But it is quite comprehensible, the amount of money lost or won depending on victory or defeat. All the spectators make bets upon the issue.

In the bazaars and streets of Pekin they sell these wrestlers at a price varying from one to thirty roubles, according to the condition of the crickets; and such is the mania among the Chinese for this game, that rich men have lost fortunes over it.

Being obliged to return with Theodor, I quitted my temple with much regret on September 12th, not having nearly finished all I wanted to do. The donkey-drivers were all impatience to return, and ran the whole way, notwithstanding the heat. They appeared to be about eighteen years old. One was strong, but awkward and silent; the other thin, but lively, bright, and an incessant talker. This lad could not be silent for an instant; he sang or talked in different voices so cleverly, that often I turned round, thinking there were at least five people behind me. When this conversation tired him, he would address all sorts of remarks to his donkey, lavishing alternately praises and threats.

We arrived at the outer wall of Pekin, and its towers and buttresses gleamed in the sun. In the town the same thick dust, the same crowd; such a din, that the only time we could hear ourselves speak in the house was when an accident, fire, affray, or such-like happened to be going on. This was the usual thing here; quiet in the streets would have denoted some extraordinary event.

On September 14th we went on foot to the Chinese quarter to see the Temple of Heaven, close to the South Gate. By following the Tziane-Mine Street we reached a large space with the walls of this Temple of Heaven on the left, and opposite to it the Temple of Agriculture. One may be close to them both without being aware of it, as they are completely hidden by walls and gardens.

The entrance gate was closed; M. Popow knocked, and was informed that no one might enter without paying. Fifteen thousand sapeques was the amount demanded; but

we bargained, and finally agreed on seven thousand, a little
more than a rouble. The gate was soon opened, and we then
entered a beautiful alley planted with thuyas and having a
second gate at the other end, which was wide open. But
just as we reached it the Chinese officials ran and shut it in
our faces. Bargaining began once more, and we at last
agreed to ten thousand sapeques, which is about a rouble
and a half. On passing into the sacred enclosure, a large
space opened out before us, turfed over and shaded by beautiful trees, but it appeared totally uncared for. On the left
we came to a building surrounded by a wall and a canal, in
which there was then no water, and this was the Palace of
Abstinence, where the Emperor fasts for twenty-four hours
before offering up sacrifice to heaven. Farther on we went
down another beautiful alley planted with trees, and reached
a terrace paved with tiles and having temples on either side
with conical blue-tiled roofs. The doors being shut, we
could only contemplate the roofs, which are, however, the
most artistic part of Chinese monuments.

And now some words about the sacrificial altar, which is
in front of the south door of the temple, fenced in by a
square low wall, painted pink and covered with aqua-
marine-blue tiles. In the interior there is another circular
wall having four doors surmounted by white marble arches.
On entering, a flight of steps leads to the altar, which is
three-storied, flat-roofed, and possessed of two terraces, the
whole surrounded by a marble balustrade. On the flat roof
there are four marble tables.

Here the Emperor offers up sacrifices to heaven, and in

one of the corners of the square may be seen a furnace behind iron bars, where the offerings of beef and mutton are burnt. We wanted to see the principal temple, but the door was shut, and the priest who was behind it went off, after pronouncing in a solemn voice that whosoever entered the temple would commit a crime. He soon came back, however, and began to bargain with us as to the price of entry. M. Popow becoming impatient, ultimately left him, full of grief and vexation that he had missed such a good chance of making money.

After all the others had gone, I remained to take a sketch, giving a general idea of the Temple of Heaven, and returned home late, to walk in the Embassy garden, listening to the distant hum of the town and the cries of the various hawkers, for in Pekin night brings no cessation of labour.

I would fain have more closely studied the singular habits of this people, but had not the chance of doing so.

I had for some time been looking forward to making acquaintance with a Chinaman of the name of Yan-Fan, an extraordinary man from every point of view, and went to his house on the 26th of September with the photographer and M. Popow, who was always ready to accompany me when he had any time to spare. Yan-Fan's house was situated in the Chinese town, not far from the Embassy. We were received by his son, a young man of about twenty, who invited us to follow him across the numerous passages, courts, and gardens, and took us into his father's study, which had glass windows, and was furnished in European style. I also observed several gas-burners. Yan-Fan was not long making his appearance, and at once apologized for having kept us waiting.   He was a man of about fifty years of age, short, rather fat, and wearing a somewhat scanty moustache.

After the usual remarks he went on to talk of science,

medicine, photography, and chemistry, but it was most difficult to sustain such a conversation through an interpreter but little familiar with the few scientific terms of the Chinese language.   To relieve the awkwardness, I asked if we might be allowed to see his house, with its gardens and courts, and whether I might take some sketches, to which he at once consented. Before going into the garden, Yan showed me a little gasometer which he had established for lighting his house. He told me that in the not far distant future he hoped to obtain the monopoly of supplying the town with gas. He had, moreover, a telegraphic apparatus, as much from the love of science as for any practical purpose, in his house; also a photographic laboratory, and a whole shed full of steam-engines which he had obtained from Europe.

There were but few trees or flowers and scarcely any vegetation in his garden, but instead there were kiosques, pavilions, artificial rocks, grottoes, staircases, bridges, aquariums, &c. I settled down to take a sketch, and to enliven the landscape Yan and his son and two of his wives consented to pose for me, the photographer reproducing a bird's-eye view of the whole. The wives were dressed in silk, with their hair artistically arranged; they were smeared with white paint and their lips with red; their eyebrows formed two black arches, and their almond-shaped eyes shone brightly. After endless compliments from Yan as to my artistic talent, I painted, at his request, some fruit and flowers on two white silk fans, and then we took our leave. We had to make haste, because on that day the closing of the gates between the Chinese and Tartar towns was to take place earlier than usual, owing to the absence of the Emperor.

On our road the Chinese, who knew that we lived in the Tartar quarter, warned us to make haste; but we were just too late: the gate was shut in our faces when we were within a few yards of it. M. Popow addressed himself in vain to the porter, who only made the key grate in the lock and gave no answer. As happens every day, there was a crowd of belated people on both sides of the gate. Close by lived a police constable on duty, and M. Popow sent me in search of that official to try and get a special permission to pass, but he was absent, and the two subordinates left in charge did not venture to take the responsibility of infring- ing the regulations, although they treated us with every mark of respect. They explained that they should thereby risk their heads being exposed on the morrow in cages over the gateway.

At this moment we were overtaken by Yan's son, sent in pursuit by his father to invite us, in the case of our being too late, to return and spend the night at his house. My compatriot would not at first consent to this kind arrange- ment, but on the young man assuring us that if we did not go with him his father would come and fetch us himself, we were obliged to accept, and the whole surrounding crowd accompanied us, out of sheer curiosity, to the door of Yan's house.

The study which we had previously visited was now lit up with gas, and in addition to the jets on the walls, an indiarubber tube led the gas to a lamp on the table.

Whilst waiting for dinner, Yan showed me his aneroid barometer, and two microscopes, which he did not quite understand the use of. He knew many chemical terms, and the properties of bodies, but having no sound knowledge of chemistry, he often seemed confused, and it was impossible for me to teach him the science in one evening.

After tea the dinner was served in European fashion, with knives and forks and plates, marked with ornamental monograms, but there were neither napkins or tablecloths. The master of the house tried to use a fork himself, although most of the time he ate with his fingers, spitting on the ground at every moment. The old servant who waited upon us breathed like a grampus. As a polite attention, dinner was followed by coffee, which the Chinese never drink.

I sketched a likeness of the master of the house, which he ran to show his wives, and they sent him back with three fans, which they requested I would embellish as a remembrance. I confess that these three fans made me realise that polygamy has its disadvantages.

At one in the morning we retired to rest, and found our beds furnished with mattresses, pillows, and blankets, but with no sheets or pillow-slips. We were no sooner awake than we were given tea, and after having drank it bade farewell to our host.

When we got back, I found an invitation to dine with the English ambassador, an invitation I was too tired to accept, and had no cause to regret, as we received a visit from Father Palladius, the Superior of the Russian mission, whose information was most valuable. This learned man, well known for his intimate knowledge of all things Chinese, recommended us to cultivate the local authorities as much as possible ; but Sosnowsky differed from him emphatically, and without any deference to the authority, character, and refinement of Father Palladius, maintained that the Chinese would put spies upon us and prevent our working; that the Chinese officials were the most disagreeable race, and that we ought to avoid them as much as possible.

Next morning we again went to Yan-Fan and examined the details of his house and outhouses. But there was nothing particularly notable in this mass of courts, buildings, and rooms. There were three reception-rooms, partly furnished in European style. In one of them was a large portrait of Yan-Fan, by a Russian artist, and in the next, used as an oratory, a little wooden model of a temple was placed on a table; on another table were cups with offerings of rice, barley, &c. In the same room, under two glass bells, were crickets fed up for fighting. The bottom of the bells was full of sand and of rice, cooked for their food. Yan appeared quite astonished when I pronounced the word *tzuitziur* in Chinese, which means "cricket."

The house was heated by means of tiled stoves, which distributed an equal warmth throughout the rooms. I set to work and drew the interior of one of these rooms, whilst Yan talked to M. Popow. He subsequently asked me various questions on chemistry, medicine, and cures, and amongst other things, if it were really true that a drug existed capable of increasing the size of a leg or an arm. It would seem that the Chinese school of medicine was acquainted with this secret, although he himself doubted its existence. He told me that certain barbers worked miracles, and caused people suddenly to faint or cease breathing, and this by pinching the scalp at the back of the head.

I ventured to doubt his ever having seen a case himself, on

which he smiled and nodded assent, saying, however, that
they did exist, and that people worthy of belief had told
him so.

I offered to submit to the experiment, and although he
was nervous about it, when I insisted he sent a servant for
this famous barber, but the former came back half an hour
later, saying he was not to be found.

When my drawing was finished, Yan took it to show to
his wives, and on his return conveyed their approval, which
was as great for foreign art generally as for mine indi-
vidually.

September 29*th*. We were to have gone by land from
Pekin to Han-Keou, but were informed that the route had
been altered, and only Matoussowsky, the interpreter, and
one Cossack, were to follow the original plan. The rest of
the mission were to go to Tien-Tsinn, and from thence by
sea to Shanghai.

I took a long walk that same day with M. Popow, and
happened to come upon a curious custom belonging to
Chinese out-door life. Whilst proceeding to the suburbs of
the capital, the Emperor was to pass along the street leading
from the Tziane-Mine Gate to the palace. The inhabitants
of the street had information to this effect from the police,
and everything was cleared away on the strength of it.
The hawkers with their booths vanished elsewhere, the shops
looking on to the main street were shut, and those running
into it barricaded with mats or draperies, so that no one
being allowed to pass, the Emperor and his suite would not
come across any living creature on their route. We afterwards

entered a bazaar, skirting the inner wall, and a crowd of natives followed us into a shop, filling it up to the counter, but it never seemed to occur to the owner to request them to depart.

I could see that he feared something might be stolen, and eventually he begged us, with many apologies and most politely, to leave the shop, as being the only way of getting rid of the crowd. The Chinese who thus entered the shop in our train would join in our talk with the shop-keeper, discussing prices, adding up sums, and so on, and trying to pick up some Russian words which perhaps sounded like their own language, repeating them over and over again in fits of laughter.

A little farther on I was attracted by a novel sight, namely, archery according to the rules of art. Although one could not help being amused by these archers, in reality one could only pity them when calling to mind how utterly powerless these bows and arrows could not fail to be against firearms, notwithstanding the time and trouble expended in the attempt to attain perfection in archery according to their standard rules.

One of them was just going to begin, and from his deliberate proceedings one might have imagined him to be fulfilling a religious ceremony. He slowly took up his bow and stood on the spot marked by the instructor, about fifteen paces from the target. He then stretched his legs as a person carrying a weight on his head and afraid of losing his balance might do, and, bending nearly double, advanced his head and chest, endeavouring to obliterate his middle as much as possible. He held the bow in his left hand, the arrow in his right, examined them carefully, and seemed to be wrapped in deepest thought, only resulting in his pressing the point of the arrow to the bow. He again looked at his weapon, ran the arrow on to the cord, and seized the latter with the middle and forefinger. Next stretching his arm out as far as it would go, he lifted the bow and arrow high up into the air, and then lowered it to the regulation shooting height. He then looked round at the spectators on his right and left with a look that seemed to say, " What is to be done ? I don't want to pull, but I must." At last he turned towards the target and began to draw the cord ; his hands trembled as he shot the arrow, but still retained his position. This done, the archer let his arms fall with the same deliberation, straightened his body, brought his legs together, and rested for a moment, but only to take another arrow and begin the performance over again.

During these manœuvres his countenance was absolutely devoid of all expression ; he was like a corpse or a somnambulist, and showed not the slightest sign of satisfaction if the shot were successful, or of disappointment if it were the reverse.

The date of our departure being still uncertain, I constantly walked in the quarter in which the Embassies were established, and in which I was consequently more likely to meet Europeans. I must confess that I was disgusted with their behaviour, as well as astonished at the longsuffering of the Chinese, and could thoroughly understand their hatred and mistrust of us. In truth, the Europeans behave in a deplorable manner: one yells and blusters in the streets, without anyone discovering why; another forces his way through the crowd by making play with his cane on the backs of the Chinese ; a third, still more energetic, slaps the people right and left; others smash the locks of the temples and force an entrance, or throw down the statues in the palace, and so on and so forth.

. It is by way of amusement that the English hunt and beat the dogs which are so numerous in the streets of Pekin. These dogs recognise a foreigner either by his clothes or his face, and run away howling the moment they see him coming. I wonder in what country in Europe such conduct would be tolerated, and whose fault is it if the Chinese call us "barbarians," adding, "very clever in various business transactions ?"

Our fellow-countrymen having invited us to a farewell Chinese dinner, I will take this opportunity of saying some words on the native cookery. The dinner was ordered the night before in a restaurant (dian). Everybody being assembled, the waiter asked whether the courses should be served Chinese or European fashion. We all agreed that he should follow the custom of the country, reserving the sweetmeats for dessert. They first served pickled cucumbers cut in slices, then tzian-doou-fou, boiled peas and beans made into a pâté of a sour salt taste; but spread on bread this combination is not unpalatable, and foreigners like it very much. Then came ham in thin slices, and what may be literally translated into " ducks' heels," or the soles of ducks' claws separated from the skin before it is cooked; it is subsequently served up cold. Next an arrangement of meat with vinegar and Cayenne pepper, which should please Americans, as it burns the throat ; pickled garlic, which they eat as we eat radishes ; the hearts of cabbages cut iu thin slices, and black radishes ; then salted ducks' eggs. These are boiled after they are salted, and then surrounded with lime for two years. These eggs were not to my taste ; they smelt strong of ammonia, but the Chinese are very fond of them. This taste need not astonish us much, for are there none among us who like cheese and game in a state of decomposition ? After these side-dishes the dinner began with a soup of swallows' nests with mushrooms and buttered eggs very finely grated. The delicate flavour of this soup somewhat reminds one of gravy soup with a faint odour of sea water or seaweed. Poached pigeons' eggs were included in this course.

These swallows' nests (in Chinese *yan-ouo*, nest from over the seas) is really the nest of a kind of swallow,* common to the East Indian Islands and to Japan. This bird makes its nest in the rocks ; the nest is semi-spherical in shape, and of a gelatinous appearance, dry and brittle. If put into water or cooked, it swells, becomes transparent, and comes away in little strips, like vermicelli. According to the Chinese, it is very wholesome food, and calculated to strengthen the consumer. Opinions are divided as to what it is composed of ; according to some it is a seaweed † thrown upon the rocks and collected by the swallows ; others

---

* *Collocalia esculenta.*
† *Fucus bursa, sphæroccus cartilaginous.*

I 2

think that it is produced from the salival glands of the bird.

The price of these nests is very high. On the sea-coasts they are sold for their weight in silver, while farther inland their price goes as high as four times that amount.

Second course.—Another very elaborate soup—sharks' fins, pork, holothurians, or "bicho di mar," the bladder of sturgeons, and other ingredients. Holothurians, which the Chinese eat with avidity, resemble leeches, and live in the corals on the shores of Australia, Ceylon, the Caroline Islands, &c. After they have been dried and smoked they constitute an important branch of the fisheries and of consumption in China; cut in slices and cooked, they look like a piece of indiarubber, and have no particular taste. They are much prized by the Chinese, who attribute most health-giving properties to them.

Third course.—Duck, with imperial rice, dressed with chestnuts, slices of ham, and holothurians.

Fourth course.—Carp, with a sweet sauce tasting of honey.

Fifth course.—Three dishes in one ; sturgeons and ham, dried fish with grated mushrooms and fish-balls.

Sixth course.—Pork, dressed with mushrooms.

Seventh course.—Boiled fowl—too much boiled, as the flesh fell off in shreds.

Eighth course.—Roast crabs.

Ninth course.—Roots of tziao baï * with sauce.

Tenth course.—Lobsters, with a sauce made from the roots of the bi-tzy (*Scirpus*).

* Perhaps nenuphar.

Eleventh course.—Sharks' fins.

We might imagine that we had come to the end, but there are four more dishes: the bladders of fish roasted, boiled cabbage stuffed with chestnuts, roast mutton and pigs' feet, with ham and holothurians.

After all these dishes of meat, fish, and crabs, followed six dishes of stewed puddings without any salt; cakes stuffed with watermelon seeds, rice, nuts, saffron, garlic, or herbs; and a sort of jelly or cream made of apricot kernels. At last we got to the dessert, consisting of the roots of a plant found in the marshes, *Scirpus tuberosis*, commonly called the water-chestnut; apples, pears, grapes, nuts roasted in sugar, tablets of apple-jelly, fried almonds or apricot kernels, and lastly tea, with which we ought to have begun, had we followed the native custom. In addition to this, brandy and rice-wine were handed to us. The latter is called Chao-Sin, from the name of the town of Chao-Sin-Fou, where it is manufactured.

To finish up the day we went to the theatre at Pekin. The plays continue all day, as they do in the booths at our fairs, and one can enter at any time. After going through three courts, where hawkers sold fruit and bonbons, we went into the gallery to be apart from the crowd and avoid notice. The piece was going on, and the audience made as much row as if they were in a market-place. Tea and nuts were served to us, and we proceeded to break the latter with our teeth, following the example of the crowd below us. The stage in this theatre did not occupy the whole width of it; it was more like a kiosk open all round, without either decorations or drop-scene. When the tables, chairs, benches, or throne, &c., had to be changed, it was all done before the indulgent public. The audience was not exacting, but neither were the unfortunate actors; witness their efforts to make themselves heard above the noisy conservations of many spectators, eating, talking, smoking, taking tea, and sometimes quarrelling and fighting. As a general rule, the audience is but little interested in what is taking place on the stage. The pit is even arranged so that the spectators do not sit facing the stage, but down the sides. The plot of the piece now being played was not very complicated. A mandarin announces to his daughter that the emperor desires to have her for his mistress; the young girl will not consent; the father insists, and is in despair at her resistance. On her side the girl knows not what to do, or how to escape this honour. A devoted servant comes to her assistance and advises her to pretend to be mad. The emperor arrives; the young girl, who acts her part, is presented to him, and then in the greatest distress the emperor leaves her. Several scenes were extremely well acted, the more so as the women's parts were acted by men. Women only go on the stage as musicians or vocalists; and the actor who took the part of the girl acquitted himself with the greatest credit.

The day fixed for our departure now drew near. The two interpreters, Andreïewsky and an old Chinaman of the name of Siuï, went by land to Fan-Tzeng, with very minute instructions from Sosnowsky and 240 roubles to travel over a distance of two thousand versts.

A farewell dinner had been given on the 8th of October

by the Ambassador, and the day after we went to the
mission-house, where Father Palladius was to conduct a
service and invoke the blessing of heaven upon us. All our
compatriots made a point of being there, and I was much
astonished to see some Chinese in the choir, who sang in the
Russian language. They were the descendants· of the
inhabitants of the town of Albazine, who were · made
prisoners by the Chinese and taken to Pekin more than two
centuries ago. They had adhered to the religion of their
ancestors, and treasured up an image of St. Nicholas, now
placed in the mission church. I felt quite overcome when
Father Palladius offered up prayer and mentioned us all by
name, for this might be the last time in my life that I should
ever be in a Russian church. After breakfast we left the
Embassy, and it seemed as if it were only now that we were
going to cross our own frontier. At last we were out of
Pekin, so I turned to cast a last look on the imposing surroundings of the capital before leaving them. Following
the southern suburbs of the town, we entered fields, a great
contrast to ours at home, which are usually so silent and
solitary. Here everything teemed with life ; villages suc·
ceeded each other in an unbroken chain, with numerous inns;
crowds of men were on foot, or mounted on asses and mules ;
vegetable vendors, fish-sellers, barrows loaded with cases
and trunks drawn by men, so that one might almost have
fancied oneself still in town. There were numbers of stone
bridges stretched across the rivers, canals, and ditches;
amongst others the famous historical bridge, Pa-Li-Kao.
Thus almost before we aware of it, we got over the twenty-

five versts between Pekin and Toung-Tcheuo, the wall of which was falling to ruins. Opposite the gate of the town two old towers leaned slightly over; the streets were narrow and the houses low and small. There was a dense crowd everywhere; many pedestrians carried bouquets; others, principally old men, held sticks with birds tied to them by a string. We arrived at the quay on the Peï-Ho, the first navigable river I have seen in China. Here, too, what animation! What numbers of big and little boats; there was quite a forest of masts. the whole surface of the river being covered with them. Some carried passengers, others took in or unloaded merchandise; but what most struck me in this mass of shipping was the orderly way in which some passed down the river, whilst others went up one by one to occupy their places, without requiring any official to maintain order. It needed a certain amount of patience for each to await his turn; but no one appeared in a hurry. Perhaps this patience may be explained by the fact that each boatman was the proprietor of his own boat, in China the boat being the home of its owner and his whole household. We now expected to find Theodor, who had been sent on with a Cossack to engage boats for our journey, and were in the act of looking for him when I noticed some one bowing to me, who turned out to be the doctor belonging to the English mission, whom I had known at Pekin. He guessed the nature of our dilemma, and showed us where our boats were drawn up on the shore. Had he not come to our rescue we should again have lost a great deal of time searching for the Cossack and the interpreter. Before settling ourselves in

our junks we went to get supper at an hotel on the quay
kept by a Russian. The house was furnished in European
taste, although built in Chinese style; the servants were
Chinese, and only knew the one word "samovar" in Russian.
They supplied us with a supper of six courses, but as we
were not hungry we carried them away with us. On
asking what we had to pay for the supper, the Chinese
replied, " Whatever you think fit ; we have no price for
strangers." On Sosnowsky insisting, they asked for two
dollars, which is nearly three roubles of silver. We had no
dollars with us, so had to take a bar of silver and break it
in bits, weighing and adding little bits to it ; but as may be
imagined, this system of payment took as long as cooking
the supper.

It was dark before we embarked on the junks, of which
there were three, with tolerably large and commodious
cabins, Matoussowsky and I taking possession of one. The
night was cool, and the river alive with people ; their voices
could be heard in every direction ; numberless lamps and
lanterns glanced about on the quay, every passer-by being
armed with one, as the town possessed no system of
lighting.

I was looking about on deck when I noticed rockets going
up from one of the boats. "They are watching over a
corpse," explained Theodor ; and I then distinguished on
the deck of the boat a coffin, and a Chinese weeping and
from time to time striking its lid. At last the time came
for us to start. The boatmen push us from the shore, using
bamboo poles to breast the river. The town disappeared

in the darkness, and the solitary shores of the river were alone visible.

October 10*th and* 11*th.* We advanced slowly. The construction of these boats differs from ours, their bows and stern being very much raised, and the deck sloping towards the centre of the ship. Most of the time during the passage from Tsung-Tcheou to Tien-Tsinn we remained on deck, and spent the night in the middle of the river, which is quite shallow.

The Chinese provided themselves with the necessary food, but we, although duly warned by our friends, did not fare so well. Once having disposed of our supper we had nothing left to eat, as Sosnowsky declined to believe that one could not always procure food in any part of China, and announced that we should manage somehow; the result being that we were one whole day without food.

October 12*th.* Weather cold and rainy; the river deserted, hardly any boats to be seen. On one of the few paddle-. boats we did meet I saw a furnace made of glazed tiles and chopped straw, equally convenient for warming oneself or for cooking.

The wind whistled in our cabin, the rain fell in torrents, so that the door had to be shut; and as it was the only means of lighting the cabin, we had to sit in darkness; so I went hungry to bed and fell asleep. The Cossacks, meanwhile, being still hungrier than we were, forced the Chinese to stop at the first village, that they might at least buy bread, on which Matoussowsky called me to get up and come in search of something to eat.

I came out of my cabin and beheld some few poor huts; in front of one of them were three benches, and this was the

restaurant. A plank was thrown out to enable us to land, and after struggling up the wet and slippery banks we proceeded to the hotel. Although a poor and wretched inn, we nevertheless were able to procure cooked pork, liver, cabbage, and bread; but as we wanted some hot things, I tried to make use of the knowledge of Chinese I had acquired in Pekin. The innkeeper being also cook in the establishment, inquired what we would have. I answered him in the two words *joou-piar* (a dish consisting of grilled mutton with garlic and sauce), but he only understood the first word, *joou*, which means meat in a general sense. He addressed us volubly, but I could not catch anything except the word *kan-kan*, which means to show; so I said *kan-kan* to him. The Chinaman left us and brought us back two bits of pork; and at last, by signs and grimaces, we succeeded in coming to a mutual understanding, whereby they promised to send some quite hot *joou-piar* on board, which we paid in advance.

October 13*th*. Beautiful weather, but cold. I shivered in my winter greatcoat, and felt quite ashamed of myself, as our Chinese were bareheaded, their chests naked, and some went barefooted. They soaked rags in the water to wipe their faces, and eat a little rice before starting.

The shores of the Peï-Ho began to wake up again, villages to appear, and boats loaded with wheat, while in the distance we could see long houses with carefully-fashioned roofs.

We were getting near Tien-Tsinn, a great centre of commerce, with half-a-million inhabitants. First came the suburbs, an unbroken line of houses along the river-banks, and on the river itself the boats and rafts increased in number, activity pervading the scene. We reached the centre of the town, where the temples towered over the houses, and where we saw the charred walls of the Catholic church; a melancholy reminder of the fire, and of the massacre of Europeans in 1870.

We halted before the bridge, which had to be opened to let our boats pass, our masts being of a considerable height; and this was done for us at once, notwithstanding the interruption of traffic caused by it. It was a special concession to strangers, as it is only opened at stated periods for the Chinese; and at this moment the whole surface of the river was covered by an immense number of boats awaiting the usual hour for opening the bridge, which we now passed under, followed by four other boats; and no one stopped them or told them that it was not their turn.

Behind the bridge long walls ran along the river, and several Chinese gunboats lay at anchor. Next we passed the mouth of the Doun-Ho, a tributary of the Peï-Ho, over which a bridge is thrown on piles; and beyond the Chinese quarter lay the European, with whole rows of houses, and several steamers moored along the banks. Farther on we came to the Russian frigate *Herminia*, and sailors of our own nationality came and took off our luggage.

A Russian merchant invited us to stay with him, and here, as at Pekin, we might as well have been in Russia. But as I wished to acquire some knowledge of the Chinese, I soon left the house, with the commander of the frigate, to wander about the town. Three other frigates—Japanese, French, and English—besides the Russian ship just named, are there as a standing threat since the catastrophe of 1870.

Let the least disturbance be attempted, and in five minutes the guns of these frigates reduce the town to dust. The Chinese are quite aware of this, and will not again repeat the drama of 1870. The cause of this disturbance has never been thoroughly cleared up, but the fact remains that it cost the lives of twenty-one Europeans, twelve of whom were women, including nine French Sisters of Charity.

Three Russians met their death: a merchant, with the wife he had only married three days previously, and a young man.

A French lady who was riding in the Chinese quarter just when the disturbance broke out succeeded in reaching the European quarter, thanks to her good horse; but as she lived in the Chinese quarter, in which she had moreover left her husband, this heroine, disguising herself in Chinese garments, returned to her home, and almost on the threshold of the house, being recognised by the shape of her feet, was pitilessly massacred.

Continuing along this quay we perceived a black cloud of smoke, which proceeded from the big American steamer *Chan-Doun*, on which we were to embark two days later. It seemed still bigger on this narrow river, and when swinging its bows round towards the shore took up the whole breadth of the river. The passengers were not numerous, but all Chinese, for they quite understand the advantage of the foreign boats (from over the seas) with wheels of fire, " ho-loun-tzouan " (*ho*, " fire ; " *loun*, " wheel ; " *tzouan*, " ship.") They use them willingly, and even have some steamers of their own. At this moment my companion showed me a

Chinese steam-yacht, the *Tzin-Haï*, and on its deck a Chinese band playing entirely on European instruments, the execution being as good as that of a European orchestra.

As a proof that civilisation begins to penetrate the Celestial Empire, I may mention that the Chinese have an arsenal here, with steam-engines, and for five years there have been no European workmen in it, even the managers being Chinese.

During ·a visit to the European quarter, I made the acquaintance of our Consul and the interpreter at the Consulate. The houses in this quarter have immense gardens and big courtyards, but between it and the Chinese town there is a debatable land inhabited by both Chinese and Europeans. Here are to be found a few shops, an indifferent photographic establishment kept by a Chinese, and the race-course laid out by the English.

Next day I gave the Chinese quarter a turn, and rode there accompanied by a Chinese servant of our host's. The streets in this quarter were narrow and dirty; the largest was transformed into a corridor, being draped across from end to end with cotton hangings. Everywhere the air was impregnated with miasma and unfit to breathe, and the traffic incessant. Crowd followed crowd; pedestrians, horsemen, palanquin-porters, barrows ; all these formed a dense mass going slowly to and fro.

I was in the midst of these crowds on a restive horse, likely at any moment to shy and crush several people at once, so I turned down the first lane to the right, in which I met a mandarin's palanquin surrounded by soldiers. My

Chinese attendant jumped off his horse at once, and held its head till the mandarin had passed.

Farther on I met an amusing procession of about fifteen masqueraders dressed up and on stilts, accompanied by a crazy kind of band. These processions are often arranged by private societies on the occasion of local fêtes.

I was at table with my host when the firing from the *Herminia* announced that the Governor-General, Li-Houn-Tzang had come on board the frigate, so I ran precipitately from the quay to the frigate, whence the guns continued to fire salutes.

I had seen portraits of Li at Pekin, and going on deck I recognised him amongst the crowd of mandarins composing his suite. He was certainly taller than the others, but his countenance was nothing out of the common. Father Palladius had, however, assured me that Li-Houn-Tzang was a remarkable man, though of humble origin. His statesmanlike and administrative qualities had raised him to high rank. He wore a blue satin robe, a cloth vest with velvet collar, and black satin boots. A tuft of two-eyed peacock's-feathers in his hat distinguished him from the others, who wore only one-eyed feathers; furthermore, he had a red coral button to mark his rank. The captain of the frigate, dressed in full uniform, most minutely explained the details of the firing, and I could see that he listened attentively to what he wanted to know, but did not seem to hear when the subject lacked interest for him.

The captain then explained the torpedoes, the use of which they were shortly to exemplify. Li-Houn-Tzang and his suite looked on with mingled astonishment and doubt, whilst the sailors began their arrangements by preparing the galvanic battery, and when it was ready they first lifted the torpedo, which was under the water, and then sank it again·

An immense crowd had collected on the quay, and the moment the river was cleared the battery was fired, which shook the frigate, and at the same instant boiled the water up to a height of forty feet at the place where the train was laid, and caused it to fall back like the jet of a fountain.

A single cry of astonishment and enthusiasm from the spectators resounded through the air, whilst the mandarin and his suite seemed much moved, for after all this had subsided a little they exhausted their vocabulary in commendation, raising the fingers of their right hands, Li at the same time begging the captain to permit him to send one of his officers to be initiated in the construction of torpedoes.

Sosnowsky and I were introduced by the captain, who explained the object of our journey to the mandarin; and we afterwards went below to the cabin, where fruit, bonbons, and champagne were handed to us. Li asked us some questions about our future journey, and was surprised that we were going to venture into provinces where the insurrection was only partially suppressed. He inquired if we had arms, and asked to examine a specimen, on which a carbine was produced for inspection, and explanations given him as to its length of range and rapidity in firing. The officers of his staff were delighted, and the mandarin made his secretary take down the name of the manufacturer, inquiring the price, and begging Sosnowsky to procure him with all speed a considerable number of the same make. Sosnowsky informed him that it would only be necessary to write to Russia to insure immediate attention to his order, on which the highly-pleased General requested that a thousand should at once be dispatched, receiving Sosnowsky's assurance that he should have them in two or three months at the furthest.

Li-Houn-Tzang would have paid down the money there and then had not the secretary of the Russian Consulate explained to Sosnowsky that he did wrong in making such engagements, owing to the political situation (China was at that moment preparing for war with Japan); that complications might arise from this affair; and that in similar cases nothing should be undertaken without the Ambassador's sanction. He even refused to translate Sosnowsky's promises, but the latter succeeded in making himself understood without his assistance, and formally promised the consignment of carbines. I heard subsequently that the Ambassador did prevent the matter from going farther.

Li then questioned us on the surveys we intended making, begged us to send him a map of Western China, and expressing his regret that it could boast neither railways nor telegraphs. He added, that if it had depended on him both should long ago have been established, but that all the members of the Government were not of the same mind as himself, and were generally determined to discourage innovations.

All this time I was drawing the scene of the explosion whilst it was still fresh in my memory, and when the sketch was finished I begged the secretary of the Consulate to offer

it to the General as a rembrance of his visit and our interview. The General seemed pleased and astonished, and
thanked me profusely with his hands folded on his breast,
while the mandarins in his suite crowded round and passed
the sketch from one to the other. The reader can already
picture to himself the fingers raised in approval. Li then
gave the drawing into the care of one of the subalterns, with
orders to take it carefully to his residence.

It was dark when Li-Houn-Tzang quitted the frigate and
after the usual salutations, got into his palanquin with closed
curtains, which four porters lifted and carried off rapidly.
After firing several rounds, the same soldiers escorted him
back. The other mandarins remained on the frigate and
prolonged the conversation far into the evening. One
of them, named Lin, captain of the Chinese Admiralty
steam yacht, and a particularly pleasant companion, had
originally been in the service of Li-Houn-Tzang, but thanks
to his industry and capabilities had risen to the high
position he now occupied. After spending the evening with
our host, where all the Russians in the place had assembled,
we embarked at three in the morning on the steamer which
was to take us to Shanghai.

CHAPTER IV.

October 16th. We are on the open sea opposite the Ta-Kow forts at the mouth of the Peï-Ho. The flat and sunken shores on which these forts are constructed retain no pleasant memories of the English commanders Seymour and Elgin; nor can the English army have much satisfaction in calling to mind those marshy shores. We now leave the Gulf of Pe-Tche-Li, and cast anchor in the port of Tche-Fou. The rough sea prevents our either coaling or unloading the cargo. An official from the steamship company has nevertheless managed to board us.

October 18th. I was unable to land or to see the town of Tche-Fou, and from the bridge could only see a row of houses, and a Chinese tower which served as the lighthouse. There were gardens and shrubberries, and farther on in the midst of fields a Catholic monastery with a very lofty church. The number of these monasteries in China seem to show that the Catholics are very anxious to convert the Chinese and lead them to the true means of salvation.

There are 12,000 inhabitants, the magnificent climate

attracting many French, English, Americans, and German merchants.

The sea now became calmer, and everyone was again astir on the ship. The sailors busied themselves with the ropes, swarmed up the rigging, or got ready the crane for the cargo. Noise and bustle prevailed in every direction, which was easily accounted for by the presence of the Chinese, who do nothing without noise. The unloading continued all day and most of the night, for we only weighed anchor at midnight.

Whilst on deck I perceived a strong smell of opium issuing from the steerage, and asked the captain to allow me to go into the cabin and see the smokers. There was no partition of cabins; it was a saloon with three rows of hammocks, one above the other, down the sides and centre. All the hammocks were occupied, and the floor was strewn with packages and food. The Chinese are so wedded to their own cookery that they never eat the food provided on board, although they pay their share. The dim light in this cabin was rendered still dimmer by the smoke. I walked round, and found that some were playing dominoes just like our own, others were having their supper, and the greater number lay smoking in their hammocks. I stopped before one who had filled his pipe and placidly went on lighting it without disturbing himself in the least, smiling at me throughout. Some of the smokers were quite young. I did not dislike this opium-smoke, but I could not have stayed long in such an atmosphere.

October 20th. A beautiful hot day, and I was walking

about on deck when some of the Chinese came up to breathe
the air, and approaching me with the utmost civility, began
to examine the tails of my greatcoat inside and out, and to
touch my boots, asking me questions I could not possibly
understand, so I spoke to them in Russian.   We all wanted
to converse, but I fancy they were even more anxious to do
so than I was.   The little town of Shanghai, where we are.
to land to-day, is at the mouth of the Yan-Tze-Kiang
(which means Son of the Ocean).   It is not very striking in
itself, but is known throughout the world as the commercial
centre of the Empire.   The English, who are a practical
people, saw the importance of this spot, and established
themselves here as far back as 1841.   This colony has now
become quite a town, and is sometimes called the " town of
palaces."   Inhabited by the representatives of eighteen
nations, capitalists, men of business, and merchants, it
enjoys all the advantages of civilisation as well as many of
its disadvantages.   We had now unconsciously entered the
waters of this immense river, the Yan-Tze; we could not see
its banks, nor those of its tributary, the Wou Soung, but by
degrees, as we ascended it, villas with conservatories, baths,
and other amenities, began to be perceptible.   The numbers
of boats and ships increased; we saw flags of every nation,
heard engines working, and horns and hammers in the
factories.   This was no question of China; it was Western
civilisation transplanted to the shores of the extreme East.
We steamed past a quay lined by immense factories, coal
depôts, and warehouses; this was the workmen's quarter;
further on we came to the European quarter, with clean

and well-paved streets, beautiful houses, and handsome equipages, and here we landed. We had seen the Chinese quarter from the deck, with its most originally shaped roofs, and a perfect forest of masts, junks, and Chinese boats, which might be counted by thousands on the river. The Russian Consul, having been apprised of our arrival, was on the look-out for us here, and conducted us to the Oriental Hotel, leaving the Cossacks to see to our luggage. We had no sooner landed than we were assailed by crowds of screaming Chinese offering us their vehicles, which were ordinary wheelbarrows, such as we use for carrying earth; or little carriages like bath chairs or perambulators. Not being accustomed to being dragged about by human beings, we preferred walking, and saw in the clean and well-paved streets numbers of carriages appointed in the English fashion, Chinese everywhere pushing Europeans about in their little carriages, sailors of every nation, and a vast number of people standing about and enjoying the beautiful weather. The hotel was kept by an American, but his staff was Chinese, and spoke English, in common with almost everyone else in Shanghai.

We took two rooms, which cost us two dollars a day each, including board, whether we eat there or not. After break-fast the Chinese brought our luggage, and I gave two dollars to the porter who had carried mine and Matoussowsky's, but as he seemed quite dissatisfied with this sum, I begged the hotel-keeper, who was standing by, to explain what he wanted, and now found out that he was informing me I had given him too much! The hotel-keeper took one dollar from

him and returned it to me, dismissing the Chinaman, who
went off doubtless regretting his honesty.

As we were only to remain two days at Shanghai, I was
impatient to see as much of the town as possible, and at the
suggestion of our Consol started off to the races, which
happened to be taking place that very day. When we left
the European quarter we got into the Mixed Town, where the
streets are wide and large. The Chinese element prevails
over the European, and this quarter is ruled by its own
laws, and owns a mixed native and European tribunal. As
we passed the judge's house, which is at once tribunal and
prison, I saw three individuals in the courtyard enduring
their most original punishment, namely, a square board
round their throats, the corners of which were fastened to
posts by means of chains. This board is divided in two, and
a semicircle cut out on the inner edges, which are then joined
round the neck of the prisoner and fastened with bolts.
This is the cangue, and is sometimes applied for a month or
more.

The crowd increased as we approached the racecourse,
and in its midst was a carriage containing six young Chinese
women. Contrary to those we had hitherto met, the natives
are by no means bashful in Shanghai, and these young
ladies did not scruple to point at the passers-by, bursting
into fits of laughter. What their social *status* may have
been I know not, but their behaviour did not speak in their
favour. There were many Japanese, Indians, Persians,
Arabs, and negroes in the crowd. Being unable to get near
the course by reason of the crowd, we retraced our steps and

went to see a monument erected to the memory of the English officers killed in 1862 and 1864, in the war with the Chinese insurgents, the *Tai-Pings*.

October 22nd. In the morning I went with Matoussowsky to draw money at the Shanghai bank. Whilst waiting we watched the astonishing cleverness with which the Chinese ring the dollars in their hands to distinguish the true from the false; there are a great number of the latter in circulation, for which reason the bank accepts none without this test. I admired the rapidity and precision of the process. In an instant thirty dollars went from the right hand of the controller to ring on another dollar poised on the middle finger of his left hand, and fell to the right or to the left according as they were good or bad. The ring of the metal was every now and then varied by the dull sound of a false coin, and the Chinese controller continued his work all the time he was talking to us.

October 23rd. I had a great wish to be present at a sitting of the Mixed Courts, and the dragoman of the Austrian Consulate offered to accompany us. As the Chinese rise with the sun, we were obliged to be there at seven in the morning. After crossing several of the usual courts we entered the hall of judgment, if an open shed with no ceiling and dusty walls is worthy of the name. The two judges, one a Chinese mandarin, the other an Englishman, were seated beside each other on a platform. A wooden railing divided the hall in three parts. Some minor officials sat in the centre division before the judges' table, and behind them were the prisoners, plaintiffs, witnesses, and police. An outer door gave access to it, and the other two divisions were open to the public. The judges at once noticed our arrival, and we were presented to them by the dragoman, and then invited to take a seat on very uncomfortable wooden benches, after which tea and cigars were handed to us, the case meanwhile proceeding. The prisoner, plaintiff, and witnesses were on their knees nearly the whole time, and when tired they sat on their legs. The opposing parties began a discussion which degenerated into a dispute, and might have ended in a fight, as sometimes happens, owing to the adversaries being side by side. The judge admonished them and the police interfered, sometimes interpreting his words or at others supplying their own.

Two cases were judged whilst we were there. The first concerned the robbery of a garment, which was restored to the owner during the sitting. The guilty party was condemned to a certain number of blows from a bamboo cane on the back, and not on the heels, as some writers assert. The punishment was immediately carried out in one of the adjoining courts. The second case regarded the concealment of a married woman who had quitted the conjugal abode, and the judge considered it of sufficient importance to send to the provincial governor. Then the Court rose, and the judge invited us to go to his house, where we found tea and various delicacies, besides cigars and champagne, the inevitable accompaniment of Western civilisation.

The judge, whose name was Tzeng, was considerably advanced in years, short, stout, not very handsome, but of a benevolent countenance. He was deeply interested in our further journey, and expressed regret that we were going into provinces where the insurrection was scarcely suppressed.

Although he made very much the same objections as other Chinese had done to our going, I saw no desire in them to hinder us, but was rather inclined to attribute their objections to laziness or want of enterprise, and to their being unused to long journeys.

Tzeng told us how the Grand Duke Alexis, the son of our Emperor, had paid him a visit last year, and had given him a watch, which he should always wear with much pride. Two hours later he returned our visit, as was customary, and made acquaintance with all the other members of the expedition, inviting the whole party to dine with him.

Having still some time on our hands, we next went to the Chinese arsenal, which is a good way from the centre of the town, but a small steamer took us there in a few minutes. Our names were sent in by the dragoman from the Dutch Consulate, who had kindly accompanied us, and the head of the establishment, a benignant though apparently timid old man, came and received us, taking us to his apartments, where we were given the usual tea, champagne, and cakes, and thence conducted over the arsenal, where there was nothing of particular interest. Originally built eleven years ago, by Europeans, it at present gives employment to 1,400 workmen, who are all Chinese, mostly from Canton or its neighbourhood.

This town, from its relations with Europeans, was the first to accept the innovations of Western civilisation. The inhabitants of Canton are therefore foremost in all commercial transactions with Europe. They occupy themselves with art and photography, and they further use sewing-machines, and supply the factories with workmen. They were the first to enter European service, to learn foreign languages, and abandon their ancient customs, such as, for instance, the mutilation of their women's feet. A woman from Canton may easily be recognised by her feet. The workers in the arsenal attain the utmost perfection, and are capable of executing the most delicate work. We could not but pity the poor attenuated, sunken-eyed creatures, reduced by hard work, insufficient food, and the incessant use of opium to this miserable condition. We next went to the Governor's house, not far from the arsenal. In China only the dwellings of the poor look into the street, for if the owner is tolerably well-off his house is hidden behind a wall, and from without only the roof can be seen. If the house is of considerable size, and the owner possessed of much land, the latter is divided into several large and small courts, passages, and corridors, and the house, which is usually one-storied, is placed in the centre or at the bottom of the court. This rule knew no exception; covered galleries with trellissed windows, shady gardens, paved courts, a pond, with its island, plots of flowers, &c. In one of the rooms was a portrait of the late Tzeng-Koou-Fan, known by his great ability, and as having been a sincere ally to Europeans. In another room was a whole collection of typographical plates, with translations of mechanics, which our good-natured interpreter, the dragoman, explained to us were quite worthless, first, from the translator's insufficient knowledge of the language, and secondly, from the very construction of the Chinese language itself.

Nine Europeans were invited to dine with the excellent Judge Tzeng, of whom five were of different nationalities. It was now dark, and men with lanterns awaited us in the first court. Tzeng himself received us in the second court, in full dress, and with a retinue of servants, all armed with lanterns.

Once within doors salutations were renewed, and tea was served in cups, which the servants handed to each person without a tray, and put down on a little table before each. Those who remained standing were handed cups, accompanied by the word *Ho-tza*, which means "Take some tea." A long table in the centre of the room was adorned with vases of flowers, fruit, and red candles; lanterns draped in red stuffs hung from the ceiling, and distributed a rosy light.

The master of the house invited us to be seated, which invitation was repeated to each individual by the servants, and after each invitation a chair or stool was brought to the table. The judge waited till all his guests were seated before sitting down himself. At the open door I saw a compact crowd watching us, and whispering together. What strange conjunctions in their social relation! On the one hand a proud and important official, and on the other a populace permitted to take its stand in the reception-rooms of this official! It was not unpleasing, although somewhat inconvenient.

More tea, which everyone refused except Tzeng, then rice-wine served in small cups, champagne in bowls, and the *hors d'œuvre*; but as yet, according to etiquette, no one touched anything. Then the host got up, and, bowing, invited us to drink, taking a goblet of wine himself. He next ordered his servant to remove his hat, replacing it by a satin skull-cap, and further, took off a carved bone necklace, the insignia of his high position. The dinner was long and elaborate, the Chinese cookery excellent.

The servants incessantly refilled our glasses and pressed food upon us, snuffed the candles with their fingers and threw the wicks on the ground, filling the hall with a very disagreeable smell.

After more than twenty courses, an interlude permitted us to walk about and smoke before resuming our seats at table. Everybody had long ago eaten enough, but the courses began again, till at length they handed the welcome rice—welcome as being always the last dish at a Chinese dinner. No one would eat any except Tzeng, who took a whole cupfull, and then ordered his servant to bring him his hat and bone necklace. When he had finished he got up and bowed to us, and we did the same thing, accepting this as a signal to depart, and taking leave of our kind host, who went with us to the door of the second court.

Instead of retiring to rest, as the Chinese do, I seized the chance of going over various institutions with the Austrian Consul, notably the dormitories or night-shelters, the baths, and smoking-halls, where opium may be procured. The night-shelter I was thus enabled to see consisted of a long room with a door opening on to the street; on the left-

hand side of this narrow room was a sort of cupboard, divided into four shelves, one above the other, and long enough for a man of average height. Each of these dens was numbered, and let for the night to passengers through Shanghai, or belated individuals unable to regain their own quarter. There were neither sheets, blankets, or pillows, for such Chinese as travel usually carry their bedding with them. Neither was there proprietor or attendant in the hall, payment being generally taken in the morning. The lower berths were occupied first ; snoring already proceeded from the row on the ground ; the next two rows were only beginning to fill, and were reached by the aid of a ladder ; the fourth and last rows were still empty. We next visited the vapour-baths, which were like those in Russia, without the cleanliness, and the entrance-door went straight into the bath-room. I could not discover where the bathers undressed. We next went to see the smoking-rooms or halls, somewhat resembling our small public-houses, with this difference, that instead of chairs and tables there were only a certain number of kangs or couches covered with cloth, fine felt, or mats and bolsters, several of which were occupied by smokers. The waiter of the establishment asked us quite as a matter of course how many pipes we should require, and on our declining returned to his post without any remark. We passed from room to room just like inspectors, examining the smokers, no one complaining of the liberty we were taking. One of the Chinese who had just filled his pipe, offered it to me in the most good-natured manner, saying *tzin-tzin*, which means, " I beg you to take it."

Each pipe of opium costs from 10 to 15 cents (100 cents go to a dollar), and the Chinese smoke two or three pipes in succession, whilst those who can afford it smoke six or seven. Their habit is to smoke three or four times a day, which costs at least a dollar a day. The number of smokers must be considerable in China, if one may accept the number. of smoking-halls in certain streets in Shanghai as a proof of it.

For smoking opium a particular kind of pipe is used, consisting of a tube a yard long hermetically shut at one end, but with a small hole on one side, into which a clay or porcelain pipe is introduced. This pipe, formed like a cup or a bowl, has an opening large enough to admit a needle. Taking a small quantity of the opium, which is soft, and black in colour, on a piu used for the purpose, the smokers warm it by means of a lamp, afterwards rolling it in their fingers. When hardened in the cooling, they warm it again, pressing the opium into the bowl of the pipe with the pin, which on being gently withdrawn leaves a passage through the opium to the opening. The smoker then lies down and applies his pipe to the lamp, holding the opium over the flame without allowing it to catch fire, and inhaling long whiffs of the smoke.

Veteran smokers by no means become somnolent, or see visions, as is generally believed; they feel stronger, livelier, and more energetic; but in time they get pains in the chest and back, their heads become heavy, their eyes fill with tears (epiphora), general debility supervenes, they become low-spirited, and seek relief anew in smoking. Opium deranges the nervous system and destroys the digestion, but the habit develops with time into a necessity. Those who cannot satisfy their craving go through terrible suffering; they feel such a need of it that work becomes impossible. They would give their last farthing, or their clothes, sell everything, even commit a crime, to procure relief from their suffering, which can only be obtained by again reverting to opium. As long as the smoker has the wherewithal to gratify his craving he does not suffer, but the more he becomes habituated to the drug the more must the quantity affording relief be increased, and then any one who is not very well off may soon ruin himself. Aware of the evil effects, he accepts physical weakness, and fades by inches; all force of will leaves him, he has no longer the power of self-control, and so goes straight to destruction. The smoker well knows that he is ruining himself and his family, and sees all the wretchedness of the situation, yet persists in the downward path, and becomes one of those living corpses to be seen in the streets, naked or ragged, waiting for death to release them from their sufferings. The results of this fatal habit are not half understood, and the evil does not obtrude itself on public notice, most of the smoking being done at night, and, so to speak, in secret.

October 24*th*. I made several purchases for my ethnographical collection. The natives did their best to cheat me by asking three times the proper price, a custom originally started by the Europeans themselves choosing to pay even more than they were asked.

October 25*th*. Thanks to the good-nature of Mr. Has, I

was enabled to visit the Chinese Town. We left our carriage at the gate and proceeded on foot. The Chinese and European quarters were like two separate worlds, and we might have imagined ourselves in a large bazaar for old clothes and trash. A great trade was being carried on in the narrow and dirty streets; one offered white mice for sale, another had crickets in little straw boxes. Every mortal thing seemed going on, even to the miraculous healing of the sick.

I halted before a brother physician, a native Esculapius, seated on a camp-stool under the shadow of a square parasol, which answered the purpose of a tent. His remedies were spread out before him on a little table—roots, herbs, animals' skulls, &c. He had a tiger's skull, a monkey's skeleton, the bark of fruit-trees, hedgehogs', vipers', and crocodile skins, horns of goats, dried bats, bears' paws, &c. For surgical instruments he had only needles and cupping-glasses, but these last were made of wood.

A wretched, emaciated creature came to consult him whilst we were looking on. I derived all the more gratification watching the charlatan from the fact that he was unaware of the presence, in my person, of a genuine physician. Putting on a wise expression and an important air, he felt the pulse, plunged one of the needles into the patient's back underneath the shoulder, and allowed it to remain there, the wretched creature patiently enduring the pain in hopes of being cured.

We then went up the ramparts to get a bird's-eye view of the town, and I was surprised to find that the Chinese

looked curiously at us as if they were not in the habit of
living side by side with the Europeans. For the first time
I heard them calling us those "foreign devils" (*yan-goui-
tzy*), or to be more exact, "devils from over the sea;"
"Look! look! the foreign devils are walking on the walls."
This did not prevent our admiring the town, which was
watered by a good many narrow canals with pretty
houses on either side, and little bridges thrown across from
one house to another. The parapets of these bridges had
mats thrown over them. After taking a sketch, we again
followed the wall, but had some difficulty in finding a way
down. We halted, considerably puzzled, but a boy seeing
our dilemma from below, ran for a ladder and propped it up
against the wall to aid our descent.

We next entered a shop for musical instruments, which
are numerous in China—wind and stringed instruments,
cymbals, bells, rattles, drums of various forms and sizes.
Some resembled our clarionets and flutes, but were much
more simple. The stringed instruments were rather like
violins, guitars, and harps, but differed somewhat from ours
in their form and strings. These last were threads of twisted
silk or copper wire. There were also bamboo whistles, used
at burials and for watching the dead.

After breakfast we went with the Austrian Consul to the
Catholic mission, about seven miles from Shanghai, in a
district called Si-Ka-Weï. The influence of the West is
again apparent. Outside Shanghai the roads are excellent,
abounding in villas and restaurants. One of the fathers
came to meet us, and offered to show us over the establish-

ment, which is as useful as it is interesting. It takes in foundlings and orphans, children of all ages, from new-born babes to those nearly grown-up, and has been established for some years. Apart from Chinese, they also teach French and Latin, besides a general notion of other subjects, but principally philosophy and theology. Neither are trade and the arts by any means neglected. We were shown the carpenters', locksmiths', and shoemakers' workshops, and the studio for painting and wood-carving, the last entirely devoted to religious subjects, intended for the Chinese churches and their members. The young Chinamen who worked in it were quite European in their manner, and it must be owned that some of them by no means resembled the Chinese type, which made their origin a subject for reflection.

The reverend father conducted us to the observatory, where he showed us a rather complicated instrument, I confess to never having heard of — the meteorograph of Father Angelo Secchi.

A branch for young girls is also established here, directed by a sisterhood, but not even women may enter.

Passing, on our return, through a populous village, we saw a head suspended from a hook in a cage. The general idea in Europe is that the Chinese are very indifferent to existence, and accept death at the hands of the executioner with the same composure as they would go to sleep. I never witnessed their expression going to execution, but from what old residents in China have told me, they hold to life as much as other men do. Do they not reckon a long life to be one of the five chief gifts of heaven?

In China the common people avoid pronouncing the word "death," neither do they like calling a coffin by its own name (*gouan-tzaï*); they generally call it "the wood" (*mootoou*).

I do not place much faith in the accounts one hears of noisy suppers preceding the extreme penalty of the law, and even were they true it would only prove that frequently witnessing the pain of death can never be of any advantage to others.

After dinner in the evening, M. Has again accompanied me to the Mixed Town, principally to see districts which in the daytime are wrapt in silence animated by noisy life at night. A compact crowd circulated in the streets, which were lit by gas, or by Venetian lanterns of different shapes hung in front of the shops. But the people, no longer in a hurry, had ceased to push and rush about as they did in the day. They were out for enjoyment, and amused themselves in the tea-houses with bands, conjurors, and singers. There were young female singers, theatres, opium-saloons, and mysterious establishments with singers, music, and opium combined, hidden in the depths of the courts in the midst of a labyrinth of passages and staircases. One might wander about for any length of time without knowing of their existence, or even being able to find them if one did not know their whereabouts. It is difficult, and even dangerous, for a foreigner ignorant of the language to penetrate everywhere; and although I did not quite believe all the tales I heard, still, I dared not entirely reject the advice of my companion.

During our walk we entered a house, the door being open, and found two Chinese women and a man in a little room. We walked in without permission, and even without salutation, as the police or those in authority might do, continuing our talk. I did not feel at ease about our behaviour, and the Chinaman did not seem pleased, or the women either, one of whom, after they conferred together, signed to us to take ourselves off. We did not wait for a second bidding, and if I relate this little episode it is only to show how one may make acquaintance with their home-life: the doors are open, and one has only to enter.

Further on we wanted to go into a theatre, but a Chinese stationed at the door gave us politely to understand that we ran the risk of some unpleasantness, and as he said we had better stay out, we followed his advice. In this quarter there were a quantity of smoking establishments, some very comfortable, others humbler, and frequented by vagabonds and beggars. Some Chinese offered to take us wherever we chose, in the hope of a reward, so I begged my companion to ask one of them to take us to some woman who would allow me to make a drawing of her feet. " Yesi! Yesi!" replied the Chinaman, imitating the English yes, and he proceeded to take us through dirty, muddy lanes and crowds of people. As we passed, we noticed a man telling tales to enliven the multitude, but not drawing a very large audience. At last we entered a house, and our guide, on explaining our wish to the woman, at once got his ears boxed, and went off without a murmur, promising us greater success at the next house he stopped at. On transmitting my request to another of his countrywomen, he again received a box on the ear, and, somewhat abashed, proceeded on his way, inviting us to follow him. In the third house he was not struck, because he was on the alert to avoid it. He was probably aware that all this would occur, his intention being rather to earn some money at the cost of a few blows than to procure me a model. His aim was accomplished, for we gave him a franc, and he then departed, expressing his regret at having been unable to gratify our wish.

Farther on, having heard sounds of a band in the same street, we decided on entering the house from whence the sounds proceeded, and went up to the second floor by a wooden staircase.

In the first room a Chinaman poured out tea behind a counter ; the second, a much larger room, was occupied by the public, exclusively male, and at the end, on a platform, were the musicians and singers. The hall was full, and there were only seats for two of us. I preferred to remain standing for the sake of seeing the public and the scene around me, but one of the audience at once got up and offered me his seat. " Tzo, Tzo, Tzin-Tzo ! "—Sit down, sit down, I beg you to be seated ! I tried to refuse, but he insisted, and I was obliged to sit down at once so as not to disturb everyone, attention being now thoroughly attracted towards us.

A humorous and not very decent dialogue was taking place on the boards between an old man and two of the singers, who accompanied themselves on guitars, the old man playing the violin. The man was quick and amusing, and, without actually understanding him, we could follow and be amused by his acting. As for the women's singing, I must confess it reminded me of cats enduring vivisection. They played their guitars fairly, notwithstanding the length of their nails and the long thimbles on the two little fingers, which coquettes always wear to protect the nails, and some-times to make believe that they wear them long according to aristocratic usage, and to make a pretence of not having to work for their living.

Directly we were seated tea was brought and a light for our cigarettes, and at the same time we had each to pay 20 cents entrance money. I undid my sketch-book, intending to sketch the stage and the actors, but I had no sooner drawn a few lines than my nearest neighbours left their places to watch what I was doing, and others further off did the same. The singers understood what was going on and hid their faces with their guitars, but the old man seemed flattered, and the public appeared charmed with this new amusement. Not being able to finish my drawing, I put away my sketch-book, and we very shortly left the hall.

I must add the fact that not one disagreeable or abusive word was addressed to us during the whole of our nocturnal walk. Was this due to the fear inspired by Europeans, or the result of the peaceable disposition of the Chinese? I leave the question to be decided by those better acquainted with the country.

October 26th. Preparations for departure by the steamer *Fire Queen* to Han Keou. Sosnowsky had started three days before.

October 27th. We had left Shanghai a good way behind us when I came on deck in the morning. The weather was splendid, and the heat increased in proportion as the sun rose above the horizon. A vast number of junks and boats were coming down the river, and on the banks the natives fished or cut reeds and piled them up on boats.

The shores of the Yan-Tze are mostly flat and solitary, but the country beyond is hilly. We came from time to time across rocky islets on which were monasteries or pagodas.

We took rather more than three days to go up the Yan-Tze-Kiang through the provinces of Tzian-Sou and An-Houï, and we now entered that of Hou-Beï, passing seventeen towns on our passage, and twenty-one pagodas, generally hexagonal or octagonal, and all badly kept. They have no religious signification, but are monuments commemorating different events.

Navigation on the river is very active, although the steamers have greatly diminished the traffic of small boats. The storms which arise on the Yan-Tze are very dangerous for boats, which on those occasions endeavour to run on to the shore till fine weather returns.

I must mention the town of Nankin, situated at some distance from the river. Since the insurrection of the Tai-Pings, it is nothing but a heap of ruins, and no trace remains of their celebrated porcelain tower. At the junction of the Yan-Tze-Kiang and the Han-Kiang there are three towns, Ou-Tchan-Fou, the capital of the provinces of Hou-Beï and Hou-Nan; Han-Yang-Fou, and Han-Keou, where we arrived on the 31st of October.

CHAPTER V.

On nearing Han-Keou, we could perfectly distinguish a row of two-storied houses standing out from the thick mass of Chinese buildings with their airy roofs; these houses, extending along a wide quay half a mile in length, and planted with willows, constitute the European quarter. We were still in our cabins collecting our things together, when we saw M. Ivanoff, the Russian Vice-Consul, coming to meet and take us to the only hotel in the town, where he had engaged rooms for us.

This hotel was by no means as clean or comfortable as the steamer we had just left, but being the only one, we had no choice, and after taking possession I hastened to become acquainted with such of our compatriots as were established in Han-Keou. They lived very much as we do at home, but complained of the excessive heat in summer and the damp of spring. With the thermometer at 30° Reaumur indoors, and 45° in the sun, all labour becomes impossible during the day, and at night the heat drives away sleep. This heat, which has a very debilitating effect, begins in

June and lasts four months, and one becomes so accustomed
to this temperature that later on 24° seems cold and 14°
gives one a chill.   The Chinese themselves pass whole days
in the sun, and often work bareheaded.   Summer is in fact
the busiest time at Han-Keou, as it is just the season for all
commercial transactions.   Such natives as are not obliged
to be out remain quietly at home, in the cool shade of their
little gardens.   The rest, if they do not wish to starve, are
obliged to carry bales of tea or sacks of coals and other
merchandise, and the mandarins and others in easy circumstances require porters to carry them about in their palanquins.   From morning to night the cries, or rather moans,
of these porters may be heard keeping up a running accompaniment to all their occupations.   We were now in
November, and they were to be seen half-naked and carrying
cases of all sorts on trucks. "O ! ho ! ho !" cries one pushing
a little way. "Eh ! hi ! hi !" answers his colleague. "E ! hui !
hui !" moans the first. "E ! he ! he !" answers the second.
"Eh ! holi !" "holi ah !" "holi !" "E ! hi !" "I ! hi !" and
so on in every tone of the same scale, a plaintive note, dwelling long on the first syllable and briefly on the others.   The
whole produces a most disagreeable effect, and our Russian
ladies tell me that when they first came they were hardly
able to endure it.

   The Russian colony included twenty young bachelors,
dealing in tea for the big Russian merchants.   They have
no plantations of their own, nor have any other foreigners,
whatever may be asserted to this effect on the tea-chests.
The tea is bought from the Chinese, and my fellow-country-

men are only the middle-men between the Chinese planters
and the Russian merchants. The Russians only prepare
tea in tablets, either in their own workshops or in those
belonging to the Chinese. Almost the whole of our colony
were natives of Kiachta or Irkoutsk ; some of them had been
pupils at the Russo-Chinese school at Kiachta.

I constantly saw M. Scheveloff, whom we had been recommended at Tien-Tsinn to attach to our expedition as
interpreter. Established for the last twelve years as agent at
Han-Keou, he employed all his leisure in studying the Chinese
language and literature, and had completely mastered them.

The very day after our arrival, several of our compatriots
invited us to make a boating excursion to see the panorama
of the three towns. Passing up the right bank of the
Yan-Tze we came on the ruined walls surrounding the town
of Ou-Tchan-Fou. A whole row of huts were built up against
the wall, and sustained by strangely shaped pillars. The
boat landed us at a terrace whence a flight of steps led up to
the ramparts, on which there was a most original tower,
called Houan-Ho-Loou. It was many-sided and three-
storied, and its corners turned up with bells ; its many
coloured cornices, its finely carved window-frames, the
colonnade running round it, the boards hung here and there
with inscriptions on them, all combined to attract our
attention.

As usual, the Chinese followed our steps in great numbers,
and I could not help remarking the difference between their
kind of curiosity and ours. A European, after he has seen
one, two, ten, or seventy Chinese, ceases to take any further

notice of them; the Chinese, on the contrary, never weary of trying to discover something new either in the clothes or possessions of a foreigner, and cannot resist the temptation of running behind him to examine the novelty in detail. This was what we were being put through. Matoussowsky was in the uniform of a Russian officer, a uniform unknown to the Chinese; moreover, he had with him an instrument through which he looked to the right and left. It was an ordinary compass, indispensable to topographers for ascertaining levels, and the pinule through which he was looking excited the curiosity of the crowd to such a degree that those gentlemen succeeded in making away with it. The alarm was given, vigorous investigations were made, and the Chinese themselves, appearing annoyed at the theft, aided the search. Schevelow and his intelligent Chinese servant joined in the hunt, but all in vain. At last the crowd was informed that 1,000 sapeques would be given to whosoever should restore the missing article. A moment afterwards the servant was told in confidence that the *thing* was to be found in the chest belonging to a priest attached to a neighbouring temple. The servant went to this priest and throwing him a packet of 1,000 sapeques, demanded the restitution of the stolen article. The priest tried to exculpate himself, but on being threatened with the police, he opened a box and took out the compass, putting the money that had been thrown to him into its place, and all this as simply and naturally as if he had merely bought the compass at a shop. No one appeared shocked by his conduct, and yet theft is severely punished in China.

Matoussowsky proceeded to take various plans, and I entered the temple, which, except in some trifling details, was exactly the same as all the others I had seen. Whilst looking through my opera-glasses at the town and its neighbourhood, the curiosity of the mob was again aroused, and I was at once surrounded by a crowd ; children and old men, well dressed or in rags, jostled around me without intending any harm, but with the keen wish to see through my glasses, if only for a moment. It was impossible for me to deprive them of this gratification. I put them to the eyes of one after another; their surprise was unbounded, and their talk incessant ; those fortunate enough to get a peep related to the others how things were diminished by looking through the big end and magnified by looking through the small end of the glasses. I was only sorry not to be able to satisfy every one's curiosity.

Whilst waiting for my colleagues, I sat down in the temple and began taking a likeness of a pale and delicate youth, with small, dirty hands, and dressed in silk. I was immediately surrounded and watched with the greatest attention and in perfect silence. As soon as the portrait was completed, every one cried *hao!* and all raised the finger ; even those who were too distant to see partook in the general delight with the portrait taken by the *yan-da-jen* (strange gentleman from over the seas). The young man who had sat to me hung about me so persistently that I was forced to give him his portrait, which he took away, followed by the crowd.

When Matoussowsky had done his work, we came down

from the tower, and went through filthy little streets to a
spot in the centre of the town called the Serpent Mount,
from whence there was a good view of the neighbourhood.
Although we were in the month of November, the heat was
still great, and we got quite tired climbing this hill, but
were rewarded by a view of the town of Ou-Tchan-Fou, the
capital of the province. The town in itself is not particularly beautiful, and is an immense collection of houses all of
the same pattern, white, and covered with grey tiles, the
edges of the roofs being more turned up than in the towns
we had hitherto visited. From such a distance it was
impossible to distinguish the narrow streets amidst the
crowds of houses; we could make out nothing but walls,
roofs, and various temples, easily recognised by their superior
height and more careful construction. The town goes
right down to the Yan-Tze, only separated from it by the
wall, which entirely hides the big river. On the left bank
are the towns of Han-Yang and Han-Keou. In a book of
Chinese travels I read that "did these three towns reckon
as one town, it would be difficult to find a larger collection
of houses and inhabitants, except perhaps in London or
Yeddo." I must confess that such was not my impression ;
but the number of vessels in the harbour was more than
striking, and I fancy could scarcely be exceeded in any
other port. There were more than ten thousand large ships,
whilst the little boats and junks were incalculable, and by
reckoning five persons to each boat, which would be rather
underrating their number, one could form some idea of the
multitude of people that lived on the water.

We beheld an immense plain, ten miles long, watered by
the Yan-Tze, some isolated hills, the same in character as

the Serpent Mount, and south of Ou-Tchou, a whole series
of lakes great and small, bounded on the horizon by a chain
of mountains.

Crossing the Yan Tze to the town of Han-Yang-Fou, we landed and went up to a hill temple, which was partly a tailor's shop and partly a warehouse for coffins containing bodies waiting to be forwarded to the birthplace of the defunct, a universal custom in China for even the poorest. I carefully examined these hermetically sealed wooden coffins, and was just going to put my hand on the putty which stopped up the holes, when one of the *hechans*, putting himself between me and the coffin, gave me to understand that the sacred ashes were not to be touched. We then left the temple and gazed on the splendid picture unrolled before our eyes : the Han-Kiang covered with boats, and on the opposite side the town of Han-Keou ; farther down, the waters of the Yan-Tze lay like an immense mirror, and the town of Ou-Tchan-Fou on the plain fading away in the distance.

We were in the middle of winter, not a very good time of year for researches in natural history, although the Chinese winter by no means resembles ours. The suburbs of Han-Keou are moreover of no interest. After one walk I knew my way sufficiently to go about the three towns, and was not afraid to venture among the peaceable inhabitants without an interpreter. ·

My drawing gave me great advantages, and by its means I made as many acquaintances during my two months' sojourn at Han-Keou as it was possible for a foreigner ignorant of the language to do, and was enabled to study all classes of society, from the official perpetually secluded in his own house, to the homeless beggar. After several days at the hotel, Matoussowsky and I gladly accepted an invitation from one of our countrymen to stay with him. From his house we had to go through several streets in the European quarter before entering the regular Chinese quarter, where the streets are narrow and unhealthy, and only consist of rows of one-storied houses with shops in front.

In the European quarter one may meet one, two, or perhaps three passers-by, but in the Chinese streets there is a compact crowd. In fact they are the open-air club, where the people meet from morning till night, and all night through. In them they transact business, work, eat, and drink, and the open streets are the scene of their everyday cares and enjoyments.

Palanquins are rarely seen, because the officials and wealthy people chiefly stay indoors. It is the poor people and the workers who fill the streets; porters with their loads on their backs or on trucks, hawkers selling eatables ready cooked, crockery, toys, ointments, &c.; workmen plying their trades; barbers shaving people in the open air; eye and ear cleaners, locksmiths, menders of crockery, all banging or ringing something to attract attention to their presence; and beggars tramping around the shops like living corpses.

Thin, mangy dogs also hover hungrily around, and share the duties of the scavengers with big misshapen pigs. We notice an artist installed at a little table in the street, not having enough light in his own house; and close by, at a round table covered with various nostrums, sits an Esculapius similar to the one we saw at Shanghai; a few steps further a *daï-fou* (doctor), seated under the shadow of a parasol,

praises his wares, which he maintains to be cheaper than
the air we breathe.

Nothing is easier than to get an insight of the workshops,
for all are open to the street; silk and cotton-weaving,
carpentering, shoemaking, metal-work, at which the en-
gravers sit in rows; bamboo-workers, artificial flower and
horn lantern makers, chandlers, and hatters. Here too are
creatures bent double over gold and silken embroideries for
the robes of officials and rich ladies; further on dyers and
confectioners. Let the reader imagine all the noise in this
Pandemonium; for, as the Chinese are not wont to speak
low, the row in the street is deafening, and it takes some
time to get accustomed to it, or to the smells and all too
realistic sights that meet the eye in broad daylight. Out-
wardly the Chinese towns present nothing but a series of
warehouses; their best architecture is hidden behind walls
and at the bottom of courts, and does not help to embellish
the town. The most beautiful edifices are the temples (miao)
and the pagodas (ta), of which the most sumptuous belong
to private establishments, which may be named clubs or
merchants' guilds. The merchants in China are a rich and
numerous class, divided in every town into societies, each of
which has its place of assembly, called Houi-Gouan, preceded
by the name of the distinguishing province; for instance—
Schan - Si - Houi - Gouan, Kiou - Si - Houi - Gouan, &c., i.e.
Assembly House of the Society of Natives of Schan-Si, &c.
All these establishments are constructed on the same plan,
and only differ in detail and finish.

Each club is divided into several courts separated by walls,

rooms for fresh arrivals, at least one little garden, and lastly
a theatre and temple.   The theatre is merely a stage, always
placed opposite the temple ; at the sides are boxes for members of the clubs and for honorary members, the general
public, which assembles on the days when there is a representation, having to remain standing in the court with their
backs to the temple.   By building temples the Chinese hope
to conciliate the gods, and the various societies spare no
expense to outvie each other in splendour and luxury ; but
as regards their construction, the genius of the architect is
allowed as little scope as that of the sculptors and other
artists, for they may not depart from rules laid down in
remotest antiquity, and are forbidden to introduce any
novelty.   However this may be, all the treasures are
collected in the temples : precious woods, marbles, gildings,
artistic sculpture ;   the tiled roofs are adorned with dragons'
heads, animals, fish, birds, &c.   The corners are spread out
and turned up at the edges.   Lanterns of strangest shape
are suspended from them, and the windows filled in with
fine paper.   The gardens of a Houi-Gouan abound with rocks,
artificial grottoes, ponds, stone bridges, aquariums, flowers
and trees.

At Han-Keou the most remarkable establishment of this
sort belongs to the merchants from the province of Tzien-Si,
celebrated for its china factories.   Meetings on commercial
matters are held in this club, as in all the others, and
banquets and rejoicings on the feast-days consecrated to
the gods of the temple, the patron deities of the province,
protectors of commerce, &c.

These fêtes are rare, the temple being generally empty
and left to the care of the priests (*heschan*) appointed to the

charge thereof: they are deplorably neglected, and left in
a filthy condition.

We had been advised, as on a former occasion at Pekin, to address ourselves to a mandarin high in authority and connected with foreign affairs, and to consult him on different questions relating to our journey. A letter written by Scheveloff was therefore despatched to Dao-Taï (the official's name), expressing our wish for an interview with him, and begging him to let us know when we could be received. The answer came immediately, and the following is the literal translation of it :—

" I am greatly pleased that these very dear guests from the Russian Empire deign to enlighten my miserable hut with a ray of their presence, and I shall await them this day, the 23rd of the 11th moon, at 3 in the afternoon. (Signed) Your younger and imbecile brother, Dao-Taï." Odd as these words " younger brother," and " imbecile," may appear, they mean the same thing as "yours obediently," ' yours affectionately," &c., &c.

We would willingly have gone on foot, but, according to Chinese etiquette, it would have been undignified even to go on horseback ; we must be carried in palanquins (tziao).

All the Europeans here have their own palanquins, and the necessary liveries for their bearers, which differ with every house. Some have blue with black trimmings, others white with blue, or lilac trimmed with red. Porters are easily hired, as there are many more than are required in the streets. When, as in this case, several palanquins are required, they may be hired in the town, so there were five palanquins and twenty porters at our door, four men instead of two for each, as etiquette required this number. The

Chinese had already found out that the Russian officials were
going to visit Dao-Taï, and had assembled in front of the
house.   One of them had nothing better to do than to run
in front of us announcing the great piece of news to everyone
on our road, and Scheveloff warned us that the whole population would turn out to see us pass.   We did in fact find
a dense crowd in the Chinese quarter—myriads of human
beings of all ages blocked the streets, leaving only a narrow
passage for the palanquins, in which we were seated in full
uniform.   They took evident delight in the procession, at
the head of which marched the Vice-Consul's servant,
carrying a packet of our huge visiting-cards, printed on red
paper, after the Chinese fashion.   Policemen armed with
cudgels accompanied him, and when their orders to stand
back or make room had no effect on the crowd, they used
their cudgels, as well as another weapon peculiar to the
Chinese ; I mean their pigtails, which they use very cleverly
as whips.   The porters shouted into the bargain, but all
their cries, menaces, or even blows could not preserve order
in a crowd excited by such an unusual spectacle.   The people
pressed towards the palanquins to get a nearer sight of an
officer in uniform ; some even sat down on the ground to be
able to look underneath.   Some wanted to accompany us to
prolong the sight; and on the crowd trying to prevent this,
discussions, abuse, and fights arose.

' I confess I found it difficult to keep my countenance, as
behoved the dignity of a foreign mandarin, at the sight of
all this childish curiosity.   Every five minutes the porters
stopped to change shoulders, which was quickly done on the

word of command, and those standing where the halt took place doubtless considered themselves most fortunate in being able to gaze on us an instant longer.

The palanquins being open in front, I could see two of my porters. They walked fast, notwithstanding the fatigue, and perspired freely, and my shame at being carried by men was modified by the cheerful mien of the honest creatures, who walked along gaily, conversing together the whole way,

and quite content to thus earn their day's wages. Those in front warned their colleagues of any obstacle, and those at the back always responded to their warning. These phrases often rhymed ; for example, " Houa-dy-hyn " (we slip), those in front would say, " Tzai-dy-vny " (we walk securely), the others would reply, " Tzo-choou-kao " (we shall stick on the left), and the others would answer, " Tzai-you " (we take the left). At length we reached the first court of Dao-Taï's house, and this was as crowded as the street, and included a barber busily shaving a customer, and an itinerant cook making pancakes. The bearers made for a triple door, but the porter raising his hand, gave a threatening cry, and they stopped short. They were quite aware that this would happen, and letting down the palanquins from their shoulders, they placed them on tressels, whilst the open door was shut. Our arrival was then announced to the Governor; a moment after the same porter who had just forbidden our entry opened the folding doors with undiminished solemnity, the bearers crying, "Tzoou!" (go on) carried us quickly into the second court, where two Chinese awaited us in their official headgear, and conducted us to a third door, and so on from one court to another. Glancing around, I noted that these courts were anything but clean; in one corner lay an old palanquin, in another a heap of cabbages and an old pair of shoes; dogs sniffed about, and squalid Chinese sat on the benches. The palanquins were finally deposited in the fourth or fifth court, and we were then invited to alight.

At the same moment the mandarin, who appeared grave and thoughtful, made his appearance by a side door. I stared at him as hard as the crowd had just done at us. Men are the same everywhere. This Manchu by no means gave me the impression of a *younger* and *imbecile* brother; he might be fifty years old; he was tall and broad-shouldered, and wore coloured spectacles. His toilet was composed of a black hat with a plume of peacock's feathers at the back, a robe of yellow satin, and over it a black satin vest, the sleeves being trimmed with sable. The Vice-Consul presented us each in turn, and Dao-Taï bowed to each with his hands folded on his breast, repeating the word "tzin" (with permission). When the presentations were over we had to pass the threshold, and after many bows the mandarin had his way, and made us pass first into a charming little court, adorned with plants and flowers, and then into a sitting-room, where, on his invitation we seated ourselves round a table.

Sosnowsky opened the conversation by speaking of the pleasure we had in making his acquaintance, of the old friendship between the Russians and Chinese, of the assistance the Chinese authorities had given us in furnishing escorts, &c., &c. Dao-Tuï, still serious and solemn, spoke very low and very slowly ; but reserved as he appeared during the intervals between the conversation, I noticed that he unbent at once when he began to listen to the talk, and that he examined us, or our uniforms, most minutely under his spectacles. The conversation was not well sustained, as Sosnowsky did not like the Chinese, and neither Matous-sowsky nor I were allowed to take part in it, so this visit became at last a real torture to us. After drinking a glass of wine and tasting the sweetmeats, we took leave of Dao-Tuï, who promised to do all that lay in his power towards our security. The chief aim of our visit was therefore accomplished. He recommended us further to call on the Governor-General of the provinces of Hou-Beï and Hou-Nan.

From all I gather, I have come to the conclusion that there is a good deal of tension in the relations between the Chinese and foreigners, and that they are entirely official ; no attempt at being on more friendly terms has been made.

The English are haughty to those in authority and rough
to the poorer classes; the Russians behave well to the people,
but never see those of higher rank unless they are obliged
to do so, and to account for this they cite the haughty
character of the Chinese.   However, as the Chinese are
masters of the situation, it would be unreasonable to expect
them to make the first advances to the unwelcome European.

Not having been able to approach any official, I begged
the Vice-Consul to present me to some private and well-to-do
individual, in whose house it would be possible for me to
observe the home-life of the Chinese.

In this way I was introduced to a banker.   His house was
at a considerable distance from ours, so I was carried there
in an open chair by two porters, one of my compatriots
going with me as interpreter.   Passing through the streets
nearest the European quarter, I repeatedly heard the words
" Yan-dai-fou " (the foreign doctor), " Yan-houa-houar-dy "
(foreign artist), which proved that I was already known by
sight.

The banker, having been apprised of my visit, asked me if
I wished to set to work and draw, and as there was not
enough light in the room, he had the paper taken out of the
windows.   His small and modest dwelling made one wonder
how it could belong to such a person ; but there are bankers
and bankers, and this cannot have been one of very great
importance.

I began to draw, but this did not by any means prevent
the master of the house from performing his toilet.   A barber
having shaved his head, undid and then replaited his tail,

and then taking it in his left hand, washed the banker's face
with the other hand, the banker bending meanwhile over
the basin.   He principally rubbed his lips with the utmost
care, much as we should rub a pair of boots.   It was in this
position that I took the portrait of my host, and he was
quite pleased with it.

Then I went into the little outer court, where a servant
had been stationed all this time expressly to keep out the
people who tried to crowd in.   By first exhorting, then scolding, and threatening them as much with his cudgel as by
word of mouth, he succeeded in keeping them at a distance
while I finished my work.   I did not, however, learn much
e master of the house as to his mode of life, owing to
rance of the language.

anker, who was most kind to me, came frequently
y sketches, bringing me tea and bonbons, and just
leaving begged for a last look at my sketches.

On my return home I was informed that we were to visit
the Governor-General of the provinces of Hou-Beï and Hou-
Nan, the brother of Li-Houn-Tzang, whose acquaintance we
had made at Tien-Tsinn.   He lived in the town of Ou-Chan-
Fou, on the opposite bank of the Yan-Tze-Kiang, so our
palanquins were sent in advance on boats.   We took an hour
to cross and go up the river, as the current had carried us
some way down.   The banks were covered by small old
houses, original in shape and very picturesque, owing to the
various additions and bamboo mats, which form part of the
material used in their construction.   A number of workmen
enlivened the scene—water-carriers, washermen, fishermen.

I even saw a small house being carried from one spot to another by means of big bamboo cylinders, on which it was propelled along. This is easily done, for the bamboo buildings are extremely light.

Walking along the quay, I remarked numbers of hollow places in the granite slabs, made by the boathooks of ships coming up the river. They are the tokens of long centuries of work, and of successive generations who have long reposed in their village cemeteries. Their descendants still carry on the traffic of the river with the same appliances as were used a thousand years ago.

Having left the ship we went up a stone staircase, followed by an immense crowd, eager to see our uniforms, which appeared so magnificent beside their poor attire. Our gold braid and accoutrements inspired respect in some of them, but others went into fits of laughter at the sight. We were carried through the streets of the town, where every one was on the alert to see our entry. I noticed that a considerable number of the inhabitants were marked with small-pox and had sore eyes; a great many besides had scurvy; indeed, the whole population seemed unhealthy.

The porters stopped before the Governor's house, and after going round the court, took us in by the opposite side. This probably was customary. Our visiting-cards were sent in, the porter's cry was heard, the great central door was opened, and our porters, taking up the palanquins, went through the second, third, and fourth courts. The door of the last was like a great open kiosk, and I learnt later on that cases were judged there. The judge takes his place on an arm-chair before a table surrounded by a few stools, while the public stand in the court.

Near the door stood several mandarins in full dress, and one of them held our cards in his hand. He saluted us with grace and dignity, and invited us to follow him into the fifth court, at the door of which this mandarin, who wore the red button, left us, without our knowing where we were to go next. After waiting a minute or two, it began to dawn on us that the mandarin himself awaited us in this court, and we looked around without being able to distinguish him from the rest, and passed him without recognising that it was he. This appeared to put him out of countenance; perhaps thought it was our foreign custom, and to see what would come next. The mandarins of his rceived our mistake, and pointed out their lord and on which we saluted him, excusing ourselves by that we did not expect to find him in this court. We were then led into the reception-room, and invited to sit at a round table.

Li-Da-Tzeng was short and fat, and of affable and bene-volent mien. He examined Sosnowsky's helmet and its white plume and decorations with much interest; also my massive epaulettes, which he even touched.

The reception-hall was more like a shed. The brick floor was covered in the middle with a red cloth. There were several rows of small tables and chairs, a wooden ceiling with lanterns, and windows draped with Indian muslin. Two large mirrors were placed on the floor, like screens, on each side of the couch; and on the walls were red and blue

boards covered with inscriptions in gilt frames. Drawings and manuscripts on long strips of paper completed the decoration of this Chinese apartment.

Li, having heard that I was a painter, begged me to draw him a picture of a railway as a remembrance, and also his portrait if I had the time, and I promised to do both with great pleasure.

The day after this visit Dao-Taï brought us a message of regret from Li-Da-Tzeng, who was unable, owing to indisposition, to return our visit, and informed us further that a gun boat was ordered to escort us on the River Han. Our Vice-Consul entertained Dao-Taï with champagne, which he evidently appreciated, but always maintained his serious expression. When he smoked he never touched his pipe : a mandarin presented it to him and held it whilst he inhaled the smoke.

We went with him to the door, and there saw the numerous suite which had accompanied him. This long procession was most singular ; therefore, taking advantage of the fact that he was also going to call on the American Consul and had to pass Scheveloff's house, I hastily took my sketch-book, and had just time to jot down the cortège.

Eight boys with fans headed the party in two rows ; at a certain interval eight more ragamuffins, walking in couples, carried red boards shaped like rakes, on which was written in black letters the dignities and offices of the mandarin. Further on four executioners, two and two ; the first struck copper gongs, the other two carried whips, ready to punish the first offender, and chains, to remind the mandarin that,

in the case of injustice or violation of the law, he may be put in chains himself; and this in China is a reality, the chains carried before the mandarin having, no doubt, been attached more than once to the feet, hands, and neck of some guilty official.

After the executioners two individuals carried a large red parasol, turn about, to shade the mandarin should he wish to walk; this parasol was trimmed with three rows of the same coloured fringe, in token of his rank. Two others carried the large "fan of modesty," to conceal the personage should he wish to change his clothes on the road, according as the weather was good or bad; and if the reader wishes to know how he achieved this, I may add that four soldiers followed behind carrying a large trunk full of his clothes on a truck, and behind them eight other soldiers on foot. Another space, and then another red parasol with a double fringe; then eight men on foot preceding the palanquin, carried by eight soldiers, and behind it six mandarins on horseback bringing up the rear of the escort—forty-eight men in all, soldiers of the garrison, and lads hired in the streets for a trifling sum, and provided with garments.

The weather was beautiful, and notwithstanding the advanced season (the end of November), I could draw in the open air without a greatcoat: we had, however, had some rainy days, and even snow. On these occasions the streets are deserted, for the Chinese do not appreciate rain, or water of any sort. It has been asserted that the best way to stop a fight between two Chinamen is to empty a bucket of water upon them, for they then cease fighting and go off to get dried.

On the 27th of November (old style) every one was occu-pied in observing the Transit of Venus through a piece of smoked glass, or in another way, hitherto unknown to me, namely, a basin of water reflecting the sun, and on its image the little spot which represented Venus could be dis-tinctly seen. I frequently went to Ou-Tchan-Fou to take views of various parts of the town; and whilst drawing the Governor-General's house everything I required was put at my service, and even things I did not require, such as tea, sweetmeats, and wine. The inquiring crowd which now surrounded me was much more polite than the street crowd, not that I could tell to what class these individuals belonged, their attire giving no clue; but in the towns of Asia it is essential to know with whom one deals, and to behave accordingly.

Wishing one day to make a drawing of the inscriptions over several of the doors in the Governor's house, I begged that they might be opened for me, which was immediately done, but only by order of an officer, it being contrary to custom. These doors are always shut, the side door to the right being alone left open, and that on the left being reserved for criminals. I was surrounded by crowds eager to watch me at work; but they were in my way, so a police-man was ordered to keep them at a distance. Scheveloff, who almost always accompanied me, repeated the remarks of the people on my drawings; some praised, and others found fault. When it was a case of copying inscriptions, I endeavoured to do it as exactly as possible, and tried to imitate their signs and hieroglyphics. The natives read them to themselves as I went along, but when they got to signs that I had not been able to copy exactly, they supposed that I was trying to write like them, but that not being able to succeed, I had taken to our own style of writing. They further took badly-copied signs for Russian letters. Sometimes great swells came to me, including the son of the Governor-General, a pale and delicate youth with black eyes, who came with his preceptor and the Governor's brother, a quiet, solemn man like a marble statue. The moment he appeared the crowd disappeared without waiting to be told, except a few of the bolder, who were driven away by the police.

When my drawing was finished the mandarins asked my leave to show it to Li-da-Tzeng, and invited us to go into the reception-room, where wine and other delicacies were brought. Li's eldest son came too, and it was he who afterwards brought me back my drawing, showed me his album, and begged me to choose some of his own drawings as a remembrance. Evidently he had undoubted talent and great patience, but his painting in the Chinese style was not very good. I made him a present of the drawing which pleased him most in my book, and he never left me all day, following my manner of working with the greatest attention. Li himself came to see me, and to remind me that I had promised to take his portrait. To-day for the first time, whilst re-crossing the Yan-Tze, I saw men rowing with their feet. It does not look very elegant, but is useful, and must require great practice.

On the 29th of November military manœuvres were got up for our gratification and in our honour. We went in full uniform to the camp on the left bank of the Yan-Tze, not far from Ou-Tchan-Fou. The weather was splendid, and several mandarins awaited us on the quay, the red button surmounting the cap of one of them betokening the rank of general. We went together to the camp, and from a slight elevation we could see lines of soldiers attired in bright red. Three salutes announced our arrival, and we then entered a long, narrow court in the camp lined by soldiers, with their pikes at their feet. The Commander-in-chief, General Liu came forward to meet us; a yellow satin vest was the distinctive sign of his rank; over this he had another for winter wear, with the fur outwards. We were at once captivated by his pleasant expression and manners. He asked us into a small room, where we were obliged to partake of a Chinese breakfast, tea, wine, and English porter.

Breakfast over, several mandarins came into the room, bending the knee to the General, who answered these salutes by raising his clasped hands to the height of his forehead, after which he presented the officers to us. Their costume was rather handsome, but quite unpractical for military men. The fur and wadding rendered it unsuitable to the season, as even we were too hot in our uniforms. These officers came for their orders, and went off again at once. A bugle gave the signal; the soldiers, unfurling their flags, marched out of camp, followed by the General and ourselves. The shooting from one flank to the other, or in isolated groups, took place by means of flag-signalling; and various manœuvres, changes of front, and offensive attacks were executed. The whole effect was pretty, but not practical. Without being a military specialist, I may state that they had all sorts of things which would be useless in battle, as, for instance, the enormous number of flags; but it was all most effective, and reminded one of a scene from fairyland.

On the 1st of December we were honoured by a visit from General Liu. The soldiers of his escort were armed with pikes and halberds, and shouted, "Make way for our master!" They then lined the streets, and stuck their arms into the ground. Liu, as an officer, came on horseback as far as the front of the house, where he got into a palanquin which had followed him, and was carried through the court to the steps.

I often went to draw at the Tzien-Si Club, which I have already mentioned, and where there were subjects to occupy one for a month at least. Like all the other important architectural monuments in China, you might pass close to it without dreaming of its existence, so carefully is it concealed behind walls and courtyards. The first time I went there the porter refused to allow me to enter, and would not even take money; but the moment that Dao-Taï provided me with an order, I was free to go everywhere. At first I thought that my working in a temple might offend the religious sentiments of the Chinese, but afterwards I saw that they cherished no respect for the house of prayer. The temple was always empty. From time to time one or two people dropped in, but more for the sake of resting in the shade, smoking a pipe, talking a little, or even idling with a friend; perhaps occasionally for the sake of observing me more closely. Sometimes they came to inquire their destiny of the gods, with the aid of one of the priests attached to the temple. The clergy had not more reverence for the temple than the laity; the priests smoked in it, took tea, dried vermicelli, twisted silk, &c. Birds made their nests in it, and even the dogs wandered about in it, and cleanliness was consequently unknown. However, everything in this temple was interesting—the idols, altars, vases, pillars, walls, balustrades; but, above all, the carved cornices and enamelled tile-roofs of all colours, arranged in every variety of design. There were also porcelain statues on the roofs, and the cornices were richly carved.

During my walks I visted numbers of workshops of all sorts, but it would be impossible to enumerate them all. I will, therefore, limit myself to the mention of such as are not in use in our own country, as for instance, the manufacture of tallow candles encased in wax. The wicks are made from the leaves of a plant somewhat similar to the absinthe plant; a thread is wound round them, and they are then suspended to a horizontal wheel over the cauldron in which the tallow is melted. The wheel being next lowered into the cauldron, is left sufficiently long for the tallow to cool and condense itself, and is then taken up with the wicks, which having remained below long enough for the adhesion of a sufficient quantity of tallow, are then sprinkled with red or white wax to prevent their running. This is simply done on each candle separately by means of a spoon over a small cauldron.

The form and weight of the candles thus obtained are fairly uniform. Two hundred *kin* of tallow usually produces two thousand candles, and employs three workmen a day to turn out that number. The process requires no preparation, and can be carried out in any house. It is true that these candles are not particularly good ; they give a bad light, smoke a good deal, and require constant snuffing, which the Chinese do with their fingers, throwing the wick on the ground, and producing a most disagreeable smell. I may add that these candles are in universal use, as there are no others; and even in towns where the Europeans have wax candles, the Chinese do not take to them, perhaps from habit, or because they are expensive. Candles made of vegetable tallow, extracted from the seeds of the tallow-tree, are also in use, but being no better they are not sought after. All their candles are fixed to the ground, or to the candlestick or lantern, by a small bit of wood stuck into the end of them.

I also had the chance of seeing how they made the straps for shoes, bonbons and dainties, head-dresses of blue king-fishers' feathers for the ladies, palm or bamboo mats, pencils for writing or drawing, and how they engraved on wood for books, and could not fail to admire the patience of these neat-fingered Chinese, whose quickness and precision almost equalled that of a machine.

It would be impossible to enumerate all the articles made in China from that most useful of trees, the bamboo: houses, utensils, furniture, musical instruments, paper, little sticks, hats, lanterns, fans, mats, sieves, ropes, instruments of torture, palanquins, summer cushions, &c. All these are made from this precious wood, as hard as iron if you want to break it or cut it against the grain, but lengthways easily divided into the finest fibres. The young shoots of this plant resemble asparagus; they are used as food, and to my mind have more flavour than that vegetable. Bamboo is so hard that it has often to be heated before it can be worked. To give the desired bend it must be heated over charcoal; next, by the aid of pincers it is given the shape required, and allowed to cool quickly. Bamboo loses its elasticity in any part that has been heated, but retains the shape given it.

Cushions are made by plaiting very thin fibres, and forming a cover for a framework also made out of strips of bamboo; or little elastic *plaques* are made in the style of carriage springs, which are kept together in a case. These make very nice pillows, and the Chinese use them a great deal during their journeys and in their houses during the summer; ·they are light and clean, and do not heat the head.

Everything made of bamboo is cheap and within the means of the poorest, which after all is not surprising, as bamboo is quite common in China, and there is no lack of clever fingers to work it. What results might not be obtained if all the energies of this hardworking people could be utilized! But many of them have nothing to do, from the want of demand for their labour. This is the more to be regretted, as the Chinese work not only with a desire to gain their bread, but with a true love of art. This people have a great future before them. Labour is very cheap, especially in the winter, when agriculture is at a standstill. During my stay at Han-Keou, the Italian missionaries, with Fra Angelo at their head, began building a church, and to guarantee it from inundation they raised the land nine feet. The necessary earth was carried more than two miles by workmen on their shoulders or in baskets, and for this labour they received less than tenpence a day. This Italian mission, composed of men and women, in two detachments, includes an asylum for children, and another for old men and the poor. Here I was able to examine the manner in which the Chinese children's feet are mutilated. The sisters, not venturing to dispense with this ancient and barbarous habit, confirmed by the custom of centuries, submit the children they bring up to this mutilation, following the regular rules of the art, and I have to thank them for initiating me in the mystery, for no European, or even Chinaman, is ever allowed to see the naked foot of a Chinese woman. This is more probably from coquetry than modesty, as there is no more repulsive sight than one of these mutilated feet. It is difficult to say whence the custom arose. Some maintain that an empress having had deformed feet from her birth, all the ladies of her court deformed theirs to keep her in countenance, and that the custom then spread to the lower classes. Others assert, and with more appearance of reason, that the Chinese being jealous of their wives, invented this mutilation with the sole object of insuring their remaining at home; but this is mere conjecture, as the custom dates from the remotest ages. It is done in the simplest manner possible, with ordinary bandages, and patience does the rest. From the age of five, six, or seven, the child's foot is tightly bound up, and this operation once begun, must be continued during the rest of its life, for if left off nature reasserts itself, and the foot soon resumes its primitive shape. In putting on the bandage, care is taken to bend all the toes, with the exception of the great toe, back to the sole of the foot. The desired result is only attained after persevering several years with this operation; the foot becomes pointed; the big toe, which alone protrudes, is further altered into being long and narrow, instead of round as Nature intended it to be. The instep becomes a hump, the heel and the toes nearly touch, and the sole is bent double. It is impossible to imagine the difficulty of walking on such feet. As the bandages are never removed, the blood ceases to circulate in the normal manner, and the skin very often breaks; these sufferings, however, are undergone with much patience and pride. The richer a woman is, the more leisure she has to attend to her feet; sometimes it comes to such a pass that she can no longer stand up. In this case her feet receive the appelation of golden lilies.

In my collection of curiosities I possess a pair of Chinese boots which are not longer than one inch and three-quarters; it is almost impossible to believe that any woman could ever have worn them. Any traveller visiting Han-Keou should seek out a certain Chinese who is most friendly to Europeans, and who never allows himself to be called anything but

Mr. Senki. He will be sure to introduce him to his wife,

Mrs. Kok-Sin Senki, whose feet he will see in satin slippers embroidered with gold, absolutely of the same size as those of my collection, which indeed belonged to that very lady, who gave them to me.

The Chinese women wear very smart shoes, into which they only put the fore part of the foot, resting it on an inner and very slanting heel.

To possess small feet is, as I have already said, one of the principal conditions of beauty in a Chinese woman. It is one of the first things a man thinks of in selecting a wife, and her merits are only enhanced by her being unable to stand or walk without support; thus Mr. Senki was very proud of his Kok-Sin. He was so fond of foreigners that he lost no chance of making their acquaintance, and considered himself much honoured if any went to see him. Imitating our custom, he never failed to present his wife to his guests, but she remained a silent witness of the conversa-. tion, as she knew no foreign language.

Among the Chinese, Kok-Sin was a beauty, and I obtained permission from her husband to reproduce her features; the .portrait was finished in two sittings. During the second her husband was absent, and I was alone with the lady and a young servant, who followed all my movements with much curiosity. This is indeed progress when a Chinese woman is permitted to be alone with a stranger. The wife and sister of our Vice-Consul knew this lady very well, and she came to pay them a visit one day in my presence. Mistress Senki seemed very timid, perhaps because she was unacquainted with any foreign language; otherwise the conversation might have been interesting. She often smoked tobacco, and teased a small dog with her foot, probably to show it off.

She could not have come up the stairs without being supported by a servant. To amuse her they played on the
piano and the organ, and even danced, to initiate her in
European amusements. She imagined a valse to be a
theatrical representation, and when her mistake was explained, she answered, " Well, my feet could never do it."
I asked her leave to make a drawing of her feet, " Another
time," she said, " and I will put on prettier boots." I then
asked her for a pair as a remembrance, and she promised
and duly sent them to me.

But let us forget the beauty and go to see the races,
organised by the English and Russians. Han-Keou was to
be favoured with a sight it never had seen before, namely
the feat of three Russian Cossacks at full gallop, loading
their guns, drawing on each other, picking up a piece of
money off the ground, &c. This caused immense excitement ;
the ladies were loud in their applause, while the shouts of
the crowd were deafening. In their excitement the English
threw any amount of dollars to see how the Russian Cossacks
would lift them at full speed.

But time was getting on. The beautiful weather was
succeeded by rain, wind, and snow ; and the sun only
appeared by fits and starts.

We had now reached the 25th of December (according to
the new style), and the English were celebrating Christmas.
It is the custom among the Chinese merchants to offer
presents on the great feast-days to their clients—either a
sugared cake ornamented with artificial flowers and fruit, or
else poultry. Thus an English acquaintance of mine

received a live turkey. We had reached the 31st of December, the last of the year, and were still here. Sosnowsky had intended going to study commercial affairs, " in the mountains," as they call the tea-plantations here, but ended by sending Matoussowsky and the photographer. I now had no companion in my room, and, as it happened, was alone in the house on New Year's Eve. It was close on midnight, and I lay reading in bed, when I was surprised by the report of a gun. For the last few days there had been ugly rumours afloat as to the rancour of the natives against foreigners, but no one paid any attention to them. A second report was followed by the sound of gongs, cymbals, and frenzied cries from the crowd, apparently coming nearer the house. This savage chorus at such an unusual hour, in the European quarter, which was usually so quiet, reminded me of the accounts of the Chinese machinations and the massacre at Tien-Tsinn, and I listened intently. There was not a soul in the house from whom I could learn the cause of this uproar, and I remained in bed until hearing the crowd approach the gates of the house, I jumped up, prepared to get my fire-arms ready and offer some resistance to the onslaught. The Europeans would be certain to resist, and I must try to join them ; but it was now too late to go down to the street. I began to dress, and felt my heart beating violently, for who would not have been alarmed at the anticipation of unequal contest with an excited crowd. Is not China a country where disturbances may be expected at any moment, and where there is but a step from peace to fire and sword ?

However, the noise began to lessen, and the crowd to go
away, and for the moment I heard nothing more. . . . . .
Some moments later I heard our European drums beating
an alarm.   No longer doubting that this was the signal for
us to meet, I took my revolver and my gun, and went down
stairs.   The row and confusion recommenced, with the addition of rockets and squibs.

Never had any of Bach's finest melodies brought back
such calm to the human soul as the noise of those rockets
did to my excited brain.   I now could smile at my bellicose
resolutions, for when the Chinese let off squibs and rockets it
is a sure sign of rejoicing, such as marriage feasts, funeral
banquets, and everything of that description.   I went
peaceably to bed again; all was now quiet, and I heard
nothing but the night-watch striking his board.   Next
morning I was informed that this nocturnal procession
might be taken as a mark of the highest consideration on
the occasion of the New Year, from such of the Chinese as
have intercourse with the Europeans.

New Year's Day was celebrated by all sorts of amusements
organised by the English : a paperchase, a hare-hunt, and
theatricals.   I joined in these amusements, so as to see the
neighbourhood of Han-Keou, which is not at all picturesque, at least in winter—a dreary plain with ploughed fields
stretching out of sight, and in some parts patches of
autumnal corn.   The soil is mostly sandy or swampy; there
are several lakes, and a few villages scattered about among
leafless woods.

It is extraordinarily difficult to learn to write the Chinese language ; it is not written in single letters, but in words, so that not merely letters but whole words must be learnt. The Chinese speak in single words, or by monosyllabic short sounds, the number of which does not exceed five hundred, and thus whereas their language is most difficult to write, no European language is so easy to speak. It is, in truth, easier to remember five hundred sounds than seventy thousand, which do not correspond to our syllables, but which are complete words. They read aloud in a jerky manner, pronouncing the word corresponding to the sign. As an example, I will give the literal translation of the passport delivered to Matoussowsky, when he was leaving for the tea-plantations, and which is called "protecting light" by the Chinese. "Russian, Consul, gives, to know, now, there is a Russian official, accompanied, soldier, three men, going to (and here the name of the localities were inserted) walk, ask, give, protection, officials, guards, towns, villages, all, in general, respectable, visit, draw, there, is no, obstacle." Which would be thus translated : "The Russian Consul announces the arrival of Russian officials, accompanied by a soldier, three persons in all, going to visit the following localities. . . . I beg every one, functionaries, town and country officials, to be respectful, to protect them, and not to hinder their going about, drawing, &c." One can easily understand that this way of writing leads to all sorts of mistakes, conjectures, and misapprehensions, as well as the difficulty of writing by conventional signs, of which there are tens of thousands.

The difficulties of the language are innumerable, especially for the compiling of a dictionary. I may be mistaken, but the difficulty of the Chinese language seems to me a more insuperable obstacle than their Great Wall, and a barrier very difficult to break through in establishing relations between the Chinese and other nations. The children take eight years to learn a thousand words. It is the same in studying our languages; the Chinese being quite incapable of pronouncing a word containing several consonants, separate them with vowels, and divide the word by sounds, as in their own language, and thus the famous Kiachta dialect was formed.

For our official visits we were obliged to have our cards printed with the Chinese hieroglyphics, and this is the transformation my name went through "Pi-a-sie-sy-tzy." As it is impossible to the Chinese to remember a word of that length, they invariably pronounce none but the first syllable, letting some qualification follow it, "Sir, great sir, great man." They never retain anything but the first syllable of a name, and the rest is consigned to entire oblivion.

A few days before our departure we went to a restaurant, where Scheveloff gave as a farewell dinner, and provided musicians and female singers. It was most interesting to have this rare chance of seeing these women closer than one ever does in Central China.

At the beginning of dinner, whilst tea was being served, the choir sang something, and then one of the performers came up to our table and presented her fan to Matoussowsky. The programme of the songs and of the singers was printed on the fan, and she passed it to each of us in turn, so that we might choose what songs we preferred. But as the name of the songstress was not written beside the name of the song, it happened that the same singer was frequently chosen. These women were by no means beautiful; two of them were young, and all had a wide compass of voice. The song which particularly pleased us, called the " Twelve Flowers " (Schi-Er-Hua), had a very original refrain. The singer imitated the cooing of a dove, and that for a considerable length of time, in the passages where the pure sound of the *r* could best be heard. These women behaved rather freely, but with decorum.

A charming young girl of seventeen played the game of Houa-Tzian, in which the loser is obliged to swallow a glass of wine, and as she often lost the game, it followed that she swallowed a large amount of wine, without, however, showing any signs of having had too much.

Before leaving Han-Keou, I ought to say a few words concerning its tea trade. In the autumn and winter the traffic in this important branch rather slackens, and one can neither see the gathering or subsequent preparation of the tea-leaf.

One of my compatriots owned a factory for tablets of tea at Han-Keou, which was nothing but a huge shed, with no ceiling, and paved with bricks. On entering it I saw a heap of tea in a corner in lumps, which workmen were breaking up with sticks. These were defective tablets of tea, which were again steamed and reduced to powder, then made up into new tablets. Another corner was full of bamboo cases, and moulds for making the tablets. In one place they were being packed up to send to Russia; in another the carpenters were making or mending the moulds. The press in which the tablets were made was in the middle of the shed, and gave work to about twenty men. The dried tea, weighed ready for each tablet, was wrapped in napkins and steamed over covered cauldrons. When it was sufficiently softened the moulds were filled with it, after being dusted with finely powdered tea blackened with soot, and finally it was put into the press. In two hours six hundred tablets were ready, and taken out of the moulds to be packed. The press is worked by means of a strong lever placed upright. At the same instant as a tablet is put into the press, a workman ascends to a height of more than six feet, takes the lever into his hands, and jumps down, describing a quarter of a circle; during this descent two men catch hold of the lever whilst it is moving, and lean all their weight upon it to make it fall. A fourth, standing on a stool, holds on to two cords, and pushes the lever with his feet, jumping on to it at the moment it passes before him. The work goes on quickly, and in one minute six tablets are ready.

There are three sorts of tablets of tea: 1st, Lao-tcha, or the ordinary tablets sent to Australasia; 2nd, Tzin-Tchouan, sent both to Siberia and Central Asia. These two tablets are made with green tea. 3rd, Mi-tchouan, blackish, for Siberia.

In one department of the factory they sift the tea and colour it. I took away some pinches of a thick layer of reddish dust which covered everything, and examined it with a microscope. The dust consisted of small fine hairs, similar to those which line the inside of the leaf of the tea-plant. The labourers in this department suffer from inflammation of the eyes caused by this dust.

They pass the tea-leaves through a sieve, of which there are eighteen different sizes, from the finest to the coarsest. The drying is done in bamboo baskets, which are put on live coals covered with cinders to maintain an equality of temperature. · Sometimes it happens that the tea having got damp, forms itself into lumps ; it is then spread on mats, and they tread on it shod with sandals.   I have myself seen this operation performed by four Chinese walking up and down on mats thickly covered with tea, their hands on their breast or on their back, whilst they stare reflectively in front of them.

I should add that in China the tea-plant is not classified into black, yellow, or green ; that neither the leaves nor the flowers have any aroma ; and lastly, that the blossom of this plant is never used: although there is a sort of tea in Russia which goes by the name of " tea-flower." What is generally mistaken for the flower is in reality the young leaf covered with a silvery down, lai-hao in Chinese.

CHAPTER VI.

WE left Han-Keou on the 11th of January, after a residence of two months, to enter upon a long journey through the rich and picturesque province of See-Tchouan, and were now making for its principal district, Tching-Tou-Fou, and for Si-An-Fou, the ancient capital of all China, and to this day a very important commercial centre. As evening approached we had made little way against the rapid Yan-Tze, but had left the European quarter behind us, and the Chinese town on piles with a forest of masts along it. At sunset we were still not quit of. the town of Han-Keou on the left bank of the Han, at the mouth of which lay another flotilla of ships laden with merchandise and passengers. After another two miles and a half we stopped for the night, as the boatmen required rest, and these boats only travel during the day. Our friends had said their final farewells, and we were to see no more of our countrymen till we reached the frontier.

One boat was occupied by Sosnowsky and the photographer, another by Matoussowsky and myself, and the third by the Cossacks and the cook's galley. These three boats were of equal size, and were divided into three divisions. The owner and his family were domiciled in the stern, the middle of the boat was occupied by the passengers, and the fore part by the boatmen. Two erections in our cabin represented beds, and between them stood a table and bench. There was scarcely room to turn round, but we could just manage to stand upright, and had a window we could open or shut at will, and a door we could close during the day and remove at night.

* After settling our things, I went up on deck to see what was going on, and found quite a floating town around us. The Chinese were invisible in the dark, but we could hear them. Children crying ; here and there a suffocating cough ; the soldiers of our escort talking together, or from time to time beating a drum ; and from the bank came the drawling voice of a night watchman ; never before had I come across so much life and activity on a river.

There were several cracks in the deck of our boat, and to stop the draught I rigged up a very practical curtain over my berth, such as the Chinese use in their travels, and made of a number of bamboo stalks joined together by small copper hinges, so that it could be opened and shut like a fan. In winter such curtains are covered with flannel to keep out the cold, and in summer with gauze or tulle, to keep out insects.

January 12*th*, 1875. We were awoke before sunrise. The master and mate went on shore bareheaded, and with straw sandals on their feet. Putting out all their strength, they began towing the boat along. The three other boats

followed in company with many others, battling against the
current; others were going down the river, which was lined
by interminable rows of brick, bamboo, or reed houses.
Further off we could see temples, and enormous brick-kilns.

Matoussowsky went on with his survey, reproducing all
the twists and turns of the river on his maps, and noting
everything on the banks. Towards twelve we stopped
opposite a village to dine and rest, and no sooner had we
halted than most of the inhabitants appeared on the banks
delighted with this opportunity of seeing the *yan-jen*, or
"the strangers from beyond the sea." Some of them had
food for sale, and we bought some rolls and two kinds of
cakes, one sweet and cinnamon-coloured, the other tasting of
garlic, and by no means unpalatable. No sooner had the
boats started than the crowd began shouting " *Yan-goüi-tzy !* "
"devils from over the sea," and shaking their fists at us.
At sunset we stopped for the night near the village of Tziaï-
Dañ, at the mouth of a little river named Sin-Hé, where we
found a lot of other boats.

January 13th. A beautiful day and blue sky; quite warm.
The banks of the river monotonous and uninteresting. To
amuse myself, and with doubtful discretion, as there were
women of the party, I opened the window communicating
from our cabin with the part of the boat tenanted by the
boatman's family. Their portion of the boat was much
smaller and less lofty than ours, which did not, however,
prevent ten of the family (ten mouths, as the Chinese express
it) finding room in it at night. It is difficult to put a name
to this den, in which all the cooking was done for the ten

mouths.   When the fire was lit its smoke filled the whole place, and attacked the eyes and lungs.

Besides the boatman and his assistant there was his good old mother, who was nearly blind, and never shifted her position, which, indeed, would have been next to impossible. They called her *lao-taï-taï* (an honourable old woman). Then there was the boatman's wife, about forty years of age, the eldest daughter, aged twenty, who, whether from modesty or shyness, as soon as she saw me, hid her head between her knees, and remained in that position as long as I was at the window, and a younger daughter, who sometimes took the helm.   Four young children, with the marks of small-pox still upon them, were at this moment in bed. Sorry quarters for invalids, but they seemed none the worse.   Such is the existence of a Chinese boatman—without comfort or room to turn round in.

At dinner-time, during our halt, I landed and found the temperature to be 21° Reaumur in the sun.   One of the brick-kilns, of which I have already spoken, was not far off, and was reached by a path leading to a terrace, where I found a sheet of water which furnished steam to the kiln, and gave the grey bricks it turned out an extraordinary solidity.   At this moment the kiln was empty, and various natives were lounging in it; one was seated near the water washing his feet, whilst another was basking in the sun.

I saluted them with " Hao, bou-hao ?   Tzy-le-fañ-le ? " which means, " Are you well or not ?   Have you eaten any-thing ? "   They replied smiling that they had eaten, and made the same inquiries.   Then two little boys of ten or twelve years old addressed me at the top of their voices, although in reality exceedingly alarmed, and ready at any moment to take to their heels, hiding behind each other at my smallest movement.

A Chinese mounted on a buffalo stopped to look at me, and the animal, usually so quiet that a child may manage it, . threw back its head and sniffed at me with distended nostrils, quite excited by the sight of a stranger. Its intentions had 'not time to develop themselves; I was just then called back to the boat, as we were going to start off again. We came across black crows with white rings on their necks, vultures and carrion crows, and the day before we had seen cranes and wild-geese. If animals were few and far between, there was no lack of human beings. They were to be seen every-where, talking together in groups, or bustling about, carrying baskets and boxes, going down the river with goods, or conveying them from one bank to another. During the next night a gun was fired to warn off the robbers who roam about the neighbourhood, and who do not hesitate to pillage the boats drawn up on the shore. At nine a drum beat the retreat, the fires were put out, and all noise ceased. Only whispered conversations were heard, and the groans of an old boatman hard-by. These boatmen lead a by no means enviable existence, as their pay for a hard day's work is only about sevenpence.

January 14th. One village succeeded another without intermission. Never before have I seen such a collection of houses without a town.

The Han now begins to be known by the name of the

Sian-Ho. This is often the case in China. The same river may be known by ten different names, changing at each district it passes through.

24° Reaumur in the sun, and hardly any breeze. We were getting near the town of Han-Tchouan, on the top of a very steep bank. The news of our arrival had spread with astonishing rapidity. The whole population forsook its peaceable avocations to rush down the rugged bank of the river. Everywhere the cry of " *Yan-jen* ! " was to be heard. Our boats were scarcely made fast before crowds swarmed on board—men, women, and children of both sexes, besides worthy old women, who, however, held themselves rather aloof. It was odd to see them limping along on their small feet to get a sight of a Russian officer, upon whom they gazed open-mouthed, their eyebrows raised with evident interest, which, without any given reason, was easily changed to anger. In short, our arrival occasioned the greatest excitement. All were keen to know who we could be and where we could be going. The boatmen and the soldiers, quite proud of being associated with us, explained that we were Oulousses (Russians) returning from Pekin to our own country. I signed to a man selling bonbons to come up, and, buying one, began to examine it, on which the crowd exclaimed, "He does not know what it is" ("Ta-bou-saio-dy "), and laughed heartily. Others screamed out, "It is good to eat ; try it." I took a handful and distributed them amongst the children, which caused a regular scramble in the crowd. Every hand was stretched out towards me, and they accepted and ate the bonbons without giving me a word of thanks.

It is not the fashion in China to say Thank you for every little thing. The man sold me all his store, which I distributed, and he then asked me two hundred sapeques. I paid him through the Cossack treasurer, who judged one hundred to be enough, and apparently judged aright, as the confectioner was quite satisfied, and had no doubt made a good profit.

Suddenly, whilst smoking on deck, I saw a Chinese at my side, who evidently meant to seize the cigar in my mouth. These free and easy manners not being customary, even amongst Asiatics, I imagined this to be premeditated insolence, intended to show his associates that there was no occasion to be polite to these " devils from over the sea." I therefore caught his arm with a strong grip, and gave him a severe blow in the eye. But quite undaunted, he jumped from our boat to the next, where Boïarsky was also smoking a cigar, and seizing it from him, rushed on shore. He was apparently delegated to bring one back by fair means or foul. Many had a turn at it, and all spat and made faces, whilst others began to cough. The river now became wider, and the landscape more picturesque, with villages nestling amongst the trees, and far away on the horizon we began to distinguish the faint blue outline of mountains.

At dusk we stopped, and Matoussowsky landed to measure the width of the river. I followed him, and as we went along asked first one native and then another their name for a poplar-tree, and both pronounced it differently, " *yan-hui*," and " *yan-sui*."

January 15*th.* A favourable wind. The boatmen took in

the tow-ropes, got back on to the boat, unfurled the sails,
and then literally rested on their oars, thankful that the
wind should do their work for them. It rose still higher,
the boats cut through the foaming water, and we should have
made a good passage had not Sosnowsky taken it into his head
to shoot, and make us stop short.

The sky was cloudy and the wind cold. The crowd of
natives shivered, although they all had wadded clothing.
To guard against the cold they actually had little fur bags
hung on to their ears. These thin and pallid creatures
gazed at us without uttering a word, but as soon as our boats
left the banks they found voice to abuse us, and call after us,
" the foreign devils," the children especially shaking their
fists at us.

The river began to wind about, and soon we turned north-
wards. The wind being contrary, we had to take in the
sails and use the towing-rope again. The birds flew very
high, usually a sign of cold and snow, but in this instance
the wind brought tempests of sand, which penetrated everywhere, and covered everything on the boat; we even crunched
it in our tea and in our food.

We stopped to dine in a large village called Sien-Toou-
Tchjen, quite on the edge of the water, so that its last street
overhung it on beams. Here again were many boats, on
which women were preparing food or sewing.

The men ate abundance of rice, fish, and vegetables, and
the children played about the deck with a rope tied round
them, so that when one fell into the water it was simply
pulled out again and put back into its place, without any

trouble being taken to dry or console it. To complete the establishment, dogs roamed about the decks as guardians of the ship.

Sometimes in passing these boats I greeted the Chinese with some of the ordinary phrases. For instance, if they were eating I asked what they ate, and they never failed to reply in the same polite way, by telling me what it was, and even showing their cups to prove that they spoke the truth. The inhabitants were all about the streets, working or taking their meals. A nuptial procession passed us—a village wedding. First came two individuals striking gongs, two others with lanterns slung on very long poles, and then four men carrying the shut palanquin which contained the bride. A group of men and women accompanied the palanquin, and four men at a certain distance carried the chests with the wedding presents. Four chests may seem a good many for a village wedding, but we learnt that the presents were generally hired to make a show in the procession.

We soon set off again. The dense population was really surprising. We passed village after village, and ever so many more marriage processions, this being the twenty-first day of the first moon, a lucky day for marriages.

The Chinese are as superstitious as we are, and, like us, have their propitious days, "on which heaven scatters its favours;" lucky days for plentiful harvests, marriages, starting on a journey, &c.

January 16th. A cold night and strong wind. Although warmly clad I preferred walking, and therefore landed, with

Stepanow, and followed the river, taking a straight line wherever there was a bend, and going through the villages on the way.

The inhabitants were all out of doors, the old people taking care of the children, and the young people working and chattering together. Cotton spread out on tables was being beaten out with flails. They were also busy drying corn and millet, spread out on mats.

Our unexpected arrival produced a sort of amazement among the villagers, so little did they expect to see any one come among them that was not Chinese. With their invariable politeness, they asked us into their houses to take tea, which I should have done with great pleasure had I had the time. Never had my short fur coat and my boots excited so much admiration. The Chinese walked all round me, lifted my coat-tails, and touched the collar and the boots, striking them gently with their nails to feel the leather.

As we were crossing a field towards the river we met a native carrying a pitcher of brandy and dragging a pig by a rope passed through its ear. His New Year's feast was drawing near, and, though poor, this man appeared satisfied with his lot. He greeted us most politely, and then pointed to his brandy and the pig, as if in explanation. He put us on the right road and offered to guide us to the river, but we only thanked him for his good intention.

"The men from over the sea seldom come to see us," said he.

"That is because you don't want them to come, but call them ' devils from over the sea.' "

"Oh, no! that is not true; we like strangers; we are very glad when they come, good people."

It seemed to me that he said this out of sheer fright, but seeing some Chinese in the distance, he could not resist calling them to come and have a look at us, and, as I happened to be taking some notes, they watched my writing with much interest. They wanted to try and write themselves with the "foreign paint-brush," so I offered them my book and pencil, but none would venture, although each tried to persuade the other to do it. A boy of sixteen was the boldest; he took the pencil and marked down two hieroglyphics, when he then read aloud. "Tain, Di" (heaven and earth), and pointed to them with his finger, this being probably the first thing he had learnt at school.

We made our midday halt at the village of Houan-Keou, and, as usual, its inhabitants soon collected to see the strangers. We happened to throw away the remains of some ham wrapped up in paper, which they straightway picked up and carefully examined; they even tasted it, making guesses at what meat it could be, and came to the conclusion that it was very good ham, and equal to their own, from which opinion we ventured to differ, as we held it to be far superior to theirs, which is thin and dried up.

When we started the crowd began to disperse, but on some one beginning to shout, they reassembled and began to run after us, screaming, jumping, and dancing. In this crowd I observed an individual without an arm, and had time permitted I would have waited to ask him how and where he had lost it. I was interested to know, for the

Chinese, being as bad surgeons as doctors, do not recognise amputation, and on principle never practice it. It is thought a sin towards the family to deprive the body of a limb.

At sunset we halted beside a village named Yui-Tzia-Keou, which we were informed contained ten thousand inhabitants. Here a great number of boats were congregated, and crowded against each other, forming a complete floating town, with its own distinct existence, the inhabitants of the boats rarely going on shore. Only the men go into the towns occasionally, either to buy food or have their heads shaved, an operation they never perform for themselves or for each other. However poor a Chinaman may be, he always goes to a barber, as they hold the trade to be ignominious. Probably this antipathy dates from the time when the order went forth to shave their heads in token of their fidelity to the Manchu dynasty, and the barber was most likely regarded as a sort of public executioner, for previous to the Manchu reign the hair was worn long, and not in pigtails.

Hardly had our boats come to a standstill when an immense crowd assembled to stare at us. Our previously notified arrival was known to the whole population, and the local police authorities came to ask if we should like the crowd dispersed. Soldiers were actually called out, but they tried in vain to send the people away; the more inquisitive persistently but quietly returned.

January 17*th.* Matoussowsky was obliged to land and measure the width of the river, and I and a soldier went with him to keep off the crowd. I then went alone to see the town, and my apparition without any escort seemed greatly to impress the inhabitants. "*Yan-jen, yan-jen,*" the one repeated to the other, and all those who could leave their work followed me, their numbers swelling at every step. Some gently touched the tails of my fur; others, like regular town-criers, informed the inhabitants that a stranger was passing down the street. On a small boy pushing me from behind, whether accidentally or purposely, the crowd reprimanded him severely, and the child disappeared.

A well-dressed young man accosted me, but not understanding what he said, I continued on my way. However, others who had overheard him insisted on my going with them, which I did, although without in the least knowing where they were taking me. It turned out that they wanted to show me a panorama. It was like those we have at our fairs, and was about three yards and a half long. They expected to astonish me with this marvel. The worthy proprietor of the panorama collected some sapeques amongst the curious, but his takings were not extensive, as most of them probably knew it already by heart. Having no money about me I refused to go in, and explained my reason to the proprietor, who begged me nevertheless to enter and see his marionettes. Later on I sent him money from the boat, but he would not accept it. .

As there were no houses on the other side of the river, we crossed over in search of a little peace and quiet. We had not been there many minutes when at least a hundred people seemed to have started from the earth and met together to stare at us. I collected some samples of the soil and a few plants, and on climbing to the highest bank at a

distance of about three hundred feet off, saw a sort of grassy
rampart parallel to the river, which turned out to be one of
those dykes which the inhabitants of the plains of Han-
Kiang raise to guard against inundation. I went up to it
and perceived a vast sheet of water divided into squares by
narrow bands of earth; these turned out to be rice-fields
submerged by the periodical inundations. Night came on
and a red fog covered the horizon. On one side of the river,
noise, care, and toil prevailed; on the other peaceful silence
and complete repose. Through the fog and darkness, both
on the quay and on the boats I could see fires of lighted
paper requiring constant replenishing. Squibs and rockets
burst forth in various directions, lanterns swung at the mast-
heads and over the sides of the boats; the noise of drums
and cymbals, which the Chinese ply with extraordinary
vigour, and guns fired from time to time, all led to the
conclusion that a fête was taking place. It was the 23rd
day of the first moon, and was evidently a feast, but what
feast I could not ascertain. The owner of my boat followed
suit and burnt a considerable number of bamboo shavings,
at the same time lighting a few candles and sticking them
into spikes arranged for the purpose on the bows of the
vessel, and every now and then letting off squibs. The
soldiers did the same, and when the fires got dim the men
began to pray, raising their hands to heaven and bowing
themselves to the earth. These prayers and offerings lasted
a good while after we had all retired, and terrible music
continued on the opposite side of the river.

On this day every head of a family who is the proprietor

of a house or a boat is expected to burn some packets of paper, candles, or fireworks. Think of the enormous quantity which must be used on one day alone!

January 19*th.* Another day's halt. As Theodor was going to the village I accompanied him, and according to my invariable rule of cultivating the natives, I got into a boat already occupied by several passengers, and thereby gave them a real treat. A good old man seated beside me opened a conversation, and Theodor translated his words.

" All men are the same, only their speech differs," said he.

" The sun shines for the whole world," I answered in a Chinese turn of phrase I had learnt by heart.

" And in your country is there a sun like ours ? "

" Not only one like it, but the same sun."

The Chinaman seemed to be astonished, but to accept the fact.

" And have you a moon as well ? "

" The same moon shines in our country."

He seemed quite surprised, and apparently wondered whether we said this only to flatter him. A crowd awaited me at the river side with deafening cries of " *Yan-jen-na !* *Yan-na !*" They might have been awaiting a friend they had not seen for years, so great was the delight with which they greeted our arrival. I landed with Theodor, and they followed us shouting "He comes ! he comes !" I then went to see some temples with most beautiful roofs, and was allowed free entry everywhere, which would not have been permitted in the towns more frequented by Europeans.

Eventually the door of one temple was abruptly closed in my face, on which I thought it best to turn back, but immediately afterwards it was partly opened, and the hechan (priest), winking his eye in the direction of the multitude, invited me to step in. This was no easy matter, as on such occasions the crowd generally forces the door. I managed, however, to pass through, with five or six of my numerous following. Those who had succeeded were in fits of laughter, but the door would certainly have been forced in if they had not been assured that I would come out immediately.

The temple was poor and sombre in comparison with others I had seen, and was of no particular interest, excepting its lovely roof. In the courts the priests were busy twisting silk into threads.

From this temple I went into another, still accompanied by the crowd, which completely filled the street; and as they ruthlessly upset the tables and baskets of the shopkeepers in their progress, much screaming, shouting, and quarrelling ensued.

I tried to find out the meaning of the inscriptions on the boards they usually carried in their processions, but neither Theodor or the priest professed to be skilled in letters, and I could get no explanation of any sort. Neither was I able to find out the meaning of the various symbolic signs also used in the processions, and at other times kept in the temples. They are stuck on long poles, and represent all kinds of articles, such as knives, hatchets, hands holding a red ball or a paint-brush, gilt melons, dragons' heads, &c.

I likewise examined the fine sculpture of the doors and

cornices and the joists supporting the stage of the theatre, all executed with the minutest care and having a series of fables painted on them. The expression of some of the faces was admirable, although occasionally laughable. Knowing how expensive carving in relief is in our country, I inquired the price of it here, and found that a sculptor is paid 20 kopecks (about sixpence) a day, food included.

I was much surprised to find European wares in some of the shops in the principal streets, such as glass, watches, soap, peppermint drops, wax candles, English needles, cottons, &c.

It is true that all these were of an inferior quality, as there is but small demand for some of these articles in China; for instance, the natives never use soap; and wax candles are dearer than tallow, and therefore less in request.

The boatmen seeing my intention of recrossing the river, all offered their boats; such passengers as had already taken their places begged me to go with them, and when we finally started they set up shouts which very much resembled our own hurrahs.

The current took us much further down than the spot where our boats were moored, so I landed to walk through the village on my way back, and began to sketch a little house built of unbaked bricks in a wooden framework.

A bench was immediately brought to me, all the inhabitants of the village clustering around me, and subsequently escorting me back to the boat.

Wandering about the neighbourhood I incessantly met

crowds of Chinese. This began to bore me, for I now knew
them so well that I never even looked at them, whereas I
was always a novelty and a new type to them, and they
mobbed me at every turn. This time they discussed amongst
themselves as to whether I understood their language or
not. "*Ta-doun-de*" (he understands), said some. "*Ta-
bou-doun-de*," said others., Next they commented on my
beard, remarking that I was still very young to grow one.
Whether intentionally or otherwise, they afterwards began
to push and hustle, and this rather alarmed me, as I was on
the edge of a steep precipice, and remembered hearing one
native say to another at Han-Keou how much he should like
to push " the foreign devils into the sea." As a matter of
fact, their bark is generally worse than their bite. But to
prevent anything unpleasant happening, I made for a small
bamboo house kept by a woman—not a very usual thing in
China, but sometimes done with the consent and approval of
the husband.

January 20*th.* Beautiful still weather. The thermometer
at 11° Reaumur. The river becoming wider and wider, the
current less rapid, and the sandy banks getting gradually
lower.

January 21*st.* A cold and foggy morning. The river
like a great lake. The boatmen pushing along with boathooks, when a slight breeze got up. The delighted Chinese
immediately began to invoke the spirits. Every now and
then they raised their eyes to heaven, calling out in a way
peculiar to themselves, and imploring the god of the wind
to aid them in sailing their boat; but the god of the wind

remained deaf to their entreaties, or perhaps was not in the humour to satisfy them.

January 22nd. A beautiful day. The village of Chaï-Yan, whose population and commercial importance almost give it the right to be called a town, was chosen for our midday halting-place. It is built on an immense plain cut up by canals, fed by an artificial pond shut in by two dams opposite each other. The first of these is opened during the spring floods to let the river-water pass into the reservoir, and the other sends the water out into the irrigating canals.

January 24th. A cold morning and a hoar frost, which reminds me of my native land. Herons fly along the edge of the water, and thousands of wild-geese pass overhead.

I now am thoroughly conversant with all the peculiarities of the Han-Kiang, one of which is that it has a much wider bed in summer than in winter. In the latter season its banks are formed by an alluvial deposit from the summer floods ; in the summer the water spreads out as far as certain dykes which follow along the river on both sides, sometimes considerably beyond its winter bed. The space between the two beds is cultivated by the Chinese in winter, and they manage to get some sort of harvest off it. They also erect temporary huts along the banks, where they sell bread, firing, and wine to the boatmen, so that they need not run up to the villages, which are often a considerable distance off.

The quantity of clay and sand deposited in the bed of the river during the summer makes it shallower every year ; consequently the water, which in summer reaches a height of thirty feet above its winter level, tends to widen, and the people along the river are forced to raise the height of the dykes. This happens gradually but surely, and the dykes which now suffice to stay the floods will in fifty years time be insufficient, and will then have to be raised to a still greater height. It is a perpetual battle with the water, and the same occurs on the Yellow River; in the winter the river seems to flow in a trough similarly formed by the banks of high dykes, and behind them is the plain, on a much lower level than the river during the summer season.

Notwithstanding every precaution, a dyke sometimes bursts, and a torrent descends on the plain which submerges everything and occasions the greatest disasters. We have reached the eve of the Chinese new year, the most important day in their calendar, and everywhere preparations are ·on foot to celebrate it worthily.

To our great regret we were to spend it on our boats in an unfrequented spot. A favourable wind permitted our sailing, and gave the boatmen leisure to prepare for their feast and their religious duties. Tan-Tchen-Kouei, the " honourable master " of our boat, as they call him, had cultivated our good-will from the very first day, and our esteem for him had been on the increase ever since. He was about forty years old and had a frank, open expression. He worked hard, but never complained of his lot or envied other men, and might have served as an example to many. He was always cheery and courteous to his family, as well as to us. His only possession was his boat, which he towed from Han-Keou to Fan-Tcheng and back from Fan-Tcheng to

Han-Keou with goods or passengers; he worked from morning to night, by the sweat of his brow to provide food for ten mouths, and was an excellent husband and tender father.

This poor man, in a 'true artistic spirit, endeavoured to ornament his boat worthily for the feast, and thereby to give it due solemnity in the eyes of his family. Giving up the helm to his second girl, he began to sweep and then to wash his boat, cleaned and decorated it with greenery, candles, and coloured paper, changed his clothes, although the change was very modest, and when everything was ready, he went up to the bows with a tray of offerings, consisting of bread, roast pork, and chicken, fried fish, and cups containing rice, water, and brandy.

Having put down this tray on the deck, he lit several candles, burnt a packet of paper, let off some squibs, and prostrated himself several times in succession. He next took a small portion of each dish and threw it into the water, emptying the cups of rice, water, and brandy into it. All this was done faithfully and reverently. The boat still pursued its rapid course, cutting through the foaming water, and the sun shone brightly upon this poor but honest worker, addressing his praises to the Creator of the universe. His prayers over, he resumed the helm, and I asked his permission to make a drawing of his decorated little abode, to which he immediately consented. Shortly afterwards we came to the village of Tan-Gouan where everyone was making ready for the feast. All business was at a standstill for three days, which was very provoking, as we had

in no provisions, being accustomed to get everything at
moment.

veral other boats were moored at this place, and amongst
rs a gunboat tenanted by a mandarin official belonging
he river conservancy. At nightfall all the boats were
minated with lanterns; they burnt paper in every direc-
or sent up rockets and fireworks. The sky was overcast
the night dark; one saw nothing but the fires and the
erns decorating the masts. The kitchens were full of
; the food for the morrow's consumption was being
ared; cocks were being slain and their blood sprinkled
the paper which was subsequently to be burnt in honour
he various gods. The noise of gongs filled the air, and
two gunboats fired salutes. Towards midnight silence
n reigned; one might have imagined that every one was
d asleep, but precisely at midnight a salute from the
boats announced the first of the year. The prayers and
tes began again, and then, according to custom, the
ng congratulated their elders, those of the same age
ted each other, the old people gave the young their good
es and everyone sat down to table.

pening the little window which looked into their part of
boat from mine, I begged our boatman to accept a few
e presents as a remembrance. I had a knife and razor
him, scissors and some packets of needles and buttons for
women, and bonbons done up in ornamental packets for
children. These unexpected presents were a great plea-
to them. All night long the Chinese sat eating and
king and talking.

January 25th. The first of the year. There was nothing to be done on the water amongst other twenty boats, and in detestable weather. A strong wind blew clouds of sand into our cabin, and everything was covered with it.

We were sitting reading and trying to amuse ourselves, when a soldier from the gunboat entered and saluted us. Theodor accompanied him with a card from the mandarin, requesting us to allow him to pay us a visit, to which we assented, and then posted ourselves at the door to receive him according to Chinese etiquette. The mandarin, in full dress, climbed into the cabin, where he bowed nearly to the ground, raised his hands and shut his eyes, without uttering a word, and composed his face to an expression of mingled fear and shyness. All this mimicry is part of the ceremonial, and rather painful to the uninitiated. We begged him to be seated, but he still remained bent double, appearing not to venture to do so. We therefore sat down ourselves, and he then followed our example, still keeping up his simulated fright and timidity. Now this man, when not paying an official visit, was perfectly simple and not in the least shy.

Conversation was difficult, but we were obliged to invent something to avoid awkwardness. We therefore expressed our regret that the bad weather prevented the people enjoying themselves, and also that we were debarred from spending the day in a town, to which he invariably replied, " Scha " (yes). After some questions about his family, and the place where he had spent his last New Year's Day, tea, snuff, and bonbons were offered him. Fortunately for us,

he then prepared to depart, but, according to Chinese custom, we had to ask him to sit down again. When he got
up he recommenced his grimaces; with his eyes lowered,
he appeared to appeal to us beseechingly, and we watched
him in silence. "Pray be seated," said I; "I beg you to
sit down." He had only waited for this formula, and took
his departure, muttering polite speeches. On deck, however, there was another check. We were all there to escort
him back, and saluted him energetically. But, motionless
and impassible, he appeared to wish to bar our passage and
prevent our going farther, and seemed as if waiting our
orders. We therefore returned to our cabin and let him
depart with a quiet mind.

This ceremonial does not come into play in everyday life,
although politeness is the rule in China. One hardly ever
meets with rudeness of any kind, and may speak to any
chance person in the streets sure of being answered by him
with all the politeness of a man of the world.

After the departure of our mandarin, we told our Cossack
to prepare our soup, which was usually done in our *lao-ban's*
kitchen by his "esteemed mother." This he absolutely
refused to do, as the mate, he said, was coming himself to
invite us to share his bread and salt, and that a dinner had
been prepared expressly for us. This being a great fête, it
was their duty to feast us. Sure enough, Tan-Tchen-Kouei
came directly after and urgently begged us to accept his
dinner and not to insult him by refusing, as, after all, he
and his children were human beings. We were very fond
of our mate, and would not for the world have distressed him

by refusing his dinner. Usually our own consisted of one
dish of meat only, with some rice or soup, but in sufficient
quantity to appease our voracious appetites. The Chinese, on
the other hand, prepare very small quantities of each dish,
so we were rather nervous as to how we should come off.
Also, without being very fastidious, we had secret apprehen-
sions as to the cleanliness of the food prepared under such
adverse circumstances. Presently the window opened, Tan-
Tchen-Koueï passed the tray through to the Cossack, and
we were soon quite ashamed of our doubts.

Instead of our solitary dish of rice, they gave us a boiled
chicken, pork with bamboo shoots, fried fish, roast pork,
different sorts of bread, meat pies, cutlets, more dressed
pork, and a caraffe of brandy. Most of these dishes were
so abundant and so excellent that we three were not nearly
able to finish them all. As a slight return, we presented
three thousand sapeques to our host, and bonbons to his
children.

After dinner the soldiers from the gunboat came to present
their congratulations. There were eleven of them, but only
two came into the cabin, making their bows and bending the
knee. The others, drawn up on deck, imitated their genu-
flections. We gave them five thousand sapeques, and
regretted we could not be as lavish as beseemed Russian
officers; but this came out of our own pockets, and not out
of the general fund, as it ought to have done.

The whole day the boatmen, workmen, and soldiers, went
about among themselves, filling the little cabins, inter-
changing their good wishes, tasting the good things which

had been prepared overnight, drinking tea and wine, and chattering and talking even more than usual; but none of them got drunk, in the Russian acceptation of the term, by which I mean that no one became noisy or quarrelsome. The children, who were dressed in wadded garments, were allowed to go on shore and play about and to let off squibs. These squibs were in little copper tubes, going off with a tremendous explosion, and I thought they were very dangerous playthings, but the children were apparently accustomed to them.

January 26th. Snow and a contrary wind obliged us to stop another day. Although warmly clad, my feet were like ice, so I went on shore to warm them, and came upon some young folk playing at ball. As soon as they saw me the game ceased, and they rushed to examine both me and my clothes. When they turned up the tails of my fur coat, I did the same to theirs. One of them drew my attention to his little cap, and as I had a soft felt hat on, I transformed it into all sorts of shapes for their amusement. One of them brought his pigtail to my notice, on which I attracted his attention to my moustache and beard. Then I began to play about with the children, running after them and letting them chase me, which gave great pleasure to small and great.

One of them, a boy of twelve, took sudden fright, and ran away in earnest. His fear was most comic, and gave me, as well as the bystanders, great amusement. I then drew a dragon, a Chinese, and a horse for them on the sand with my stick, and a boy traced three hieroglyphics, and asked me if I understood them, which I did not.

"*Tian, Di, Jen*" (heaven, earth, man), he explained, and pointed at me as he said the last word.

" I am not a man, but a foreign devil," said I.

All the grown-up people made signs in the negative, and cried with one voice, " Aïe, Aïe, Aïe ! " (No, no, no ! man, good man."

" Your countrymen call me a foreign devil."

" No, no ! it is not true ; it is not possible that they can have said it."

Others came from the village and asked me the usual run of questions, to which I had learnt the conventional answers. They generally referred to my age, my nationality, and also from whence I came and what I sold. The boy who had run away came back from the village and hid behind the rest till I ran after him and caught him, on which he asked my pardon with clasped hands, and made the rest shriek with laughter.

To-day paper was again burnt on the boats, and a good many fireworks were let off, the gunboats at the same time firing salutes.

January 27th. Frost, and although only one degree, in the open air it was very perceptible. The boats were covered with hoar-frost. Not a soul to be seen about. Everyone stopped indoors, having covered the boats with mats to keep the cold out.

January 28th: The same weather. The Chinese expected a thaw, and were getting the ice off the decks to prevent its flooding the boats. We had gone twenty-five *li*, and although it was not late we were obliged to stop, as the men could not tow for long on the slippery ground. We were not far from the big town of Añ-Liu-Fou, but it was not visible from the river.

January 29th. Another stoppage, owing to the bad weather. The ice was beginning to melt and drip, soaking everything—our beds, tables, &c., which was unpleasant, but unavoidable.

January 30th. The boatmen were themselves getting wearied of the inaction, and decided on going, but the ground was so slippery that they had again come to a standstill.

January 31st. The wind had fallen and the sky cleared. The thermometer stood at 13° Reaumur in the sun. We were meeting more boats than ever; they had probably been detained by the bad weather of the last few days. With their sails unfurled to dry, they advanced majestically in rows or in groups, and gave the river a most lively appearance. The melted snow ran down in streams to the river, just as it does with us in the spring.

We met some fishermen in a boat to which it would be difficult to put a name. Two tubs were joined together by a small joist, to which was fixed a transverse plank giving balance to the whole. A small bench was fastened to the joist, the fisherman was seated upon this, and lowered his legs into one of the tubs, and rowed with one oar. The river was still wide, but its banks began to be higher, and the poor boatmen were forced to climb up and down the hills, slipping and tumbling at almost every step. Farther on we came to some rapids. Through the breaking of a rope of our boats, it was carried to some distance by the current before it could be stopped.

February 1st. 20° Reaumur in the sun. The banks of the river got steeper and steeper. In the distance we could see pagodas on the hill-tops, and although so isolated from the world, the temples were nevertheless surrounded by walls. To-day we again met many boats, and not one passed us without its owner expressing surprise at the sight of the *yan-jen.* Most of these boats were not larger than our own, but every now and then one of much larger size passed us laden with merchandise. On one of them I counted as many as twenty-three men on deck at dinner, and in the forepart of the ship at least ten heads peering forth to gaze upon us.

February 2nd. We neared the town of I-Tcheng-Sian, which is at a distance of three quarters of a mile from the river. On the left bank is a very rugged granite crag and a stone quarry.

Here we halted for the night. I joined two Cossacks, Theodor, and a soldier, and set off on a foraging expedition. We went through fields of beans and peas, and I was amazed at the quantity of crows and magpies in them. Generally birds are very quiet in China; they do not know a gun by sight, and several times I have noticed their astonishment on seeing another killed or wounded. They fly around wondering why the other bird does not follow them, and without the least knowing the danger they are in themselves. If a gun goes off, the birds merely change their tree, and allow you to get up to them again.

We soon reached the suburbs of the town of I-Tcheng-Sian, with its wall and gate surmounted as usual by a tower. A canal surrounds the wall, and a stone bridge with a single arch leads to the gate. The children playing about the canal were the first to see us and give the signal of our arrival. A noisy crowd awaited us at the gate and followed in our wake down the narrow street, no cleaner than usual in Chinese towns, and the crowd no less inquisitive. Their pleasure and satisfaction was equalled by their curiosity, and the crush became greater at every step. The Chinese soldier went off with the Cossacks to lay in provisions, whilst I and Theodor went to the local police station to send off a letter to Fan-Tcheng, where our two interpreters were to await us. Whilst Theodor went into a house to get change for a bit of silver, I waited behind a wooden paling outside, leaning against the wall. The surging crowd increased, for all wanted to get a close look at me; the paling gave way under the pressure and was broken to pieces, and some boys who were astride upon it fell to the ground, upon which some set up shouting for satisfaction, whilst others yelled because they were being suffocated, and here and there quarrelling for a good place arose. I remained grave and composed, although from time to time I could not help smiling. The Chinese observed the movements of my lips, and shouted with laughter. Someone in the crowd threw a piece of bread at me, but I did not appear to notice it.

Meanwhile Theodor had again joined me, and we resumed our walk. Our advent was energetically heralded, so that none should miss the chance of seeing a *yan-jen*. This is done to a certain extent all over the world, but none surpass the Chinese in their open satisfaction at being able to spread abroad some new thing. Followed by all this crowd we reached the *yamin*, a small and dirty edifice in which everything was old, even the officials belonging to it.

One of them was most desirous of talking to me, and appeared to believe that I knew their language perfectly although I pretended for some unknown reason not to understand a word of it.

After giving our letter to a subordinate, we went on down the street, meaning to leave the town by another gate. We came upon a very picturesque triumphal arch in ruins. None of the inhabitants could tell us in whose honour it had been erected. There are similar monuments in every direction, and their history is equally unknown.

Farther on we came upon a temple in ruins, its court deserted and grass-grown, its tank empty, and its gate blocked up. None but the birds and bats dwelt therein.

" Whose temple is this ? "

" The temple of the great Koun-Fou-Tzy," several voices in the crowd replied.

For two thousand years this name has endured, and it certainly will never be forgotten. Some visiting-cards were to be seen hanging over the doors of the houses, where they had remained since the New Year.

The sun had nearly set by the time we reached the gate, and those who followed us could not venture to go any - farther, as the closing of the gate might have compelled them to remain all night outside the walls. The crowd diminished, and two men who were with us to the last, after bowing respectfully, took leave of us at the gate. I then found out that these were police agents, who had been with us the whole time without our being aware of it.

Many Europeans holding the Chinese to be very suspicious of foreigners, might herein fancy a system of supervision, but I merely saw a delicate attention in it to strangers, which civilised nations might do well to imitate.

February 3rd. Pedestrians, cavaliers, and even palanquins made the banks of the river as lively as the streets of our biggest towns. Quantities of men and children lounged about on the grass, many dressed in white in sign of mourning; others only wore white turbans. I could not find out the cause of all this mourning. Perhaps an epidemic had increased the mortality in this district. A favourable wind permitted our sailing, but at a point where the river was very shallow we stuck on a sandbank, where washing the sand for gold was going on, but we did not wait to see the process.

February 4th. We arrived at Fan-Tcheng, on the Han, a most important commercial town, and we could now see the surroundings of town and garrison, with its wall crowned by towers and kiosks, decorated with pikes and flags in honour of our arrival; farther on a long and solid quay, pagodas, and some frail-looking houses. Where the quay terminated the houses were raised on stone foundations. Red paper cards were glued on all the houses, with various inscriptions, and prayers for the owner and his household, obscure prophecies or flattering announcements, such as,

"The grandfather, father, and son, all three learned men."
The red colour denoted that all was well in the household.

On the river a whole flotilla of boats and bamboo rafts
went up and down, and piled on the banks was wood for
masts and thick planks for coffins. A great crowd moved
backwards and forwards, pursuing its avocations, and one
could not help being struck by its poverty and squalor.

It had evidently collected on the strand to greet our
expected arrival, and the more courageous soon began
climbing up our boats. One set, if sent away, was immediately replaced by another, and we were forced to invoke
aid from the gunboat, but it availed nothing; they would
only wait for a favourable moment to return to the charge,
and this not from impertinence, but from sheer, over-
mastering curiosity.

Theodor was sent into the town in search of quarters and
of our interpreters. Whilst awaiting his return, I had
begun to draw the view of the quay from the bridge, when
a stone the size of an egg was thrown in my direction. I
put it beside me, in a place where every one could see it.
The crowd were very much disgusted by this cowardly
attack, and it was not repeated.

On his return, Theodor brought us the local mandarin's
card, and his appologies for not being able to come and see
us, owing to the recent death of the Emperor.

This was startling news to us, for the young Emperor had
died without heirs, and civil wars and disturbances might
very likely arise. We had already heard that he had the
small-pox, but he was reported convalescent, the crisis

having been got over.   It seems that on this occasion 1,500 roubles' (£250) worth of sacrificial paper was burnt by one of the court physicians.

Theodor returned with four of the military police dressed in white—that is in mourning—to protect us from the crowd.   It turned out that our interpreters had gone off to Han-Keou, and thereby missed us.   Andreïewsky had left a letter warning us to be very prudent, in view of the growing hate of the Chinese for foreigners.   We paid no attention to this warning, as he was one of those people who always made mountains out of molehills.

It was decided to keep on the same boats as far as Lao-Ho-Keou, and there to get others more suitable to the upper part of the Han.   The military boat was to leave us here and another to replace it, and the mandarin in command came to visit us.   He was a young man from Hou-Nan. We offered him bonbons and a cigarette, which he twisted about for a long time in his fingers without knowing what to do with it.   Everything was now ready for our start had we not been obliged to wait for the missing interpreters.

February 6th.   Cold, dark weather. · Hail, and the boats covered with mats.   Not one of the inquisitive mob was to be seen on the shore;   the barometer of Chinese curiosity had never hitherto fallen so low.   Our Cossack came to inform us that as Sosnowsky did not wish to proceed in the same boat, he had hired a larger one in which we could all travel together;   our boatmen were accordingly dismissed, and were in the greatest despair.

Matoussowsky was bidden to wait on our chief, and soon

returned to confirm the news. We then went to examine
this boat, which certainly was bigger, but very little adapted
to our pursuits.

As the new year's feast lasts two weeks, we found it most
difficult to procure provisions.

We went into the town for dinner, accompanied by our
Cossack and a police agent, and begged the latter to take us
to a decent, not too far distant, restaurant. We struggled
along through black and slippery mud, and except a few boys
following us, not a creature was in the streets.

This was the only place in China where I saw the use of
pattens among the natives.

The police agent took us to a poor little inn where a
quantity of workmen were eating vegetables, vermicelli, and
bacon; others were having tea; but on the Cossack
explaining that we wanted something rather better, he took
us on a little farther, explaining that every other place was
shut up on account of the feast. There was not much to choose
between this and the last place, but to avoid collecting a
crowd we went in and ordered such food as we required to
be brought to the boat.

At length we espied a big courtyard through an open
door, and at the end of it trellised gates. I was going to
ask what these gates were, when the Chinese standing
about asked us to enter, and after going through two courts,
we found ourselves in a restaurant, where they undertook to
give us dinner.

The police agent stood outside and warded off the crowd
with his club, but several individuals braved his blows, and

ished themselves in the room next to us. We had to
ome time for the dinner, which consisted of slices of
ork, a hash of cold salted fowl, mutton, and pickled
ge, a thick paste like mastic, and soup like dishwater,
efore each of us was placed a bottle of vinegar. The
rant-keeper would name no price, and insisted on our
our own discretion. We gave him a thousand
ues, with which he appeared amply satisfied, and we
lves did not think a rouble and a half (five shillings)
for four people, as we had enough for the policeman
he bargain.

Chinese outside hastened to announce that the
ers had dined and were going back.

went into some shops on our way back, and found
is foreign goods—glasses, watches, lamps, wax candles,
les, &c. We even saw stuffs of Russian make.

ning back from an expedition in the afternoon, we
. an excited crowd on the banks, and our Cossack
ined that the big boat hired by Sosnowsky was the
t of their attention, as our things were just being
d to it. The Chinese had found out that this boat was
ke us to the town of Han-Tchang-Fou, and that the
r boatmen who had been engaged to go as far as
Ho-Keou, were very dissatisfied at being left in the
They had lost both time and money, and perhaps
have some difficulty in finding fresh passengers to
Keou.

ey knew that an instalment had been paid to the new
whose boat was utterly unfit for the navigation of the

L. I.   R

upper Han, and marvelled that he could so unscrupulously take the risk. They jeeringly predicted his destruction, and tried by every conceivable means to make us understand the danger which threatened us, recommending us to forfeit the money rather than lose everything we possessed. Our own *lao-ban* having been told that we should still retain him, came to add his voice to the rest, and, backed by competent advisers, tried to explain to our colleagues that the boat could not go farther than about a hundred miles. This advice was evidently quite sincere, for no one had anything either to lose or gain in the matter; the former boatmen, who were the only exceptions to this, looked on in silence.

February 7th. The gunboat was now to return to Han-Keou. The mandarin came to take leave of us, and received the gift of a *papier-mâché* ewer and basin. He returned it, saying he had no use for it, as he did not know what it was for; the soldier who brought it notified, however, that his master would be very pleased to accept something else; such as a watch, for instance. The mandarin came into our cabin afterwards, and we thanked him for his good offices, gave him our photographs, and at his own request I embellished his cardboard basin with drawings, after which we parted for ever. In the evening, going along with Matoussowsky, we met children carrying lanterns of the strangest shape—monster heads of men, birds, fish, dragons, &c. Some of them threw dice for coloured eggs like those we have at Easter. This was a remnant of the new year's feast.

February 8th. To-day the military commandant of the Fan-

Tchang camp came to see us. A very agreeable man, but much less communicative than those whose acquaintance we had hitherto made.

I asked him if he had ever met foreigners before? and what struck him most about us? To the former question he replied in the negative, and answered the latter by saying that our tight clothes and beards astonished him more than anything.

We then asked why his compatriots did not travel, as it was so useful to go and study other people's habits? He agreed to this, but objected that they were too far off, and that it was too cold in our country. I recommended that they should make railroads, and need not fear the cold, as our houses were well heated; to which he replied that he would go if his Emperor sent him, but that he could not go on his own account, being in the service. Upon our requesting to be allowed to visit the camp, he begged us to go with him there and then, which we willingly consented to do. It was close by, and was surrounded by an earthen rampart, with two exits. The soldiers drawn up in the yard were being drilled with English words of command; at least we took his word for it, as we should not have otherwise guessed it.

On our arrival they presented arms with great precision, and hastened to meet their commandant, who went in, surrounded by his officers, and begged us, in accordance with their customs, to enter his abode. Unlike the towns, which are very dirty, this camp was carefully kept and very clean. The soldiers' quarters were equally clean, but some were full of a thick smoke, the frequent cause of sore eyes among the soldiers.

We presented a carbine to the commandant, as Li-Houn-Tchang at Tien-Tsinn had asked us to do, and explained its use.

At our request a target was brought, and we asked the officers to shoot at it with the gun. One refused, and another fired in a way that showed us that he had no idea of shooting at a mark. A few of the soldiers could shoot tolerably at a distance of two or three hundred paces. The Chinese are almost totally deficient in this essential branch of military art, but they could easily be taught. This was the last day of the feast. At night the town became very noisy; we could see the sacred fires being lit, and on some of the boats the men prostrating themselves, and raising their eyes and hands in prayer to heaven.

February 9th. As usual I went out to draw, followed by a mob, and stopped to admire the piled-up roofs of a cluster of most irregularly-built houses. I should not have been able to draw, on account of the crowds, had not two soldiers kept them off with clubs. I found out afterwards that these soldiers belonged to our future escort. To-day the commandant, the aide-de-camp, and several subalterns returned our visit. Several among them, having heard that I was a doctor, consulted me about various maladies, chiefly eye-diseases, and I promised them some remedies. They expressed themselves in very unflattering terms about their own doctors, and expressed their regret that they could not have foreigners (*yan-daï-fou*).

" But you could have good native doctors ; only you must establish schools ; five years are necessary for the study of medicine."

Sosnowsky backed me up by adding that the science of medicine was no easy matter, and required as much study as the science of war.

Before going away, the officers invited us to an entertainment in their quarters, but in the meantime we had accepted an invitation from a Mahometan merchant, a descendant of those Mussulmans who had emigrated from Eastern Turkestan and become Chinese in every respect except that of their religion, to which they had adhered. They married Chinese women, gave their daughters to Chinamen, and lived in exactly the same way ; nevertheless, a smouldering hostility which had always existed between the Mussulmans and Chinese, ended in the almost total extermination of the former. Only a few escaped the massacre and continued to dwell in peace. There are a few Mahometan mandarins in the service of the State. The master of the house was sixty years of age and very thin ; his hair was grey and his eyelids drooped, which gave him a trick of throwing his head back when he looked at anything, like people who leave their spectacles on their noses. In greeting us he took our hands and pressed them to his heart.

• We entered a small court by the back-door of the shop, and from thence went into an almost dark reception-room, the only light in it being derived from a very small hole through the ceiling. We were at once requested to take our seats at table, Theodor and our host having a long discussion as to precedence. One interpreter to four people was quite insufficient, so that when one of us was speaking the others could do nothing but eat. The sons and nephews of the merchant had several times attempted to enter into conversation with us, but no one seemed at ease.

The dinner was served in Chinese fashion, and was excellent. Amongst other things there were pancakes, only eaten once a year, on the 13th, 14th, and 15th days of the first moon, on which occasion every one, from the emperor to the poorest beggar, is expected to eat them. The latter have to procure them as best they can; if unable to make them at home they must buy them; but no one could tell us if this custom had any religious significance.

February 10th. Our party is increased by a new member, as one of the soldiers returning to Han-Keou in the gunboat, on which he filled the post of cook, preferred going on with us in the same capacity to serving the State any longer. If I mention this not very important fact, it is only to show the ease with which a Chinese soldier may quit the army whenever he chooses. He has only to inform his own commanding officer of his intention and no difficulties are made; he is given his discharge and his clothes, and is then free. The very day he entered our service we unexpectedly received live poultry, mutton, bread, and nuts from the commandant of the garrison, who perhaps had been told that our living was very frugal. Our chief sent him two bottles of champagne in return, which had been given us by our compatriots.

Time went on, and still we awaited the interpreters. I

wandered about the town every day by myself, as Theodor was required to be always in attendance on our chief. The natives became quite accustomed to me, and called me the "foreign painter," or "painter from over the seas." They were even more occupied with my pencil, or "foreign paintbrush," than with me. Although unable to run after me like the men and children, as soon as they heard the cries of "He is passing! he is passing!" even the women posted themselves at their doors to get a sly peep.

Passing along with my numerous suite, I saw a frame from which depended what appeared to be yellow threads. I took them for skeins of silk, and on stopping to examine this curious erection, found it was designed for the manufacture of vermicelli, which hung on it in thick strips. Next to the vermicelli a baker was established in the open street, and kneaded his dough in the most original manner. A quantity of dough is thrown down on a low table, or sort of wide bench, set against the baker's house; the baker then seats himself on one end of a long bamboo pole (the other being fastened to the wall of the house), and proceeds to spring up and down, backwards and forwards, on his bamboo in such a way that it kneads the dough, and stirs it thoroughly in all parts.

Just as I thought of going back, several of my Chinese suite insisted on taking me in an opposite direction. From their talk I could only gather the word "*hao-kan*" (worth seeing), and then they took the lead, quite delighted that we had understood them. We soon came to a rather remarkable temple above the gate of the town, and I at once set to

WASHING, SCALDING, AND KNEADING DOUGH.

work to draw it, but the ever-increasing crowd frustrated my attempts, notwithstanding the efforts made to keep a space clear by those more immediately around me. They began to hustle, and two handfuls of sand were thrown at me. This was severely rebuked; but fearing that, as often happens in crowds, these pleasantries might turn to violence and uproar, I decided on going back. I was obliged to chastise one man after he had twice thumped me on the shoulder.

February 11*th.* The military manœuvres took place to-day at our request. At nine in the morning an orderly was sent to announce that all was ready, and that our presence was awaited; but our chief delayed going till eleven o'clock, which was the more unfortunate, as the Chinese are the most punctual people in the world.

When at length we reached the camp, all the mandarins were assembled in a group, but not one of them was in uniform, and the Commandant was pointedly absent. I heard afterwards that he had got tired of waiting for us, and had given the officers orders to change their clothes. It was quite apparent that our free-and-easy conduct had annoyed them, for no one came to meet us, and we were very coldly received.

The soldiers of this garrison were armed with percussion guns, and had been drilled by European instructors. After the manœuvres were over I visited the barracks, which were built of bamboo; ceilings, walls, and roofs were all bamboo. Each bed had curtains to protect the men from gnats, mosquitoes, spiders, scorpions, and other insects.

The good Chinese, having already forgotten our morning's behaviour, invited us to a dinner prepared on purpose for us. The Commandant joined us, and every one was pleasant and cheerful. Knowing that we did not use chopsticks, they had sent for our knives and forks, which to our surprise we found ready on the table for us. After dinner they brought in cups full of hot water and grey rags, but we declined to use them, saying that it was not customary with us.

The mandarins' quarters consisted of only one room each, furnished with a bed, a table, a trunk, and some chairs. They all had pots of flowers, inscriptions on their walls, and maps of China, but of Chinese origin.

The Commandant's room, to which we next adjourned, was exactly the same; and whilst we were talking I noticed that the mandarins took it in turns to go to lie down and smoke their pipe of opium.

One thin and yellow man with hollow cheeks smoked nine pipes in my presence. He owned that it was wrong to do so, but could not give up the habit, for the moment he did so he suffered terribly. This officer begged me to tell him of some remedy, and I was sorry that I could do nothing for him. If I had been remaining any time I should certainly have tried some treatment. After a talk with him I was convinced that opium brought him no sleep, any more than those dreams which it is supposed to bring; on the contrary, after smoking he became livelier and more active.

The Chinese questioned us on Russia and its climate, its towns, and industrial products apart from textile fabrics, &c. They asked, moreover, what pay officers received; and our

chief, who did not at all approve of those sort of questions,
answered that an officer of his own rank received from 12,000

to 14,000 silver roubles (£1,925 or £2,245 16s. 8d.).   The
Chinese appeared evidently to think this very handsome pay.

Many invalids consulted me, and I bade some of them come to me for remedies, but I had to refuse to take portraits, as I had only a limited amount of time at my disposal. We thus spent the whole of a beautiful day at the camp, but at night a tempest arose which lasted till morning.

February 12th. Bad weather all day.

February 13th. Continued bad weather.

The son of the Mahometan merchant with whom we had dined came to call on us, and as soon as he had entered took off his shoes and sat in his socks. Being very near-sighted he wore spectacles, but without their being suited to his sight. Unfortunately I had none with me, and I recommend all travellers to provide themselves with some, as they might find them very useful.

February 14th. Better weather, our boatmen longing to set out; we could not, however, start without our interpreters. I went to a pretty temple on the outer wall, overlooking the river, on a sort of promontory. The porter at once shut the door behind me, that I might admire everything alone and in peace. Workmen swarmed at the foot of the wall, shouting in their usual style, and every now and then I looked through an embrasure, thinking that some disaster must have happened, but it was nothing ; they were only dragging trunks of bamboo out of the river, which they had brought down as rafts. Others were carting away straw, and some women were quietly washing linen. Presently the keeper of the temple took me by the coat-sleeve, and led me to a small adjacent room, where a man sat playing an instrument which I had overheard in the distance. The musician hastily rose to greet me, begging me to sit down beside an exceedingly hot stove. I asked him to continue playing, and to testify my approval held up the middle finger of my right hand ; but he disclaimed all merit, and waved his hand in the negative. His most primitive instrument, called *er-tzyn* by the Chinese, that is "two stringed," consisted of two segments of bamboo, one longer and thicker than the other, joined together at right angles. The first served as a finger-board, the other as a sounding-board. Two silk strings and a bow completed the instrument. He produced all sorts of sounds by the skilful manipulation of his bow ; and one time I could fancy a distant voice singing, at another it seemed to exactly imitate the song of a bird. I could hardly believe my eyes or my ears, and could have stayed all day listening to him, had I not been obliged to rejoin my colleagues, and visit the Commander-in-chief in the town of Sian-Young-Fou, situated on the further bank of the Han, opposite Fan-Tcheng.

Two mandarins came to escort us, and we took two of the soldiers from the military junk to keep order in case of need. One of these mandarins had a great many wounds on his head and face, received in a fight with a band of insurgents which had committed many crimes, and whose chief had designs of seizing Pekin and taking possession of the throne. He was utterly routed, his band dispersed, whilst he himself fled and disappeared from the scene.

The town of Siang has all the appearance of a fortress ; its granite quay rises above the water to a height of about ten feet, and is built in ridges, which are, however, so narrow

that it would be difficult to obtain a footing upon them.
This quay terminates in a small ledge following round the
ramparts. In 1268 Houbilaï-Han, the founder of the Mongolian dynasty, laid siege to the town, a siege which lasted
five years. The street leading to the gate of the town was as
narrow and dirty as all other Chinese streets. The inhabitants stood in groups at their doors to see us pass, and many
followed in our wake. We soon reached the residence of
the Commander-in-chief, and went through four courts into
a little room, which we found empty. This was not the
usual Chinese habit, as they generally come to meet their
visitors ; the mandarin who accompanied us said that the
Commander-in-chief must be dressing. But I afterwards
heard that this reception was preconcerted, in return for our
being two hours late in going to the camp, and we were
made to feel how disagreeable it was to be kept waiting, even
for a much shorter time than two hours. We went through
several more courts and rooms ; in nearly the last, one of the
inmates made himself known to us as the chief. This is the
Chinese custom, as from the similarity of dress in all classes,
one never knows to whom one should address oneself.
There was a good deal of European furniture in the room—a
couch beside the *kang* ; two clocks, one of which was on the
wall ; and four candelabra, with glass globes, all of which
were presents from the English at Shanghai. A bureau also
appeared to be of European manufacture. The governor was
a very singular person, about forty years of age, tall, strong,
and quite unlike the Chinese type, and this dissimilitude was
increased by his long hair. During the period of mourning

for an Emperor the mandarins do not shave their heads.
He wore his cap on one side, and not on the back of his
head. Neither were his manners those of a Chinese
mandarin; they may possibly have been formed on those of
some European acquaintance. When we took our leave after
dinner, he went with us to the second court, another
mandarin to the third, whilst another went with us all the
way to Fan-Tcheng.

When we got back, Theodor came to inform us that he
was going to leave us, and return to Han-Keou. He would
not divulge the reason of his unexpected departure, and we
could not persuade him to remain, although we offered to increase his salary, and let him eat at our own table instead of
with the Cossacks. All that we could obtain from him was
a promise to remain until Andriewsky and Siui returned.

February 15th. A visit at ten o'clock from the *ti-dou* whom
we had nicknamed the "Ataman brigand," owing to his
cavalier manners. He was on his way to the cavalry
barracks, and begged that we would send the photographer
to take his likeness on horseback. The head of their can-
tonment asked us in return to dine with him. The camp
was not so well arranged as that of the infantry; both the
officers' and soldiers' quarters were smaller, and not so clean.
Many of the men were suffering from sore eyes, doubtless
the result of the smoking logs in their rooms. I marvelled
that they they could remain in such dense pungent smoke;
it attacked ones eyes and throat, and made them sore for the
rest of the day. The soldiers were fed on rice and vegetables, and were given meat only at very rare intervals.

The grey-haired commandant was evidently a great lover of nature, as he had borders of flowers, tanks containing various aquatic plants, besides an aviary full of rare birds, such as larks, quails, starlings, partridges, pheasants, &c. His thirty pigeons had a house to themselves, each pair having a separate division. Throughout dinner our " Ataman brigand " ordered everybody about as if he were in his own house, and swallowed a great quantity of strong wine. This was the first occasion on which I had seen water handed round after dinner for washing the hands and face.

We expressed a hope that we should see our friends some day in our own country, to which the *ti-dou* replied that he did not like long journeys by sea, and that if ever he came it would be on horseback. He knew a great deal about horses, and had a very fast trotter, which, at our request, was saddled and brought round. ·

After dinner we went into a room belonging to the Commander-in-chief, and I took a pipe and began preparing the opium. Our "Ataman brigand" took it from me, telling me I was not doing it properly, and showing me how to proceed. I asked him if he smoked, and he denied doing so in a way that left no room for doubt, but not very long after he lit a pipe to show me how it should be smoked.

A few minutes later, his horse being ready, he jumped up and went out, bidding us follow him. He then mounted his strong little animal, and darted off at a great pace, as if seated in an easy chair. He took several turns, and dismounted, with a glance towards us to see what we thought of his horse. I showed him the finger of my right hand, which appeared to please him greatly. We then returned indoors, and during our talk he inquired the strength of the Russian army, on which Sosnowsky stated it to be a million in time of peace, and three millions in time of war.

February 16*th*. Everyone knows that the Chinese train cormorants to fish. I had long sought an opportunity of seeing this, and happening when on deck this morning to see two Chinese in a boat with some of these birds, I hailed them, and begged them to take me with them, to which they assented with pleasure. They had five cormorants perched on a piece of wood covered with straw, to which they were held by one claw; a straw ring encircled their neck, and they appeared eager to set to work. We rowed a long way up the river, and then let the boat drift down broadside. The Chinese unfastened the birds, when some of them dived into the water without any further bidding; others had to be unceremoniously pushed in, but all followed the boat, plunging and diving to a great depth, and sometimes remaining a long time under water. Their owner stimulated them by words and exclamations, and they appeared quite to understand him. If they came to the surface without any booty they seemed quite disappointed, panted hard, and snarled like dogs. One came up with a fairly big carp, on which the fisherman set up shouts of delight, and rushed to assist the cormorant, who held the fish firmly in its beak, although it struggled violently for freedom. The cormorant tried to get the carp's head into its throat, to swallow it before it could be taken away from it; but with one hand the fisherman seized the bird by the throat, and with the other took

the carp away. The bird was evidently accustomed to this, as it showed no ill-humour, only shook its head repeatedly, washed its beak to get rid of the taste of its prey, and began all over again. They came to the surface constantly with fish. When it was a small one they swallowed it, but the ring round their necks prevented its passing into their stomachs, and the Chinese catching hold of them made them return the fish, and sent them back to their work. One cormorant would wait patiently till another had been attended to. If the fish was very small, it was occasionally left till two or three were collected in their throats, and then they were all removed at the same time. Sometimes the fish taken was so big that another cormorant would immediately go to the assistance of its companion and help it to hold on. At other times they quarrelled and wrangled amongst each other, and thereby lost their prey, which they never succeeded in re-catching. Some fished energetically and others indolently, notwithstanding the encouraging cries of their master, who would feign anger, and shout, and scream, and jump about till he got them to do as he wished. After an hour of this the birds were given a rest, and were taken out of the water and put back on their perch; they breathed hard, with their beaks wide open, and then spread out their wings to dry like sails, and scratched their heads. During this rest they were given nothing to eat, as they only fish well when hungry. Half an hour afterwards they began again, and this time when a bird brought back a big fish it was given a small one as a reward or an encouragement. The cormorants never deserted their own boat, even when we were passing many other boats pursuing the same avocation, and the men always knew their own birds, which seemed a difficult matter to an uninitiated eye.

When they had done fishing, the men took me back to my own boat, and asked me to choose the biggest fish, but, as on other occasions, they would fix no price. I gave them five hundred sapeques, rather more than two shillings, with which they seemed quite satisfied.

Their style of duck-hunting is most original. After sunset they throw several hollow pumpkins into the water where the wild ducks collect; the birds, which at first view these pumpkins with distrust, soon become accustomed to them, and swim unsuspectingly around them. The sportsman then gets into the water with a belt fastened round his waist and his head adorned by a pumpkin, through which holes are pierced to enable him to see. He then lies in wait, up to his neck in water, watching his opportunity among the un-suspecting ducks. When one of them goes near enough to the sportsman, he catches it by the claws, draws it under water, wrings its neck and hangs it to his belt. As the ducks are used to seeing each other dive they never notice a few of their number disappearing off the surface, and only take fright when they see the man get out of the water.

February 17th. Our interpreters have at length arrived, and Theodor has left us, although I tried again to induce him to remain. Instead of two days, we have been a fort-night at Fan-Tcheng. The owner of our boat ran into the town to lay in provisions, and recommended us to do the same, as henceforth the villages are at a greater distance from the shore. We further purchased some little mirrors, brass buttons, needles, and wax matches to distribute as presents among the river folk. Although glad to get on, I was sorry to leave the unpretending huts on the Fan-Tcheng quay, the good people who collected every morning round our boat, and even an unfortunate dog which had got into the habit of coming to us every day for his breakfast.

We left the town with a favourable wind, and therefore with sails set; Matoussowsky and I on our own old boat, and the rest on the new one of which such evil had been prophesied, with a military junk accompanying us. We stopped at a short distance from the town, as we could not have reached the ordinary halting-place before nightfall.

February 15th. A beautiful morning, a blue sky, and the sun as hot as in summer. We set out, and our boatmen went at a good pace, but we soon lost sight of the bigger ship. The river became very wide; its banks, at first flat and sandy, now became higher and rocky, with caves running back into them. On an overhanging ledge stood a temple which seemed likely to crumble away before long, as the water-springs incessantly undermined its foundations, notwithstanding the support given to it by solid brick masonry. At sunset we stopped at the village of Pou-Heou, and Matoussowsky set to work to measure the rapidity of the river. The inhabitants had not been made aware of our advent, and for the moment seemed stupefied, but overcoming their astonishment and fright came and talked to us.

We answered them in Russian, and the conversation thus came to a standstill. The steep and clayey soil made the river banks almost impracticable, but the Chinese held out their hands and helped us to climb. Farther on I happened to look up at a tree with dried pods on it, and as they were out of my reach one of the Chinese climbed the tree, and not even throwing them down at me, took a branch between his teeth and brought them to me, refusing to accept anything for his trouble. As we came back to the boat I began to wonder how we were ever to get down the banks again, but as we approached the little path I discovered to my surprise that steps had been hollowed out to make it easier. Not knowing who had been good enough to do this for us, I thanked them all for their delicate attention, and offered them money, which, however, they firmly declined. I could not help contrasting this in my own mind with the French " pour-boire," the German " trinkgeld," and the Russian " naa-tchi," which is exacted for the smallest service.

Night came on, and there were no signs of the other boat. We consulted our boatman, who said it had probably halted further down, and so we retired to rest.

February 19*th.* A beautiful day with mild delicious air. After waiting a long time for the other boat, it at length passed us and took the lead.

The district became more and more mountainous, the population still more densely massed, and I had no difficulty in believing that the Celestial Empire counts three hundred million souls.

The large boat again fell behind, so we decided to stop at a place where the sand was being washed for gold. Nine natives were working at it when we came upon the scene to disturb and frighten them. Their expression seemed to bid farewell to their gold, and showed that they should count themselves lucky if they themselves got off unharmed.

After the presence of our boatmen had somewhat reassured them, we asked them to show us their gold and their mode of washing it, to which they replied that they had only just begun work, and therefore had as yet found none. Our boatman, however, impressed on them that we had no sinister intentions, and they finally produced a box containing two small bits of gold about the size of peas. This was melted gold. The natural gold, which they showed us on a tray, had crystals in it as fine as sand. For a trifling royalty the Government feus out land in lots where the sand has a gold deposit. The tenant marks out the limits of the piece conceded to them with posts, and instal themselves with their companions and workmen.

After removing the upper layer of sand, which never contains gold, they fill baskets with the pebbles forced by the water to a depth of half a yard, and place them at the top of an inclined plane arranged with troughs across it all the way down. The water emptied into the basket passes between the pebbles, taking with it whatever sand and particles of gold may be amongst them, and the latter, being heavier than the sand, stop and are deposited in the troughs; whereas the sand falls into a tray, which is most

carefully submitted to a second washing. The gold particles are taken out of the troughs with the aid of pincers.
The process is thus of the simplest kind, and a workman can
wash nearly a thousand pounds' weight of pebbles and sand in
a day, counting himself fortunate if he can get gold to the
value of about a shilling out of it; usually much less is taken.
These are certainly not to be compared to our gold-mines,
and the diggers look as poor as all the other peasants. In
Russia no one would even undertake such labour, but the
Chinese do it cheerfully, more especially as in winter agri-
cultural labour is at a standstill. If, on the one hand, the
Han-Kiang produces little gold, on the other it possesses an
inexhaustible store, the same quantities having been found
in it for centuries.

After thanking the Chinese, we returned to our boats,
accompanied part of the way by the principal digger,
probably in recognition of our honesty.

The sandbanks now rendered the navigation more difficult, as it was well-nigh impossible to get free if once the
boats ran foul of them. Boats belonging to the river
conservancy were placed at regular intervals, or rather
where there was danger, each being commanded by a
mandarin.

February 20*th*. The river now forked into two branches,
and wound round a large sandy island. Our boats followed
the left branch, employing tow-rope, poles, and sails, all in
their turn. We were a numerous company, as twenty boats,
with their sterns very high out of the water, went along
with us. The boatmen, while working their poles, uttered

groans enough to break one's heart. About a mile from the
river, the town of Houang-Houa-Sienn, with its battlements,
gate, and tower came in sight, and at last we halted at Lao-
Ho-Keou, a large commercial village, where we were obliged
to change boats, as our old friend Tan-Tchen-Koueï con-
scientiously and formally refused to go beyond it, having no
further acquaintance with the navigation of the river.

CHAPTER VII.

February 20*th* (continuation). The Han now entered the
mountains, and the change of feature was most striking. We
cast anchor opposite the town of Lao-Ho-Keou where there
were already numbers of boats. In less than five minutes a
crowd had assembled, but a couple of policeman at once
appeared and put an end to the curiosity of the public, who
knew only too well that the policemen's clubs would be
employed without mercy. Matoussowsky and I took a turn
in the town whilst awaiting the arrival of our colleagues,
and the policemen accompanied us, the one marching before,
the other behind us.

They were attentive and zealous to excess, making incessant play with their canes, which fortunately were not
very thick. Scattering the crowd and ordering off even
those who kept their distance, the two made more noise
than all the rest put together.

The streets had no particular feature, but were dirty and
full of bad smells, so we returned very shortly to our boat.

The quay and embrasures in the walls were crowded with people. They had found out I was a doctor, and many invalids were brought for me to cure.

Fortunately, as I had no interpreter to refer to, most of their complaints were external, and I had plenty of remedies with me. But it was not so easy to come to an understanding about their internal sufferings. At night we preferred remaining on board to lodging in the town.

February 21*st*. A day like summer, 17·8° Reaumur in the shade, 28° in the sun.

The commander of the gunboat which was to accompany us from Lao-Ho-Keou paid us a visit, and I then tried to find a new boat for our own use. None of those I saw quite pleased me, but there was no choice, and I engaged one for the sum of 200 roubles (£32 1s. 8d.), including everything, to go a distance of rather more than six hundred and sixty miles. The owner was to find men and feed and pay them ; the wages of each man came to 8,000 sapeques (about 33 shillings) for the whole journey. A large number of sick people awaited my return. Their principal maladies were cutaneous affections, sore eyes, stomachic complaints, and rheumatics. Whilst examining the eyes of one of them, he tried to take my cigar from my mouth. I knocked his hand away, upon which he soon showed the white feather and got well jeered at by the crowd. I had been warned not to permit any liberties if I wished to ensure their respect, and to accomplish this I had to be haughty and reserved. The mob was uncivilised and rude, and did things that no single individual would venture upon.

The whole day was taken up prescribing for the sick, and at night a new Chinese servant came to us to help the Cossack, who acted as my interpreter, and could not do everything. This Chinaman, of the name of Tjchou, volunteered his services, but would fix no salary, which it appeared was the Chinese habit. He only asked for 200 sapeques (or .12s. 6d.) to buy suitable clothing; as to his wages, they were to depend on our appreciation of his services.

We decided on engaging him, on which he ran into the town and shortly returned in new clothes to pay the customary homage, kneeling and bowing three times before each of us, not excepting our Cossack.

February 22nd. Splendid weather, 17° Reaumur in the shade. We now changed our boat, and the exchange was scarcely for the better, as although the boat we were now to inhabit was deeper and more spacious than the last, it was much older and dirtier, and was impregnated with a smell of smoke. Insects and spiders abounded therein, and any number of mice.

After a thorough cleaning we endeavoured to exterminate these unwelcome inmates by means of insect-powder. We next put down mats and covered the sides of the cabin with muslin, and our abode then looked fairly habitable. The owner of the boat seemed a good sort of man; we also liked his assistant, who was educated and intelligent, and we therefore hoped that all would go well with us.

February 23rd. We were to depart from Lao-Ho-Keou, but the mast of our boat was not ready, so we begged Sosnowsky to go on without us, which he did at daybreak, unfortunately leaving no orders for the police, so we were left unprotected. As ill-luck befell, the populace perceived that we had no one' to protect us, and very soon became bolder. Beggars, sick people, and idlers besieged the boat; the confusion was such that I declined to prescribe any longer. At one time I was alone on the boat with the owner's wife and children. On the waterside the people talked vociferously, and by attentively listening I could make out that now that I was alone they intended to take me by storm; and I then saw that a considerable number had forced their way on deck, some well-dressed, others in rags, and that they were staring into the cabin. At first I begged them very politely to leave me in peace, but finding that they turned a perfectly deaf ear to my request, I went on deck and spoke to them, putting on a severe expression, and helping them back to the shore. They went off slowly and jeeringly, and as I remained on deck some stones were thrown at me, and one of them struck me on the shoulder. I was now at a loss how to proceed. To go down to the cabin would be to give in, for which reason I decided to remain where I was till the crowd remained quieter. I had no sooner gone into the cabin than I heard loud shouting and laughter. About twenty of them had jumped on deck and were trying to come in. My coolness exasperated them. In reality I was considerably enraged, but I pretended indifference and continued writing. They persisted in speaking to me, plucking me by the coat, and offering me meat and bread for sale. If I stirred they drew back a few steps, but only to return to the charge, mockingly showing

me their eyes and heads as if they were ill, and some of them
tried to get into the cabin. But when I suddenly got up
their courage fled, and they all made as fast as they could
for the water. To put an end to this joke I took my revolver
out of its case and kept it beside me, after which not one of
them dared to come near me, although they continued shouting when at a safe distance.

We were now to leave the old boat, and we parted from
this worthy family with mutual regret.

The inhabitants of Lao dispersed seeing we were about to
depart, and only a few boys followed us with abusive epithets.
The boatman was to join us lower down, and whilst we
waited for him I had time to sketch a bit of the village and
the boats on the river. Seeing us halt, the surrounding
inhabitants rushed into their little boats, rowed with all their
might to get a nearer sight of us, and came on board with
as much coolness as if they had received an invitation to do
so. Our Cossack was obliged to repulse them with a boathook.

February 24th. The new boatman was certainly not equal
to our old friend Tan-Tchen-Koueï, but was as idle and stupid
as the latter was hardworking and intelligent. He neither
knew the river or its neighbourhood, which was especially
inconvenient to Matoussowsky, who depended on him for
information on certain subjects.

The mountains became higher and higher; the soil alter-
nated between yellow sand and reddish clay, and we now
came on barren rocks. The river was shallow and full of
sandbanks, making the navigation most difficult. The towing

became very arduous, not only owing to the sandbanks, but on account of the steepness of the path, which is only practicable from steps being cut out in the rocks. Our poor men were obliged to climb the rocks or descend into the ravines just like chamois. The proprietor, who was here called *taï-goun* (it was even considered an insult to call them *lao-ban* in this district) never moved off the deck all day, being occupied in making a bamboo cable. This sort of cable was much the strongest; the rocks and the force of the stream made it impossible to use the ordinary rope.

February 25th. The Han now wandered for miles through a mountainous district, and temples crowned the summits of the hill closing in around us.

Frequent stones of various forms and colours now emerged from the water; absolute silence prevailed, broken only by the occasional cries of the men towing, which re-echoed from the surrounding hills, and were not unlike the groans of a sick person.

. The introduction of steamers would be a wonderful thing for these poor people, condemned to such hard work. They, however, dread the innovation, as this towing is their only means of subsistence, and they prefer straining their legs and arms with this painful labour to being deprived of their means of livelihood.

We stopped at the town of Tziun-Tjoou or Tzyn-Tjou, situated on the right bank of the Han, which here changes its name to Tzyn-Ho, and here we overtook our chief's boat.

February 26th. The river meandered along with many turns, and was more like a great lake enclosed by mountains.

The scenery reminded us somewhat of Switzerland, with the difference that it was on a much larger scale, and that every-

where the band of man was apparent. In the ravines and on the slopes of the hills the inhabitants had built perpendicular walls, and then filled in the intervals with earth.

They thus formed terraces and miniature fields. Through our opera-glasses we could see the owners hoeing and raking in the fields and gardens ; and this was the panorama which unfolded itself unceasingly before our eyes. Our boat often stuck fast in the sand, and it was then curious to observe the way in which our boatman went to the aid of the men towing, who were hidden on the hillside. Putting his interminable cable on one side, he took a long bamboo boathook with an iron spike, stuck it into the bottom of the river, and planting his feet firmly on the deck, jerked himself violently backwards to such an extent that his back actually touched the deck. He simultaneously uttered a strident cry, which sounded as if a red-hot iron had been applied to his back ; and repeated the same manœuvre until the boat was freed. Then with a calm smile he resumed work at his cable.

The windings of the river became more and more tortuous. The rocks and mountains gave a grand and wild tone to the scenery, and enormous blocks closed in the river. These rocks are all granitic, covered with mosses and lichens ; they take every shade of blue, green, and violet. Although they appear at first sight inaccessible, narrow pathways exist which are used by the men, and wind up and down among the rocks. It was sometimes quite alarming to watch these poor creatures climbing and jumping at the peril of their lives. To slip was to be hurled into space, but they always found something to hold on to, and managed to get up and continue their work. The rope often caught on the stones, and at every minute they had to raise or lower it, and watch that it did not get cut. This was truly hard labour, and yet

the poor Chinese seemed to take quite kindly to it.   The
men divided the task ; some towed, whilst others protected
the rope from any accidents.   I could watch their skill from
the boat, and I soon ceased to fear for them, having acquired
a certainty that no harm would happen to them.

There were, however, spots that these active creatures
could not pass, and they then took in the rope and rowed
.across to the opposite shore, jumping on the bank one after
the other, unwinding the rope as they went, and scaling the
mountain, looking to us like little black spots in the distance.   When we halted at night they squatted down on
the sand, and smoked a sort of greasy tobacco whilst waiting
for their supper.   Later on they rigged up a sail as a tent,
and lay down to rest.

The land is gratuitously parcelled out by the Government,
and then the people settle down and cultivate it.   In my
walks I frequently came upon small houses perched among
the rocks, like birds'-nests, and saw some lime-kilns, with
adjacent cabins for the workpeople.   There were apparently
no animals except bats in this region.

February 27th.   To-day we saw the first swallow, the har-
binger of spring.   The birds sang in the hills, and the leaves
burst forth on the trees.   But spring in China has not the
charm it possesses with us.   In reality it succeeds the
autumn, and not the severities of winter.   We approached
Yun-Yang-Fou, and our arrival was greeted by a salute
from a gunboat.   This town, situated on the left bank of
the Han, is surrounded by a wall, outside which there was a
suburb of small houses built in terraces.

The gunboats having drawn attention to our arrival, an immense crowd collected, and all the boats in the place swarmed around us. In no other town had the crowd reached such a pitch or shown so much curiosity. More than ten thousand pairs of eyes were all turned in the same direction. Their high cheekbones and open mouths were quite as curious a spectacle to us as we were to them.' The police agents had come to protect us against the crowd, and without loss of time I hailed a small boat and went down the river to a suitable point of view, whence I obtained a sketch of the quay. The police agents were most obliging, accompanying me, and holding me up under the arms like a bishop when I was going on or off the boat.

Later on we were visited by two mandarins, and as conversation was difficult, we showed them all our things to amuse them. At the sight of my rug, travelling bag, and drawings, the mandarins fell into ecstasies of delight. We next went into the town, where the streets were exceedingly dirty and muddy from the recent rains. The soldiers who went with us made it their duty to help us along, as we slipped at every step. There was nothing the least curious in the town, unless it were a small temple containing the statue of a god, said to be very ancient. This statue was fashioned in clay, and fairly well modelled; the costume resembled that of the warriors of olden times. I was beginning to make a sketch of it when the onlookers brought me a bench and sat down beside me. One was called Tchen, and was introduced to me as a brother artist. He was

dumb and very ugly; but I asked him to sit down beside
me, and then began to draw. Everyone expressed admiration; the poor artist especially showed his approval by
inarticulate sounds and profound bows. When I had finished
drawing he placed himself in front of me, and contemplated
me as if I were a divinity. Noticing that I wanted to smoke,
he took my hand most respectfully and led us into his room,
where we sat down and got a light. I begged him to show
us his drawings, but he blushed and shook his head. On my
insisting, he brought out a piece of stuff folded as we fold
our maps, and opening it showed me some things which he
had drawn. Like all pictures by Chinese artists, the figures
were very small, and had mottoes written over their heads to
explain the subject. I complimented him upon them, but
he shook his head, pointing at me, raised the middle finger
of his right hand in sign of his admiration for me. When
we left he went to the door with us, and signed to the crowd
to show us the greatest respect. He remained standing
there for a long time looking after us, and waving to us as if
he were parting from old friends. As we went back we
passed through the cemetery, where all the graves were of
the same form, built of bricks in the shape of a tent. Before
leaving, we had a visit from the commandant of the town,
accompanied by his three children, a boy and two little
girls, who were not the least shy.

After leaving this place the river became less rapid, and
the mountains forsook the banks of the river. We had to
use boathooks to get on, and one of them wounded a big
fish, which struggled a long time on the surface of the water.

One of the Cossacks threw himself in to try to get a hold of it, but did not succeed.

· The villages followed each other in uninterrupted succession, and we stopped opposite one for the night. Some of the natives came out to see us, but held themselves timidly aloof, and when I went towards them they ran away as if the devil were at their heels, and returned no more.

March 1st. A dull sky and high wind, 10° Reaumur. The river became narrower, the stream more impetuous, and blocks of granite appeared out of the water. There were a great many boats on the river, and the Chinese on their decks seemed to be taking no notice of anything around them. A man on one of them lay on his back smoking his pipe, and chanced to look our way. It was amusing to see the rapid change which came over his countenance. After the first moment of surprise, he called his colleagues to let them have a look at the *yan-jen*, and wondering if they were under the influence of a dream, they rapidly spread the news among their neighbours. Again we halted to wait for the other boat. Matoussowsky landed with the Cossacks to measure the width of the river, whilst I uprooted some plants and took some samples of rocks. When I got back I found some Chinese installed on deck, but they were quite well-behaved, discussing my cigar, and speculating whether I was smoking tobacco, and whether it was strong or mild. After smelling the leaves they came to the conclusion that it was very strong foreign tobacco. To their great delight, I gave one of them a cigar which he tried to smoke, and after coughing violently, handed on to another. They all had a turn, till they made their eyes water with .its strength, and finally＊ restored it to me, as if they imagined I should finish it !

After classifying the plants I had collected, I again landed, and began looking at a pagoda in the woods through my opera glasses, which at once excited the admiration of the Chinese, and they lost no time in testifying the greatest desire to have a look. I yielded to their wish, and they all took them in turn with childlike delight, exceedingly astonished that the same pair of glasses could magnify and diminish things. These country folk were very well behaved, as all the Chinese are when they are not in great numbers; but the inhabitants of the Celestial Empire are completely different in a crowd to what they are when isolated. When I again returned there were others on deck, and to my surprise some children, including little girls, amongst their number, who are generally very shy. I took the portrait of one of them, but her over-zealous friends stuck her down so close under my nose that it was most difficult to manage it. Moreover, it made her shy to be so near a "foreign devil." After a few minutes she got tired and cross, and made faces and stamped her small foot. I made her understand that her portrait would soon be done, but . before I could even give her a little present she ran away off the boat. I succeeded, however, in producing a good portrait, much to the satisfaction of her friends, who pronounced it to be exactly like her. Her parents were on their way to Han-Keou, and had halted for the night. The father was a merchant, gifted with unusual common sense, and had no prejudices concerning strangers.

In the evening the gunboat arrived, and its commander came to see us with no very ostensible object. On entering our cabin he made a military salute, without uttering a single word, and began inspecting our effects, touching and examining everything, and showing his pleasure by signs. If I had not previously heard him speak, I should have imagined him to be dumb, and his antics reminded me of those of a monkey. After completing this minute inspection, he took leave of us. The rest of the party caught us up during the night, and we decided on remaining where we were.

March 2nd. Rain.

In the mountains we could see black holes, and were told they were caverns hollowed out in the rock, where in olden times hermits spent their time in solitude, flying from the temptations of the outer world.

The wet weather prevented my plants drying; it made them all mouldy, and some were entirely wasted. The damp of the boat spoilt everything; the rice was worthless, the tobacco covered with mould, and the paper all stained. We advanced quite slowly, which allowed Matoussowsky to take plans. Information about the Han was given us by the men and translated by our Cossack, who from perpetual practice, and the use of the dictionary of which I had made him a present, was now quite an adept in the Chinese language. He was more useful to Matoussowsky than to me, as my profession required a still more intimate knowledge of the ins and outs of the language. He was very amusing in the choice of his expressions ; thus he would say :. " In the tenth moon the water of the river sits still·on the earth, and makes the greatest play in the seventh and eighth moons."

In the evening the mandarin from the gunboat, and one of his soldiers, came to hear the concertina played, and, laying their heads together, they examined the instrument all round. The mandarin raised his finger in token of his approval, as usual never uttering a syllable, and tried to play on it himself, so as to acquire some knowledge of the construction of the instrument. I recommend travellers to take a few with them. They may come in as very valuable presents.

March 3rd. We reached the first rapids. The mountains re-echoed the noise of the waters dashing up against the rocks. There were·numerous boats on the river, towed by eight or ten men, and loaded with merchandise ; others were managed with enormous oars, having five or six men at each of them. They sang at their work, and one man reciting in a sad, drawling voice, was joined in the chorus with a cry of " Huo-â !" which the ravines and mountains re-echoed a thousand times. The villages became more and more numerous, the houses better built, and the vegetation richer. The houses were pleasantly shaded by trees and bushes ; temples and farms were scattered over the wild cliffs and brightened up the landscape ; the trees were covered with flowers, and this remote corner of the earth was altogether a most charming resting-place. At nightfall little lights marked where the various habitations were dotted about in the hills.

March 4th. Bad weather and very cold. The soldiers constantly landed and walked after the boat to warm themselves. My attention was attracted to the piety of one of them, so rare a commodity among the Chinese. Before every temple—and they were very numerous—he knelt, and seemed to wish to testify his religious feeling; but I soon discovered that he was a regular rogue and thief. In China, as in our country, the passers-by deposit their offerings in the temples. The pious thief contributed his mite, but directly after doing so, seized the poor Chinaman by the hair of his head and tugged at it without the smallest provocation. He then made some imaginary accusation against him, and pretended to compromise the matter by exacting perhaps ten or even a hundred sapeques from the poor creature in exchange for the single coin he had offered to the gods. He had repeated this performance several times before I effectually put a stop to it by threatening to denounce him to his chief.

We subsequently halted opposite the little town of Baï-Ho-Sian, on the right bank of the Han, and the most picturesque town we had hitherto seen. Situated on an arm of the mountains, it spread out in the form of an amphitheatre on one side and went down into a ravine on the other. An ancient crenelated wall surrounded it and wound up and down the unequal surface; from it arose a beautiful three-storied pagoda. But the Chinese towns are so constructed that they are best seen from a distance, and most of the charm vanishes as you draw nearer.

Having found out that we were to remain here some hours, I went to explore the ravine with a police agent. The principal charm consisted in the extreme irregularity of the building, which followed no plan beyond the fancy of the owners; if a passing wish seized them for a door, balcony, or staircase, it was immediately gratified. There were houses with five stories, and each story had its own outer staircase. Other habitations, being built up against the mountain, had a door to each floor which opened straight out on to the winding path.

March 5th. The navigation became more and more difficult owing to the rapids. Gunboats could go no farther, and in exchange eight soldiers were allotted us to follow our boat on shore.

It was impossible to get through the rapids with the same number of men, so we were obliged to have recourse to the landsmen, who were forced by the soldiers to help us. If they showed any disinclination to assist us they were dragged along by their pigtails and forced with blows to do the work. Such scenes were most unpleasant, but it was impossible for us to interfere. The temporary helpers were paid 500 sapeques, with which they appeared quite satisfied, and then returned to help the others.

We now made our entry into the province of Cheñ-Si, or rather Chañ-Si, words which mean "west of the mountains," in contrast to the name of Chañ-Toung, "east of the mountains." It is usually called Cheñ-Si to distinguish it from

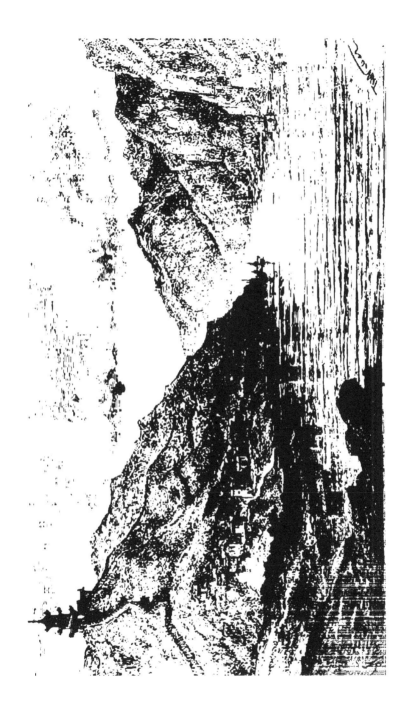

another province in the north of the same name. The limits
of the frontier are marked on each side of the river by
slabs of stone bearing inscriptions.

March 6th. Special preparations for a dangerous channel
which we could now see in front of us. The water became
a foaming torrent dashing up against the rocks. The men
rapidly climbed the hill, the rope tightened, and we began
to advance. The men towing us had passed the rapids long
before, but at last we got successfully over and proceeded
quickly on our way. As far as Lao-Ho-Keou we had our
friend, Tan-Tchen-Koueï, who knew the neighbourhood;
and now we had Sin-Van, a simple workman, but well-
educated, clever, and possessing a thorough knowledge of
the country. He pointed out all the towns and the principal
industries of their inhabitants, and gave us every sort of
information.

March 8th. During the day we stopped opposite the village
of Tjchan-Tjcha-Ba. Van informed us that the inhabitants
of this village were mostly employed in making paper from
the fibre of a tree called *koou-schou* (*Aralia papyrifera*),
and offered to give us the opportunity of seeing this industry. We climbed up the steep banks, and directed our steps
to a small house papered white on the outside, and surrounded
by a nice little garden. Behind the garden a wall supported the terrace belonging to the next house, on which
were strawberry-beds, peach, and other fruit-trees in full
blossom. Houses with their terraces, gardens, and flower-
beds were scattered over the mountain-side, and groups of
Chinese women, with their hair artistically dressed, sat talk-

ing together on the grass. We got over the paling of the first house, where everything was scrupulously neat, and the apparition considerably alarmed a son of the Celestial Empire who was working on, the steps, and became as white as his own garments. Born in the midst of his native mountains, which he had never left for a day, and living exactly the same existence among his own neighbours from one year's end to another, this was really not to be wondered at. If we ourselves had been brought up in the same way, the sudden apparition of two total strangers, starting as it were from the earth, might have had the same effect. On seeing his perturbation, Van succeeded in reassuring him by explaining who we were and whence we came, and he then very civilly invited us into his house. The paper factory, if one might thus designate the little house, only consisted of two rooms, and gave employment to five or six workmen. The process by which the fibre or bark of the aralia was turned into paper as fine as silk was most simple. Previously ground together with lime, the fibre was left for some time in a furnace; the whole mass was then hammered out and flattened into wide strips, which were rolled up and cut into little lumps, just like sausages. All these lumps were then pounded in a mortar by a primitive mechanical hammer till they formed a compact mass and a sort of paste. This paste was next put into a basin of water, in which it dissolved. In the next process they took a bamboo sieve with very fine parallel fibres and plunged it into the basin, quickly removing it again. The water ran through, leaving a fine layer of the paste spread over the sieve. They then turned the sieve over, pressing it on to a sheet of paper, to which the new leaf adhered. A fresh layer was added to the first, and so on till they came to a thousand, when the whole was pressed and dried, and the paper was ready. It is called *koou-pi-tjy*, that is, paper made from the bark of the *koou-schou* tree.

There are a great many different kinds of paper in China, and the leaves vary in shape, size, thickness, and colour according to the material used. It was most curious to see paper manufactured out of bamboo, cotton, silk remnants, herbaceous plants, and the hair, or even intestines, of animals.

When we had seen everything we thanked the kind master of the house, and went back on board to continue our journey, cut short on this occasion by violent and contrary winds, which forced the boatmen to stop work. There was nothing for it but to wander off with my gun, and I shot a very pretty Chinese magpie (*Urocissa Sinensis*). On my return I was surprised to find that I had been followed the whole time by one of the soldiers of our escort. I could not make out whether he was merely obeying the orders of his chief to protect me against the crowd, or whether it was the police supervision against which I had been warned, but in which I had not placed much belief.

Matoussowsky and the Cossack had long since retired to rest. It was a peaceful, beautiful night, and I was gazing on the moonlight from my bed, with the windows open, when I heard some one knocking at the door, a most unusual event at that time of night.

It turned out to be our servant, Tjchow, and as I could not understand a word he said, I had to waken the Cossack to find out what he wanted. He had come to warn us to be on the alert and to load our revolvers, for there were brigands on the river who had recently pillaged a boat and assassinated the occupants. He warned us that if the soldiers of our escort sounded a bugle, we should have to get up and prepare to defend ourselves.

We followed his advice, loaded our pistols, and returned to bed, but not to sleep, as a nocturnal attack might prove really dangerous.

March 9th. We got throught the night quietly, and no one came to disturb us. We rested in the middle of the day opposite the little town of Sin, or Siun-Yan-Sian, situated on a low mound, which seemed as if thrown down by chance among all those high mountains. From the river this town had all the appearance of an amphitheatre, built as it was on three semicircular terraces.

There were only about ten boats moored opposite the town, a most unusual circumstance, but I learnt subsequently that, owing to the force of the stream, they all took refuge in the Sin-Ho, a small river skirting the town. We found the navigation most difficult, and were towed much farther up the stream and then rowed across, but had to be towed up a second time before we could land. The town had no special peculiarities ; the houses were very small, and it boasted of three red temples; a tower and a wood in the midst of the town crowned the top of the hill.

Very few of the inhabitants troubled themselves to come

and' see us, for the town was at a considerable distance from the Han, and they had to cross the Sin-Ho to reach us. Those who came were very rude, laughing at us and calling us "foreign devils." Notwithstanding this reception, I was just going into the town when a message came that we were to start the moment a courier arrived with some letters.

News spreads in China with astonishing rapidity, notwithstanding the absence of telegraphic communication. For instance, how in the world did it come to be already known here that a courier was to arrive from Han-Keou with letters and parcels? It was not the result of imagination, as it was stated that he was to arrive immediately, and was close by, which turned out to be quite true, and the courier soon appeared with letters from Russia, forwarded by our kind friends from Han-Keou. In the central provinces there is no regular post; all official correspondence is managed by an especial staff relieved from point to point; sometimes a single runner is sent the whole distance. Money and letters reach their destination with extraordinary precision. People who have lived for years in China assure me that they have never known a case in which letters, parcels, or money have been lost or stolen. Those casual postmen are hired at private offices, which fill the place of post-offices. They take charge of all private correspondence. Considerable sums of money and valuables of all sorts may be unhesitatingly confided to them. We took the runner on board with us, intending to answer our letters and send him back next day.

March 10*th.* Another rapid, almost a cascade, so tremendous was the fall of water. The men towing were upon the .hillside, dragging us by the bamboo cable. We advanced so slowly that the boat almost seemed to be at·a standstill. Nevertheless, we were really moving; by degrees the rapids were left behind, and the boat once more breasted the stream. For the first time I noticed the remains of ruined forts or castles in the mountains. They testified to that terrible time when civil war drove the inhabitants from their houses, and forced them to take refuge in these inaccessible spots.

March 11*th.* Warm weather. The character of the country had entirely altered ; the mountains had disappeared, and the banks were sandy and stony. The bed of the Han now became very wide ; on the right bank the suburb of Sin-Añ-Fou appeared, and shortly after the town itself, with several temples overlooking its walls. Behind Sin-Añ-Fou were more mountains, with clumps of trees and bare tall trunks dotted about the latter, looking exactly like columns in the distance. We halted opposite the town on the left bank, and a crowd of natives descended on our boat. We oon sent them off, but they showed no signs of annoyance. We were waiting for our chief's arrival, when a police agent came on board to ask who we were, where we were going, and how many we numbered. He wished to know if we were those strangers who had been expected for some time, and for whom they had orders to prepare quarters. We explained to him that this last would not be necessary, as we did not intend to reside in the town, and begged him to thank the local authorities. Our colleagues arrived shortly

after, and we crossed to the opposite bank, where a number
of rude and mannerless people assaulted our boat, and
obliged us to keep out from the shore to escape the sand and
stones they threw at us. Amidst this crowd I suddenly
perceived Ma, the son of Fan-Tcheng, the Mussulman with
whom we had dined. He jumped on to the shoulders of
the nearest man with bare feet, and was thus carried to our
boat. To our great surprise he informed us that Sosnowsky
had invited him to accompany him as far as Sin Tioon, and
perhaps farther, as he knew the country, and he then left
us to go and see the chief. Next morning he came and
asked me to go with him into the town, which is a quarter
of a mile from the river at low-water. We walked that
distance over sand and stones till we reached a solid rampart
of earth and masonry, which protects the town from the
summer inundations. The wall dominates it, and a stone
staircase leads to the gate, on passing through which
another staircase leads down again into the principal street,
which is considerably below the level of the upper terrace
on the ramparts.

The principal street is straight and narrow, and most
picturesque; and the pretty shops, beautiful roofs, quantities
of signboards, and crowds of men all carrying parasols
presented a very characteristic view of Chinese life.

In this street we met an old man brandishing his cane
right and left. I imagined he was trying to excite the
crowd against me; however, no one paid him any heed. He
seemed surprised at the crowd surrounding us, and his eye
happening to fall upon me, he raised his stick. The blow he

intended for me caught Ma on the head. I asked if he
was hurt, but he reassured me, and told me that the old man
was a harmless lunatic who had lived here a long time.
Either this madman was really not dangerous, or else,
judging by his being allowed to parade the streets by himself, he was absolutely without relations. In China, where
there are no lunatic asylums, every family is responsible for
damage done by any lunatic belonging to it. In some cases
this responsibility is very great, as any assassination per-
petrated by a madman is punished by death.

We went through the whole town, and came on a fine
tower rising from a wall at the opposite end. Just as we
were entering, the door began to shut in our faces, but at
the same time we heard a voice bidding us to come in
quickly. We stepped inside, and the door was then shut,
as the crowd was not to enter. There were only a few old
men, and the priests of the temple with their friends, inside.
I let them touch my clothes, and sat down to draw the
principal street. The crowd below uttered frightful threats
and yells, but no one heeded them, as it was only their
usual style of conversation. They managed to discover that
I was drawing, and then nothing could restrain them from
throwing themselves on the door and insisting on its being
opened for them. The police vainly threatened them with
their clubs, and as the door was not very strong the priests
of the temple thought it imprudent to prolong their resistance, and gave in to the populace, who now swarmed into
the tower with savage shrieks. Any one else might have
been frightened, but I had by this time become so accus-

tomed to their noise that it did not discompose me in the
least.

Without wishing to boast of my courage, I recommend all
who travel in China to mix unarmed in the crowds. A
weapon would be useless, and probably harmful. It would
be of no use to lose patience or seize a revolver; one would
be certainly worsted, and to fire a shot or two would only
diminish the chance of escape. I had noticed that the
crowd had a certain amount of respect for a defenceless man,
and felt flattered by the confidence placed in them. I was
therefore able to go steadily on with my drawing, fully convinced that, although they might come to blows among
themselves in their endeavours to get a good view of my
performance, I myself should escape unharmed.

A few minutes later five policemen in full dress came
and took up their position around my chair. They had
been sent by the authorities to protect me, and brandished
their clubs at all those who wanted to get too near me, even
following this up with blows. Ma went to see Sosnowsky,
and suddenly returned in a terrible state of mind just as we
were going to bed.

Not being able to make out anything he said, we sent for
the Cossack, who explained that the chief refused to take
him with us, stating that he had not engaged him, and that
he had no need for his services, whilst Ma insisted on the
contrary that he had been asked to come, and that in view
of this he had given up his place, and spent a good deal of
his money in overtaking us. He further advanced that he
should be ashamed to return with the news that he had been

sent away after being engaged by the foreigners. It was a most painful and disagreeable scene, and we were unable either to console him or exonerate ourselves, as he included us in the general condemnation.

March 13*th*. It is just a year since I left Petersburg, and behold I am now in Central China, walking the streets of Sin-Añ-Fou under a parasol, and accompanied by Chinese soldiers driving a crowd of rioters before them.

Matoussowsky and I thus came in for a very comic scene. A poor creature, well advanced in years and half naked, was jumping and careering about for all the world like a young calf, and muttering all the while to himself, "I will see the strangers; I will see them, too!" Then he jumped about with increasing excitement at the thought of meeting the strangers, looking forwards for us, without any idea that we were just behind him.

The crowd and the officials were all laughing at him, and when he asked where we were, one of them struck him on his bare shoulder and said, "Here are the foreigners; look, quick."

He turned round, and not expecting to see us so near, a sudden change came over him. He was as much frightened as if two tigers were just going to spring at him; all his light-heartedness disappeared, and he was rooted to the ground pale and speechless.

The "foreign men" could not resist smiling as they passed the Chinaman, who speedily disappeared in the crowd.

Matoussowsky went to take a plan of the town, and I

meanwhile walked about and drew the most interesting of its buildings. A fine continuous rain necessitated my using an umbrella, and my new friends showed great zeal in my service, drawing in their chairs, and either holding my own parasol over my head or one belonging to themselves.

Sin-Añ-Fou is two distinct towns; the old town, Tziu-Tjen, is nearest the river, and Sin-Tjen, the new one, is farther off. I walked all round the ramparts of the former, and found them well kept and paved with tiles. I was not able to visit the second town, dominated by a beautiful tower.

March 14*th*. We left Sin-Añ-Fou in dreadful weather, rain and wind. Fortunately the latter was in our favour and enabled us to sail our boats. The soldiers of the escort could not keep up with us, so we took them on board.

We had often remarked the absence of respect the soldiers showed their officers when off duty, and therefore were not astonished by their treating us in the same way.

These *brave tigers* of the Chinese army lay about in the most extraordinary attitudes, on their backs, or with their feet up in the air, violently scratching their legs, with their pantaloons raised above the knees. They suffered from scurvy, and came to me one after the other for remedies. I gave them each an allowance of sulphur and ointment, and explained how they were to be used. These details may be uninteresting, but are characteristic.

Our presence did not the least embarrass them; they sang or played pitch and toss, from whence arose quarrels and endless rows.

The wind soon went down, the rope was resumed, but the

rain continued, and the poor men with their bare heads and
feet found it impossible to keep warm. We halted out of
pity for our boatmen, but they gained little. They had no
warm clothing, so could only sit shivering and coughing.

March 15th. The same horrible weather. Violent rain.
The pilot announced that the water had risen four *tji*, about
five feet, and the stream became yellow and turbid.

March 16th. Continuous bad weather. As our chief's boat
was still behindhand, we went up the hill to see the coal-
mines. After going about twenty paces down the mine we
were obliged to retrace our steps, owing to the darkness; the
workmen were absent, and we had no time to wait for them.
The mine has been worked during the last sixty years, and
its length is about eight *li*, or two miles. Two deep ruts
worn into the rock by their wheels testify to its age. The
coal is taken away on little two-wheeled wicker carriages.
At the mouth of the cavern we came upon an apparently
limpid stream, but it left a deposit of brilliant yellow on
everything it came in contact with. A very pleasant Chinaman, who had shown us the way, pointed out a disused coal-
pit on the opposite bank which had taken fire through
some imprudence. The subterranean conflagration appears to
have lasted three years, and the mountain is riddled from
top to bottom with three great black holes. We took some
samples from the mine, and subsequently proved that they
contained a superior quality of anthracite.

March 17th. Better weather. The rapids became more
and more frequent and difficult to surmount. We had constantly to take extra help from the shore. The landscape

was beautiful. Bamboo woods and brushwood cov
hills and a quantity of trees quite unknown to m
birds sang from morning till night. This would
be an inexhaustible field for the naturalist.

Our chief's boat continued to labour along, always
hand, greatly to our satisfaction, as we were thus en
collect plants and birds.

The inhabitants were gentle, peaceable, and very
to help us in every way. I went up a narrow path f
of Yan-Ho, a charming nook where eve
ed of happiness and well-being, and the
that I was picking flowers, began gatherin
inging them to me; then observing that I
ing plants, they climbed the steep hills and
ry sort of plant, with branches of trees which
self have reached. I could not understand wh
o tell me about the plants; probably they d
edicinal properties, their use as nourishment
itions attached to them, which are very
a.

e same village Van showed me a temple, cal
Tjy-Doun, and informed me that it was erected on
where in remote ages a stream of rice and water had
" Nowadays," he added, regretfully, " there are
streams."

I continued my walk across private property with
freedom as if it were my own, and shot birds close u
houses or in the fields.

Several Chinese accompanied me, their curiosity

l by my gun, which they saw could bring down even
nllest birds at a great distance and on the wing. The
nt I began to take aim they stopped their ears and
the other way; but after the shot was fired they
to run like pointers and setters. Thus I got several
I should otherwise have lost, as there were quickset
s to climb, and various very stiff obstacles. After
ing for the wound, which was often hidden amongst
athers and showed no trace of blood, they were dis-
to attribute magical properties to my gun, and to
e that the birds were killed by the noise of the report.
complimented me upon my weapon and upon "my
and and correct eye." I also saw the rice-fields, which
s season seemed more like small ponds covered with

en fields are to be prepared for the cultivation of
the agriculturist principally devotes his attention to
ng the water into them from the highest point, so
t may descend from the higher to the lower terraces
le waterfalls.

night I went back to the boat. Sosnowsky's craft had
d, and the onlookers seemed not so much astonished at
ight of strangers as at the *ma-yan-tchouan*, which is
name for that particular kind of boat. Notwith-
ng the lateness of the hour, they hung about ex-
ng their amazement that it had got so far and that
wsky should still intend to proceed in it.
rch 18th. We now came to a rapid, where we required
lp of thirty men from the village. A fresh rope was

fastened to the top of the mast, and the old one was put to its base. The arrangements were divided among two sets, one going along the right bank, and another along the left. At a signal from the pilot, they set to work, chanting their habitual chorus, and we advanced slowly with our bows high out of the foaming water. If our ropes had happened to break, our boat would have infallibly been smashed to pieces against some stone, but we had the new rope which our *tai-goun* had worked at so assiduously.

The river was not very wide, and we could easily have swum to shore at the risk of a few contusions; but the possible loss of all our effects was our real cause for anxiety. At last we were out of danger, and we halted to give our men breathing time before they went to the assistance of the big boat. We watched the whole thing curiously, and our Van, boathook in hand, took the command of the party. The proprietor's energetic and intelligent little wife transmitted the orders from the shore, working and superintending everything herself.

To my surprise, the proprietor himself took the helm; each worked with all his might, and with the energy peculiar to the Chinese.

To do the proprietor justice, he never sought to put himself forward, but seeing the superiority of his assistant, Van, he always gave up the management of his boat to him, fulfilling his instructions without hesitation.

The town of Tsy-Yan-Siañ is situated on the left bank of the Han, not far from the mouth of the Jin-Ho, or Rin-Ho, with its limpid green waters. The inhabitants annoyed us

greatly by climbing on the boat and standing on the plank leading from the boat to the shore. Our servant, Tjchou, tired of sending them off at every moment, drew away the plank just as one of them had his foot upon it, even giving it a shove. The other, furious, screamed out, "Hit him!" and the crowd re-echoed the cry. A stone was thrown at Tjchou, and the multitude rushed at the boat, intending further retaliation. The moment I showed myself their anger turned into fright, and they dispersed on every side, but only temporarily. From the opposite bank a boatload of people tried to board our vessel, but the Cossack prevented them, calling out in Russian, "Kouda, kouda," which means "Where are you going, where?" These words caught the fancy of the populace, and when a second boat tried to come up to us they screamed at the pitch of their voices, "Kouda! kouda!" holding their sides with laughter.

March 19*th.* Hearing that we were to remain a whole day at this place, I decided on going to see the town, accompanied by an agent of police. We reached it by a pathway lined by houses built on overhanging beams. In some places this path became a flight of stone steps.

After leaving the inhabited regions, I climbed much higher up the hill, and gazed on the beautiful view extended at my feet.

On going still higher, I suddenly came upon another town, with the usual wall, towers, and temples. It was only the upper quarter of Tsy-Yan-Siañ, which I now entered, to the great delight of the women and children.

At least thirty clients awaited my return to the boat. The

fame of the foreign doctor had been spread abroad; but having before had experience of the futility of giving ·advice, owing to my ignorance of the Chinese language, I contented myself with prescribing for those whose maladies were external and required no examination.

March 20th. We started off again, and whilst our boat waited for Sosnowsky's, I took my gun, went towards the hills, and got a specimen of the little *Suthora Webbiana.* The note of this bird is most original, and has two distinct intonations; the first prolonged and muffled, as if coming from afar; the second short and loud, and three tones higher than the other. The path followed the river, and where it was steepest there were steps hollowed out in the rocks. At one period I went up about a hundred steps to the edge of the hill, from whence I beheld Sosnowsky and his companions contemplating the removal of chests and cases, which were being opened one after the other and their contents spread out to dry. Either the boat had a hole in it, or else had been swamped. I hastened to return, and heard from Matoussowsky that we should remain here till the things were dried.

March 21st. A beautiful morning and fine weather. Our boat was separated from the scene of the accident by a projecting rock, and thus we were unable to see what was going on upon it. Our Cossack, who had gone to it, came back with the news that four of the eight men had departed, owing to their having had to drag about the baggage all the day before without being allowed a moment even to eat. They thought that at least they would receive payment for their extra trouble, but on receiving nothing, had gone off.

We inquired what the head man intended to do, as we could certainly not proceed with only four men, and were informed that he wished to go into the town to get others, but that he had no money, and that the chief, saying he had nothing to do with it, would give him none.

We were two miles from Tsy-Yan-Sian. I had time enough to make an excursion into the hills, but on enquiring for a soldier to accompany me, I found that they too had all gone into the town. They possessed neither money nor food, and had imagined that our chief would at least have given them dinner or proposed some sort of payment. Having received neither the one nor the other, they went off home, promising, however, to return.

All this was very unpleasant, and we gave our Cossack orders to pay a hundred sapeques every day to all the soldiers of our escort, whether they required it or not, and without reference to what they were to receive when they finally left us.

The interpreter, Andeïewsky, came soon after with orders that we were to start for Han-Tchong-Fou, the last station on the Han. The others were to go back to Tsy-Yan-Sian, and from thence by land to Han Tchong-Fou.

" How! by land ? " exclaimed Matoussowsky, " there is only a footpath, and no highroad between these two towns. You ought to go to Ha-In-Sian, where there is a road. As for us, how are we to proceed without passports or escort ? But I will go and explain all this to the chief."

However, on going to Sosnowsky, he was only told to mind his own business, and that he was mistaken on every point.

The Chinese joined their entreaties to ours, and tried to persuade Sosnowsky to change his plans, even delegating a Cossack to be their mouthpiece, but the latter merely received a severe reprimand for his pains.

There was nothing more to be done, and after their departure I went into the hills with Van to botanize and search for insects. He assured me that golden pheasants abounded in this region. We met a native carrying the plumage of two of these birds, which he sold to me for sixty sapeques (about threehalfpence). Van returned to the boat, and I continued botanizing not far from a very tidy village, surrounded by gardens, and planted with orange-trees, spreading palms, banana-trees, &c. The labourers in rice-fields, seeing me collecting plants, showed the greatest interest and came promptly to my assistance, or if I killed a bird they at once ran and fetched it for me.

Suddenly I heard the children scream "Tou! tou!" and saw them point out a hare making for the mountains. I fired and killed the hare, on which they ran and brought it to me in triumph. They were most anxious to know if we ate hares in our country, and on their informing me that they did in theirs, I gave it over to them, and returned on board.

The weather was warm, and although the temperature of the water marked only 13°, I proceeded to bathe. The Chinese looked on with horror, for they only bathe after the beginning of June, and are at no time enthusiastic about this amusement.

The Cossack now came to announce that the others were retracing their steps. They were still a long way off, but the Chinese knew of it already.

March 22nd. We continued on our way up the river, and came upon another rapid. The soldiers fetched eight men from the neighbouring village, and promised them a reward. When our boat had got past we paid them; but our chief was of opinion that the boatmen should have paid them, so they fell between two stools, and departed dissatisfied.

The heat was suffocating. A thick mist hung overhead, and the men towing frequently stopped to appease their thirst with tea. Towards evening a heavy shower forced us to stop.

The men arranged a tent with a sail, covered it with mats, and lay down to rest. They sleep with no clothes on, and do not wrap themselves in the bedclothes as we do, but make a bag out of them into which they get, leaving either their heads or their feet out of the bag. When two individuals get into the same bag, one keeps his head inside and his feet out, and the other has his head out and his feet in the bag. Before going to sleep they smoke opium. Seeing me appear, the men seemed rather confused, and tried to hide their pipes, as if in fear of rebuke. I reassured them on that head, and begged them to go on smoking. To my great regret I saw Van also smoking opium.

March 23rd. A splendid day; the air delicious after the

rain. We came upon a few unimportant tea-plantations. We halted in the village of Han-Van-Tchen to procure provisions, and I landed with my gun. The score of Chinese who surrounded us dispersed in every direction at the sight of the *tchian* (gun), but after the first moment of fear they returned and asked me questions, as we went along, as to my country, my age, my name, the price of my gun, &c. Having killed a specimen of the *Motacilla Sulphurea*, I returned to head-quarters, and proceeded to stuff it. The natives were quite surprised that I could occupy myself with such a thing, and they had a long discussion as to whether my scalpel and scissors were of silver or steel. Great praise was awarded to the foreign workmanship, as being superior to the Chinese.

On seeing various skins I had dressed, one of the natives ran home to get two other skins, and after asking six thousand sapeques, he gave them to me for a thousand.

This evening when we halted near the village of Sse-Ouo an acccident occurred which might have had a sad ending. Our boatman's little girl, aged twelve months, fell into the water; they got her out in a second, but the whole thing was characteristically Chinese. Seeing the child slip into the water I rushed to its assistance. But one of the men, without stopping his talk with two companions, seized the child and passed it up to its mother, who took it on her knee and continued her conversation with her husband as if nothing had happened. This cool way of taking the matter greatly astonished me; it almost seemed as if infanticide had been intended, and yet opportunities abounded if this woman had really meant to make away with her child. Infanticide is said to be very prevalent among the Chinese, especially among the poorer classes, or in families in which there are only girls, as they are supposed to drown the latter. I can only say that never once during our long journey did we come across one single body in the water. I never even heard such a thing alluded to, and yet I came in contact with many poor and necessitous families.

March 24th. I sketched two soldiers of our escort and our pilot Van, whom I loved and esteemed. This man was bright and active, notwithstanding his fifty-three years, and remarkable for his intelligence and cleverness. Nothing escaped his small half-shut eyes. He made a favourable impression upon us from the first, and had now become quite a friend. We stopped for the night in a most deserted spot. The mountains were steep and barren. We were told we might expect brigands, and were advised to fire a few shots to frighten them. The shots resounded from crag to crag like the rumbling of thunder. "Schan-inn" (the voice of the mountains) Van called it, to reassure me, thinking I must be frightened.

March 25th. Early in the morning the Cossack came with orders from the chief not to set out till after matins. The boatman replied that we must hasten onwards, that the river would shortly become exceedingly dangerous, and that after all we could pray while we were going along. The argument appeared unanswerable, and we were allowed to start.

The river became in truth most difficult to navigate.

Whilst Van kept careful watch, and tried to escape the
rocks, the men who towed us went along the mountain path,
bending nearly double, catching hold of the bushes, and
jumping from one stone to another. The soldiers lay on
deck warming themselves in the sun, and one of them wrote
out the names of the plants I had collected in Chinese. We
could see the landsmen working in their fields under the
shade of bamboo-trees, and others fishing by a process
hitherto unknown to me. They were throwing bunches of
grass or twigs into the river, attached to a string. The
fish slipped into these, and then all that was necessary was
to pull the string quickly to shore, and land both fish and
twigs together.

Another proceeding was almost as ingenious : in a shallow
part of the river, but where the current was strong, they
turned an old boat up, and filled the part under water with
stones to prevent its being carried away, the bottom of the
boat facing the stream. Thus the water in the boat was
quite smooth, and once the fish got into this haven they did
not seek to leave it. Every now and then the Chinese came
and took out the fish with their hands.

March 26th. Town of Che-Tsouen-Chien, surrounded with
a wall surmounted by towers. As soon as we arrived I
sallied forth with a police agent. After drawing one of
the towers I went on farther, my attention being attracted to a frame at which worked a big, strong woman,
nicely dressed, and rather pretty. The frame, on which
she was making blue cotton laces, was placed upon two
little tables with drawers, and roofed over by an awning

f grey cotton. Its mechanism was complicated, but mos
ıgenious.

I stopped to watch this woman at work, and to draw tl

was not the least disturbed by my proceedings. Turning the winch-handle, she put nine threads in to work, three for every lace, and thus obtained three laces, each a yard and a half long, in less than one minute. The laces were smooth, strong, and even.

. The inquisitive beings that followed me could not comprehend why I should trouble to draw the frame, but they were pleased to see the woman's likeness, and the drawing of the table and the threads. It was all duly examined and taken in, to be subsequently talked over with their friends. The woman herself seemed very flattered at having attracted the attention of the stranger. I did not leave without buying some of her laces.

Farther on I met a very well-dressed Chinaman, and remarked the respect with which the crowd treated him. He came bowing towards me, and the police agent presented me to him, saying, " Da-jen " (great lord). The people always treat their mandarins in this way, without either mentioning their name or their dignities.

This personage was the chief of the district, and a Mussulman. He took me by the arm, and we walked on together, exchanging a few ordinary remarks. He invited me to take tea with him, asked for one of my drawings as a souvenir of my visit, and made me a present of two pots of flowers. When I got back to the boat the flowers were there before me, and half an hour afterwards the mandarin came himself with his little girl of seven years old to see me. He had previously been in command at Laū-Tcheou-Fou, a district on the Khami road, occupied in his day by insurgents, but

now quite at peace. We gave the little girl bonbons, scis
and a piece of soap.

March 27th. Although we had been urged by every
to take different boats at this point, it was decided tha
should continue on the same. Even the owners begged
to be taken any farther, as their boats were unsuitable
the future navigation of the river.

March 28th. A beautiful day; the air fresh and
Just as we were to start we were begged to wait, as
proprietor of Sosnowsky's boat declined to pay the men
of his own pocket. Sosnowsky therefore set out to se
for mules, and gave the boat up. Our men were not s
to rest a little, and our proprietor, usually so silent, rema
that we should long ere this have reached our destin
had the other boat not kept us back.

Just as we were going to depart, three mandarins arr
one of whom carried a sounding-line. He began a conv
tion with our chief, which degenerated into a regular tu
Of the two interpreters, one did not understand a si
word, and the second was incapable of translating
Russian. At last we made out that they took us for co
band merchants trying to smuggle our goods. All that
needful was to show them the passports given us by
Chinese authorities, but Sosnowsky obstinately declined
this, and a very disagreeable scene took place in consequ
The mandarins insisted on our baggage being exam
We begged them to go on to our boats and see for t
selves that we were not merchants. Politeness and coo
of demeanour immediately changed the character of

interview ; they cast a glance round our cabin, and at once announced that we might depart in peace.

I collected some flowers for my herbarium to-day—*Wisteria Chinensis* and China roses. I had picked such a quantity that I had enough to decorate our cabin, to the great delight of the Chinese, who are all lovers of flowers. The wild and steep rocks now gave place to gentle slopes, on which the soil was cultivated and fertile. We again saw men washing for gold, and a naturalist might have formed an immense ornithological collection from the multifarious specimens of birds to be found in this region.

END OF VOL. I.

PRINTED BY J. S. VIRTUE AND CO., LIMITED CITY ROAD, LONDON.